THE POLITICS OF CRIME PREVENTION

The Politics of Crime Prevention

BRIGITTE C.M. KOCH
Institute of Criminology
University of Cambridge

LONDON AND NEW YORK

First published 1998 by Ashgate Publishing

Reissued 2018 by Routledge
2 Park Square, Milton Park, Abingdon, Oxon OX14 4RN
711 Third Avenue, New York, NY 10017, USA

Routledge is an imprint of the Taylor & Francis Group, an informa business

Copyright © Brigitte C.M. Koch 1998

All rights reserved. No part of this book may be reprinted or reproduced or utilised in any form or by any electronic, mechanical, or other means, now known or hereafter invented, including photocopying and recording, or in any information storage or retrieval system, without permission in writing from the publishers.

Notice:
Product or corporate names may be trademarks or registered trademarks, and are used only for identification and explanation without intent to infringe.

Publisher's Note
The publisher has gone to great lengths to ensure the quality of this reprint but points out that some imperfections in the original copies may be apparent.

Disclaimer
The publisher has made every effort to trace copyright holders and welcomes correspondence from those they have been unable to contact.

A Library of Congress record exists under LC control number : 97077390

ISBN 13: 978-1-138-34436-5 (hbk)
ISBN 13: 978-1-138-34439-6 (pbk)
ISBN 13: 978-0-429-43854-7 (ebk)

Contents

List of Figures		*vii*
List of Tables		*viii*
Preface		*ix*
Acknowledgements		*xi*
1	Introduction	1
2	The Home Office as a Whole	27
3	The Home Office Departments	59
4	The Police Service	91
5	The Probation Service	125
6	Crime Concern & NACRO	141
7	National Representation for Local Authorities	157
8	Conclusion	171
References		*191*
Appendices		*207*

Figures

2.1: Overall Home Office Structure, April 1996   29

4.1: Crime Committee: ACPO Crime Strategy   103

Tables

1.1: Police Sub-Divisions By Number Of Positions Filled, Total Number of Police Officers Surveyed, Total Responses And Response Rate — 12

1.2: Number of Positions Filled, Total Responses, And Percentage of Officers Included In The Research By Sub-Division And Rank Of Police Officer — 13

1.3: Boroughville's Sub-Division's Uniform Patrol And CID By Number Of Police Officers Surveyed, Number Of Responses And Response Rate — 14

1.4: Number of Positions Filled by Total Responses, and Percentage of Probation Officers Included in the Research by Rank of Probation Officer — 15

2.1: Crime Prevention Expenditure (£m) — 50

3.1: Type of RPU series by subject matter for the period 1980-July 1997 (number and column percentages) — 65

3.2: Cost of External Current Research Projects in the Research Programme Publications by Subject Matter (1984/5-1994/5) — 66

3.3: Number of Publications in the Crime Prevention Unit Series by Subject Matter — 80

4.1: Number of Police Officers by Percentage of Police Officers by Type of Crime Prevention done as part of their day-to-day activities — 119

Preface

This research examined how national crime prevention policy was structured, organised and determined in England and Wales between 1979 and 1997 with a particular focus between 1995 and 1997.

The research examined the agencies that were in a position to influence national crime prevention policy. They included: the Home Office, the police service, the probation service, Crime Concern, NACRO, local authority associations and the National Community Safety Network. The relationships between these agencies were addressed, as well as the role of political ideology in national crime prevention policy.

Several issues were addressed in the research. These issues aimed to:

1) investigate what crime prevention means at the national level;
2) study the nature of crime prevention policy making;
3) examine the role of the individual in making things happen;
4) investigate the extent of political ideology in crime prevention policy;
5) investigate the influence of politicians on policy making;
6) examine the relationship between political ideology and research/practice;
7) examine trends that have occurred over the past fifteen years;
8) investigate how national crime prevention is organised, including the role played by national crime prevention (sub) committees;
9) determine the prominence of crime prevention within each agency examined in this research;
10) examine the role of each agency in crime prevention policy making;
11) determine who has responsibility for crime prevention;
12) investigate whether national instructions for local practice are consistent with national practice;
13) investigate whether issues raised at the national level in this research are also applicable to local level research done by others;
14) to determine whether perceived roles of local police and probation officers in Boroughville are consistent with national findings.

The methods used within the research included reviewing the literature; interviewing key crime prevention policy makers; analysing internal documentation such as annual reports, pamphlets, training materials, internal letters or memos, minutes to meetings, and publications from the organisation itself, and finally; surveying both police and probation officers in one city (named Boroughville in the research) through the use of a questionnaire.

Results of the research showed that over the past eighteen years in England and Wales, national crime prevention policy was very much influenced by Conservative party ideology and by the identity of the Home Secretary and the Minister responsible for crime prevention. This not only affected policies, but also the selection of advisors. Crime Prevention since 1979 has very much focused on situational approaches. Criminality prevention or offender oriented approaches has received much less attention in comparison. Under the Conservative government, crime prevention was assigned to the police service, although other agencies were recognised as playing a role.

The research suggests that national crime prevention policy is forever changing. Structures change within organisations and people (including political figures) change every few years. These changes that occur at the national level affect policies which filter down to the local level and influence the types of crime prevention activities that receive central government funding.

Although national policies do influence local practice through funding, the practical responsibility of the Home Office in crime prevention has been dispersed with the establishment of the Single Regeneration Budget and Crime Concern. The tactic over the past few years is one of diminishing the role of the state, and increasing the notion of individual responsibility.

Acknowledgements

This research was designed to provide insight into crime prevention policy in England and Wales during the period 1979-1997.

Having read the acknowledgments in Maureen Cain's (1973) book that she completed her doctoral thesis while "boiling nappies on the gas stove" was of great inspiration in my own work. I do hope that one day, this work will inspire another "mum" to complete her studies.

Having said all this, this book would not have been possible without the help and time that so many provided, and to whom I owe much gratitude. However, due to the fact that confidentiality was assured, it is not possible to thank these people individually. Nevertheless, I do greatly appreciate the honesty and openness and information provided by those interviewed. In some instances over five or six hours were spent, explaining various aspects of crime prevention policy, or in developing the questionnaires to be sent out to police and probation officers. I do sincerely hope that these people recognise themselves in this paragraph.

Many thanks also go to all the police officers and probation officers who took the time to fill in the questionnaires and to the services themselves for granting access for this research. Here again, the author is tempted to thank a few key people, but since the services surveyed are to remain anonymous I do hope that these people know who they are.

Dr. Trevor Bennett, my supervisor, was also instrumental in completing this research. His comments and support throughout the years are greatly appreciated.

Finally, I would like to thank those at home: my husband for his continual encouragement, support and confidence; my son Alexander for his patience; and my daughter Rachel who waited until I finished my work before coming into this world (she was born within hours of my completing my PhD).

1 Introduction

Crime and crime prevention theories are influenced by the social and economic context and have evolved over time. This is linked to the society we live in and to the politics of the day (Sykes and Cullen, 1992). Bottoms and Wiles (1996: 10) indicated that "the development of contemporary forms of crime prevention can best be understood as part of a much wider process of change in contemporary Western societies".

The following account of changes in the social-economic context since World War II is by no means exhaustive and the reader is referred to Bottoms and Wiles (1995, 1996), Savage and Charman (1996), and Hogwood (1992) for more detailed accounts.

After World War II, the role of the state became one of provider of last resort (for example through the welfare system). This ultimately displaced the economic role of the family and voluntary social organisations. In 1973, the world went into an economic crisis initially triggered by oil price increases, which eventually led governments to become more aware of spending growth. Since World War II the cost to the state of acting as 'the provider of last resort' as a share of national income has steadily increased. This is true of every developed country.

Savage and Charman (1996: 40) state,

> the capacity of governments to finance the public sector, and in particular 'social expenditure' or the 'welfare state', was placed under increasing pressure. Variously defined as the 'fiscal crisis of the state' (O'Connor 1973; see also Johnston, 1996) or 'overloaded government' (Brittan, 1975), depending on one's theoretical and political stance, the conflict of ever expanding public expenditure and a decreasing capability of government revenue - mainly fiscally-based - to fund it, became increasingly acute.

Now governments to the left and right are trying to redefine the appropriate functions of the state. The push by both major parties in Britain is towards individual responsibility and away from state dependency (e.g., see Sherman, 1996). Savage and Charman (1996: 53) maintain "constraint in the public sector is unlikely to be abandoned whichever political party takes Britain into the next millennium". This affects criminal justice policy and more specifically crime prevention, both via funding constraints and changing political priorities. As Graham and Bennett (1995: 1) argue, "the role of the state has increasingly diminished and it has become accepted that neither the government nor the police can tackle crime alone".

Within the domain of criminal justice, recorded crime rates increased steadily from the 1960s until 1992. Taking this fact into account with the following trends in crime prevention is helpful in understanding the current characteristics of crime prevention in England and Wales.

In the 1960s prevention was mainly based on rehabilitation and treatment. In 1966, the National Association for the Care and Resettlement of Offenders (NACRO) was established. During this period, resource constraints were not a major issue, and there was a belief in the government's ability to solve social problems.

The economic crisis of the 1970s coupled with the criminological findings from the United States from Martinson and Wilson led to great pessimism. Martinson (1974: 34) declared that there "is very little reason to hope that we have in fact found a sure way of reducing recidivism and rehabilitation". Wilson (1975) claimed that there was not a lot one could do about crime because we could not change human nature. Wilson (1975) and others believed crime could not be eliminated. All one could do was to try and manage it. This (a) opened the door for managerialism, and (b) shifted the focus in crime prevention away from the offender to the victim and the opportunity for crime. The middle of the 1970s was thus a turning point both for criminology and for the economy.

During the 1980s in England and Wales, the emphasis in crime prevention was placed on utilising situational or opportunity reduction strategies in designing communities and rebuilding neighbourhoods. The notion of local agencies working together with local people was popular and the period was characterised by an emphasis on multi-agency co-operation. Initiatives such as the Five Towns Initiative, and Safer Cities were launched by the Home Office.

This change in crime prevention policy, coupled with the fact that in 1979 the Conservative party came into power, prompted "a reaction on the part of some sections of the socialist academy in Britain to the general experience of Thatcherism" (Taylor, 1992: 95). This lead to left realist criminology. Left realist criminologists pointed out the social injustices of Conservative government policies and highlighted the fact that criminology was drawn "into the wider political realm and <that> crime control must inevitably become part of a comprehensive political programme. For too long we have pretended it could be otherwise" (Matthews and Young: 1992: 21).

This notion of crime and politics is examined within this research. This research also draws on left realism in that "it draws freely on a tradition of critical theorizing which aims to demystify and dereify social relations" (Matthews and Young, 1992: 4). In other words, the author attempted to demystify or clarify how crime prevention policy making is structured organisationally and to investigate the role of social relationships within the decision making process.

During the 1990s one has, so far, observed a move away from communities and multi-agency co-operation to a much more localised, targeted and short-term approach to crime prevention. To use King's (1989: 300) adjectives, the values of "consumerism, individualism and self-reliance" are strongly advocated along with the emphasis on individual responsibility. Technological anti-crime products are recommended from alarm systems to Closed Circuit Television systems (CCTVs) to more effective computers and programmes for the police (e.g., for crime pattern analysis). The role of detection as a last resort for crime prevention initiatives is also emphasised (see for example, Anderson, Chenery and Pease [1995]).

The term 'multi-agency' was replaced by 'partnership' by the Conservative political masters, and the role of the community was replaced by the role of the individual. Statements such as "least attention has been given to social crime prevention" (Bright, 1991: 64), and "if one surveys the publicity literature disseminated by the Home Office ..., the overriding theoretical implication seems to be that most crime is a product of opportunity and the way to prevent crime is to reduce opportunities" (King, 1989) are found to be true in this research.

Given that a new government came into power in May 1997, it is possible that the focus on prevention will shift more towards a focus on technological advances combined with the notion of focusing on the 'at risk' population (as per David Farrington and Ken Pease).

According to Ruggiero (1992: 123), within criminology "we are witnessing a process of politicization. This is a function of changing political imperatives and the attempts to create a one-dimensional society aimed at constraining critical discourses". "The priority is assigned to quantitative as opposed to qualitative research" (Ruggiero, 1992: 125). This ties in with managerialism and the idea of having strategic plans, mission statements, and key performance indicators to measure aspects of efficiency and effectiveness (see Bottoms, 1995; and McLaughlin and Muncie, 1994).

This research takes account of these developments in attempting to understand the context of crime prevention between 1995 and 1997. In determining how crime prevention came to be what it is today, Cohen's (1985) five models of rhetoric and reality were considered. Thus, key organisations involved in national crime prevention policy making were examined, professionals within those organisations were interviewed, the political ideology of the Conservative party was examined as was the power of the state in policy making; and finally, the structure of crime prevention policy was explored.

Before diving into the research findings, this chapter examines the purpose of this research in more depth. It also discusses the methods utilised for the research and theories of crime prevention which are particularly relevant for the analysis and definitions of crime prevention. Finally the structure of this research is summarised.

Purpose of Research

This research was done to understand how crime prevention policy was determined in England and Wales. The aims were to determine:

1) Who influences crime prevention policy at the national level?
2) How is crime prevention at the national level structured?
3) What the role is of these various organisations in crime prevention and what they actually do?

This research explains how crime prevention policy developed from 1979 until mid 1997 at a national level. This was done in order to illustrate how the prominence of crime prevention developed and to illustrate how crime prevention was conceptualised between 1995 and 1997. Agencies that actively played a part in national crime prevention policy making were identified, and the manner in which they influenced national policy was examined.

This research examines the relationships between the key national agencies and the people involved in national crime prevention policy making - a task which has not been undertaken before. It analyses official and unofficial documents and includes interviews with key persons involved in the process. It is an in-depth examination of national crime prevention policy making as opposed to a commentary.

While conducting the research many themes were investigated. These themes aimed to:

1) investigate what crime prevention means at the national level;
2) study the nature of crime prevention policy making;
3) examine the role of the individual in making things happen;
4) investigate the extent of political ideology in crime prevention policy;
5) investigate the influence of politicians on policy making;
6) examine the relationship between political ideology and research/practice;
7) examine trends that have occurred over the past eighteen years;
8) investigate how national crime prevention is organised, including the role played by national crime prevention (sub) committees;
9) determine the prominence of crime prevention within each agency examined in this research;
10) examine the role of each agency in crime prevention policy making;
11) determine who has responsibility for crime prevention;
12) investigate whether national instructions for local practice are consistent with national practice;
13) investigate whether issues raised at the national level in this research are also applicable to local level research done by others;
14) determine whether perceived roles of local police and probation officers in Boroughville are consistent with national findings.

The research did not evaluate actual crime prevention initiatives or projects, nor did it focus on one particular form of crime prevention. Tertiary crime prevention (defined later in this chapter) was ignored in this research. This was not a conscious decision of the author, but rather the result of interviews and sources analysed which did not consider tertiary forms of crime prevention to fall under this heading. Generally speaking, tertiary crime prevention fell under the headings of 'prisons' or 'probation'. The fact that tertiary crime prevention fell under the heading of 'probation' was one explanation why the probation service's role was questioned by policy makers and politicians within the field. In this research, the author examined the potential role of the probation service in primary and secondary prevention.

Methods

In conducting this research a decision had to be made on who or which agencies affected National Crime Prevention Policy. An obvious starting point was the Home Office since it determines national crime prevention policy for all of England and Wales. In speaking to Home Office officials and by reading through the literature, it was obvious that the police also had a role to play at the national level by giving advice to the crime prevention minister and the Home Secretary. This was done through Her Majesty's Chief Inspectorate of Constabulary, ACPO, The Home Office Standing Conference on Crime Prevention, the National Board for Crime Prevention, and the National Crime Prevention Agency.

Only national organisations which included crime prevention as a part of their remit were examined, thus eliminating all local initiatives involved in crime prevention practice. Although the 'Business Sector' was recognised as playing a large role in crime prevention, there is no organisation which represents the entire industry's interests. For example, in the National Crime Prevention Agency only Vauxhall Motors and J. Sainsbury Plc are represented.

In the end the researcher was left with the Home Office, the Police Service, the Probation Service, Crime Concern, NACRO, and the Local Government Association. Those interviewed agreed that these were the agencies most influential in crime prevention policy making, albeit to different degrees. This is specifically in relation to the role of the probation service and NACRO. More shall be said about this issue later in the research.

Funded national programmes such as Safer Cities were not analysed in this research since they were considered to be a consequence of policy as opposed to a policy making instrument. Where pilot crime prevention initiatives were introduced and evaluated (e.g., the Five Towns Initiative),[1] their effects on policy making itself were considered to be minimal since the 'second' phases (e.g., Safer Cities Phase I and Safer Cities Phase II) were introduced before evaluation results were available (Interview).[2]

The methods utilised in conducting the research included (1) reviewing the literature; (2) conducting interviews; (3) analysing internal documentation; and (4) distributing questionnaires.

Reviewing the Literature

In reviewing the literature on crime prevention in England and Wales, sources such as journals, books, pamphlets, and conference speeches were used. The sample of information reviewed for this research was based on literature which was classified under terms such as prevention, reduction, causes of crime, measures to tackle crime and so forth. The limitation of this process was that because crime prevention policy was specifically examined rather than policies which might affect the likelihood of offending or an offence being committed, a whole field of documentation was ignored (e.g., education, psychology or sociology [in regards to family structures and relationships], social services, and housing). Although the documentation which was ignored could be considered to be related to crime prevention, it was not classified as such. It was therefore ignored in this research.

The strength of this method was that by only examining documents classified under the heading of crime prevention (and its variances), an indication of what was understood as 'crime prevention' was achieved.

The result of this review revealed that very little information was available on crime prevention policy-making at the national level in England and Wales. Bright (1991) and Jones, Newburn, and Smith (1994) recently touched upon the issue, but not in a manner that made the mechanisms of how everything works understandable. Other articles on crime prevention policy in England and Wales include Laycock and Heal (1989), Heal (1992), Heal and Laycock (1988), and Rock (1994).

Information could be found in some journals and books on individual Home Office departments, on the Home Office as a whole or on some

---

[1] See for example, Liddle and Bottoms (1991).

[2] See for example, Ekblom (1996).

individual organisations. However, no information could be found on how these organisations all worked together or were interconnected, and who in these organisations had responsibility for crime prevention.

The author therefore decided that in order to determine what these organisations actually did and how they were all interconnected, the organisations themselves had to be contacted. Interviews were conducted with those responsible for crime prevention and documents of the various organisations analysed.

Interviews

Interviews were conducted in order to begin filling in the gaps that exist within the literature. The interviews were held in a semi-structured format with key 'crime prevention policy makers' at both the national and local level.

Seven police officers (1 Constable, 1 Sergeant, 1 Inspector, 3 Chief Inspectors, and 1 retired police officer) explained the mechanics behind policing and helped to prepare the questionnaire. These interviews were conducted between 1992 and 1994. Twenty-one individuals were interviewed with respect to crime prevention policy making. In total, twenty-eight individuals were approached for information in relation to this research. Second and third interviews were conducted with some of the interviewees in order to update the author on changing events. The information that came from the interviews were consistent amongst all those interviewed.

Due to the prominent positions of most of these people, confidentially needed to be assured. Most people are still working in the crime prevention field and their honesty in the interviews was not to be exploited.

The interviews were very helpful, not only by what the interviewees told the researcher, but also in that it allowed the researcher to obtain internal documentation that would most likely not have been made available otherwise. In other instances, the interviewees directed the author to internally published information.

Where possible what was said in interviews was compared to what exists in publications (e.g., the opinion of an interviewee that the Probation Service receives less attention by the Home Office in regards to research can be substantiated by the fact that in analysing Home Office publications, the probation service received little attention compared to areas related to Policing, Courts, and Prisons).

One might argue that "if a researcher has a stake in a particular hypothesis, he/she may see evidence to support the hypothesis in spite of the best intentions" (Stern, 1979: 73). In this research the author did not begin with a hypothesis. The author considered this research to be an explorative study rather than a hypothesis-testing study.

In interviews one has to be aware that "the information collected sometimes depends on who gathers it, or on how, when, or where it was collected" (Stern, 1979: 81). In this research the author was the sole interviewer. The author cannot guarantee that the same answers would have been provided had another researcher asked the same questions, or if interviews were conducted in a different manner.

Analysing Internal Documentation

The internal documentation analysed included annual reports, pamphlets, training materials, internal letters or memos, minutes to meetings, and publications published by the organisation itself. All the minutes of the ACPO sub-committee on crime prevention were analysed from its inaugural meeting on 4 September 1986 until 25 May 1995. These minutes are not available to the public. The analysis of these minutes therefore contributes information to the field of crime prevention and policing that had in the past not been available.

As will be evident in the research, these documents revealed much information about the organisations in question. An organisation's publications were considered important in that they are the means by which the 'outside world' develops an impression of what the organisation is about. The documents provide an illustration of what the organisation is trying to convey to the public.

In analysing internal documentation, references were made to political ideology. In order to determine political ideology Conservative party manifestos were analysed. This was an important part of the research because "policy change and formation are inevitably a political process, <and thus> applied research must necessarily address the political realities within which it is conducted" (Judd, Smith, and Kidder, 1991: 338).

The term ideology is not an easy one to define. As McLellan (1986: 1) states,

> Ideology is the most elusive concept in the whole of social science. For it asks about the bases and validity of our most fundamental ideas. As such, it is an

essentially contested concept, that is, a concept about the very definition (and therefore application) of which there is acute controversy.

Although a definition of ideology could not be found within the literature that applied to this research, it is possible to suggest lines of thought that were connected to the term when the author used the word. First of all, as Marx argued, ideology was connected with idealism (cited in McLellan, 1986: 10) and with "the superficial or misleading way in which truth is asserted" (McLellan, 1986: 18).

Secondly, as Locke and Montesquieu argued, ideology "concealed the real nature of social and economic relationships" (McLellan, 1986: 14). Thirdly, as Engels argued, ideology "derives its form as well as its content from pure thought, either his own or that of his predecessors. He works with mere thought material, which he accepts without examination as the product of thought, and does not investigate further for a more remote source independent of thought" (cited in McLellan, 1986: 23).

Finally, as Habermas argued, ideology was considered to be "the study of systematically distorted communication" (McLellan, 1986: 78). The meaning of words was therefore considered to depend "heavily on the conditions under which it is produced and those under which it is received by its readers or hearers" (McLellan, 1986: 72).

This research utilises discourse analysis to determine ideology. Thus it analyses the language of the documents in an attempt to "uncover ideological implications in the apparently innocent structure of sentences" (McLellan, 1986: 70). The work of Foucault (1969) and Cohen (1985) are also utilised in this process. In analysing the documentation, sentences were not taken at face value. The author considered who wrote the document, who published the document and the reason why it was produced at that particular time. In some instances, messages conveyed through publications were discussed in interviews by those people who wrote them or were involved in its production.

The documents were also used to verify, where possible, information gained in interviews. The Home Office research publications, for example, were categorised to determine trends as to which subjects were considered of importance over time. In addition to the author having gone over the categorisations twice, the author asked a financial economist[3] to categorise

---

[3] Under ideal circumstances, the author would have asked a criminologist to categorise the publications. However, due to practical constraints this was not possible.

the publications according to the methods stated in the appropriate section. The following percentages of accuracy (reliability) were achieved.[4]

- 83% (327 of the 395 articles were similarly categorised) for the Home Office Research Bulletins;
- 83% (79 of the 93 papers were similarly categorised) for the Research and Planning Unit Papers;
- 76% (41 out of 54 publications were similarly categorised) for the Crime Prevention Unit Series.

The categorisations for the first two checks utilised a different categorisation than the later one. The later one was categorised prior to the other series'. The author asked the economist how exactly the publications were categorised. In many instances it was done by title alone. The author therefore amended the method of classification section to reflect the fact that in most cases the articles were referred to. This might partly explain the percentage differences amongst the publications. Due to practical constraints, not all the sources categorised could be checked for reliability.

Furthermore, the author gave copies of various sections of this book to the organisations in question. Their comments were then incorporated into the final version of the chapter. This was done as both a measure of reliability and validity.

Questionnaires

The final method utilised for this research was the distribution of a self-completed questionnaire to police and probation officers of all ranks in one city.

The purpose of the questionnaire was to explore whether 'national' findings were consistent with opinions and attitudes at a local level. This was done to determine whether national statements, mostly made by very senior officers who no longer work in a police station, reflected the views of those working on the practical side. Although the questionnaire findings are not necessarily generalisable to all of England and Wales, they can at

---

[4] The process of double checking the author's categorisation was done upon completion of the research for the purpose of receiving her doctorate degree. The author updated the research upon completion to bring this book up to date. The added material was not double-checked by anyone but the author.

12   *The Politics of Crime Prevention*

least begin to explore the possibility of consistency or inconsistency between national and local levels.

A guarantee of anonymity and confidentiality was given to all respondents, where neither the police force nor probation service surveyed would be identified. For this reason the author has named the area which was surveyed "Boroughville".

Distribution Of Questionnaires for the Police When this research began there were two police sub-divisions in Boroughville (called sub-division C and D by the author). These two sub-divisions have since merged. The questionnaires for the police were thus conducted on two separate occasions.

One part of Boroughville was surveyed in July 1993 (Sub-division C). All police officers and one half of the CID officers were surveyed. This resulted in 90 questionnaires being distributed. 74 of the questionnaires were completed producing a response rate of 82% (See Tables 1.1, 1.2 and 1.3 for a detailed breakdown of response rates). A chi-square test was

Table 1.1 Police Sub-Divisions By Number Of Positions Filled, Total Number of Police Officers Surveyed, Total Responses And Response Rate

	Sub-division C	Sub-division D	Total
Total Number Of Positions Filled	145	136	281
Total Number Of Police Surveyed	90	103	193
Total Responses	74	76	150
Response rate	82%	74%	78%

Table 1.2 Number of Positions Filled, Total Responses, And Percentage of Officers Included In The Research By Sub-Division And Rank Of Police Officer

	Number of Positions Filled	Total Responses	Percentage of Police Officers Included In The Research
Sub-Division C			
Chief Inspector +*	3	3	100%
Inspector	7	4	57%
Sergeant	20	13	65%
Constable	115	54	47%
Total	145	74	51%
Sub-Division D			
Chief Inspector +*	2	-	-
Inspector	7	5	71%
Sergeant	25	18	72%
Constable	102	53	52%
Total	136	76	56%
Total: Boroughville			
Chief Inspector +*	5	3	60%
Inspector	14	9	64%
Sergeant	45	31	69%
Constable	217	107	49%
Total	281	150	53%

*: Includes the ranks of Chief Inspector and Superintendent.

calculated which illustrated that the distribution of questionnaires over ranks in sub-division C were not significantly different from the distribution of the population over ranks.

The survey for sub-division D was conducted in September 1993. In this instance all 103 police officers on duty within a 24 hour period were

Table 1.3 Boroughville's Sub-Division's Uniform Patrol And CID By Number Of Police Officers Surveyed, Number Of Responses And Response Rate

	Sub-Division C		Sub-Division D	
	Uniform Patrol	CID	Uniform Patrol	CID
Number of Police Surveyed	76	14	88	15
Number of Responses	60	14	65	11
Response Rate	79%	100%	74%	73%

surveyed. The rank of Chief Inspector and Superintendent were excluded from the survey. The Chief Inspector felt that it would be more appropriate to hear from other ranks. Seventy-six completed questionnaires were returned resulting in a 74% response rate (see Table 1.1). A chi-square test was calculated which illustrated that the distribution of questionnaires over ranks in sub-division D were not significantly different from the distribution of the population over ranks. Table 1.3 shows the response rate of uniform patrol officers versus CID.

Distribution of Questionnaires in the Probation Service The questionnaires for the probation service were distributed in February 1995. They were distributed to the 42 probation staff working in Boroughville. After one reminder in March 1995 to return questionnaires, the author received a total of 31 out of 42 (74%) completed questionnaires.

Table 1.4 illustrates the break-down of those that returned their questionnaires by rank. Although the total number of questionnaires distributed in the probation service is low, in comparison to the police, one can at least suggest that the findings are applicable to probation staff in

Table 1.4 Number of Positions Filled by Total Responses, and Percentage of Probation Officers Included in the Research by Rank of Probation Officer

	Number Of Positions Filled	Total Responses	Percentage of Probation Officers Included In The Research
Chief Probation Officer / ACOP	4	4	100%
Senior Probation Officer	4	4	100%
Probation Officer or Deputy Warden	19	13	68%
Assistant Warden	4	2	50%
Community Service Officer	4	1	25%
Probation Service Officer	7	7	100%
Total	42	31	74%

Boroughville. To try and generalise the findings to the entire county or country would not be suitable. The questionnaires are therefore only to be used in an exploratory fashion and no firm conclusions may be drawn.

Theories of Crime Prevention

In order to understand crime prevention policy making today, the building blocks of criminological theory and their modern expressions need to be reviewed. The concept of preventing crime is not a new one, and concepts from over 200 years ago are still evident in policy making today. Within the field there are numerous theories of crime prevention. In order to understand current thinking about crime prevention both classical and positivistic criminology need to be understood. The two theories were essentially the building blocks for modern criminological theories and represent the founding paths that define debates within crime prevention today.

Classical criminology focused on the act of crime and positivistic criminology focused on the offender. Although these theories still apply today, these terms are not readily used. The debate between the crime and the offender has, however, continued to this day, except that the terminology has changed over the years.

The modern expressions of these two theories can be translated through situational prevention (or opportunity reduction as Rosenbaum, 1988 would suggest), and criminality prevention.[5] A further discussion of the terms used within the domain of crime prevention follows this section. First, the theories will be described.

Classical Criminology

In 1764, Cesare Beccaria, dubbed the father of Classical Criminology, published *On Crimes and Punishment* which was condemned by the Catholic church in 1766 (Vold and Bernard, 1986: 24-25). Beccaria's theory is renowned for providing justification for punishment to this day.

The offender was perceived as being rational and unwilling to live responsibly. Punishments were based on the crime committed and

---

[5] Although there are many other crime prevention theories (i.e., environmental criminology, rational choice, routine activities, Skogan's theory of disorder and neighbourhood decline, Structuration theory; Control theory; and theories connected to aggressiveness or other behavioural traits) they can, generally speaking, be affiliated within the two approaches.

prevention was based on deterrence. Beccaria stated "the end of punishment, therefore, is no other than to prevent the criminal from doing further injury to society, and to prevent others from committing the like offence" (Beccaria, 1963: 47 cited in Mueller, 1990: 3).

He believed that the punishments should be swift and proportionate to the act of crime and the harm done to society. Since the punishment for committing a crime was proportionately high, the potential gain from committing the crime would be perceived as not worth it. Some of these themes are evident in crime prevention policy today.

Beccaria's work also included a section on preventing crime. Beccaria declared:

> It is better to prevent crimes than to punish them. That is the ultimate end of every good legislation. ... Do you want to prevent crimes? See to it that the laws are clear and simple and that no part of it is employed to destroy them. See to it that the laws favor not so much classes of men as men themselves. See to it that men fear the laws and fear nothing else. For fear of the laws is salutary, but fatal and fertile for crimes is one man's fear of another (cited in Vold and Bernard, 1986: 24).

The major limitation of Beccaria's work, was that his focus was on the act of crime and he considered all individuals to be equal. Thus a two year old was as equally liable as a twenty year old. Although it is no longer considered that all individuals are equal, Beccaria's focus on the act of crime, having a punishment to fit the crime, and the notion of deterrence are still very significant in crime prevention theory and policy today. For example, one could say that 'situational crime prevention theory' is a modern expression of classical theory.

Positivist Criminology

After Beccaria's work was published, other theorists searched for the causes that regulated human behaviour through observed correlation. Their theories came to be known as positivist criminology. They considered individuals to be determined by factors such as biology, psychology and social position.

Positivism in comparison to classicism focused on the offender rather than the act. Since positivists had "an image of man as fundamentally constrained", persons were not considered responsible for their actions (Matza, 1964: 5). "Instead of punishment, they require treatment or other forms of correction" (Matza, 1964: 7). Limitations of the positivist approach included the fact that criminality was still not perfectly predictable. Not all persons with the predictable factors were deviant. Some were capable of behaving 'normally'. Furthermore, it did not explain why criminality was generally not permanent, but rather a period in an individual's life which most people outgrow. Although theorists might not necessarily consider themselves as positivists, many of their theories have evolved from positivism, in particular those connected with criminality prevention.

Situational Crime Prevention

As stated earlier, situational crime prevention could be considered a modern expression of classical theory. 'Situational crime prevention' is a term that has been used very loosely to refer to theories based on the act of crime as opposed to the offender. It is connected "with neo-classical, conservative ... criminology" (Walklate, 1996: 16). Graham and Bennett (1995: 47) stated that it "is based on the assumption that people choose to commit crime and that the decision to offend is influenced by situational factors". This is consistent with classical thinking. In order to avoid adding to the confusion of the meaning of 'situational prevention', only the work of Dr. Ronald Clarke is addressed. He was essentially the founder of the situational approach in England and Wales.

Clarke (1992: 3), stated that the concept of situational prevention was introduced in the mid 1970's, the first classification appearing in Clarke and Mayhew's (1980) *Designing Out Crime*.[6] Clarke (1992: 3) declared that situational crime prevention "refers to a preventive approach that relies, not upon improving society or its institutions, but simply upon reducing opportunities for crime".

Situational crime prevention was defined as comprising,

opportunity-reducing measures that are,

1) directed at highly specific forms of crime

---

[6] Bennett and Wright (1984: 16) suggest that situational crime prevention has continuously developed since the publication by Sutherland and Cressey (1955).

2) that involve the management, design or manipulation of the immediate environment in as systematic and permanent way as possible
3) so as to increase the effort and risks of crime and reduce the rewards as perceived by a wide range of offenders (Clarke, 1992: 4; See also Clarke and Mayhew, 1980: 1).

Examples of such measures include 'target hardening' approaches such as better locks and bolts; technology such as alarm systems, CCTV, breathalysers, and speed traps; guards, neighbourhood watch and utilising resistant materials to prevent vandalism.

Clarke (1992: 5) stated that the development of situational crime prevention was influenced by Newman (1972) and the concept of defensible space, and by Jeffery (1971) and the concept of crime prevention through environmental design (CPTED). Later on, the theory of situational crime prevention was influenced by Goldstein's (1979) 'problem-oriented policing' (Clarke, 1992: 7).

More recently the rational choice perspective has been incorporated with situational crime prevention. This perspective assumes,

> offenders seek to benefit themselves by their criminal behavior; that this involves the making of decisions and choices, however rudimentary on occasion these choices may be; and that these processes, constrained as they are by time, the offender's cognitive abilities, and by the availability of relevant information, exhibit limited rather than normative rationality (Cornish and Clarke, 1987: 933).

The reader is referred to Clarke and Cornish (1985) and Cornish and Clarke (1986) for further information on this perspective.

Criminality Prevention

Criminality prevention is not a single theory. According to Rock (1994: 151), the term was initiated within the Home Office. It is a term associated with theories about offenders (as opposed to the act of crime) and research based on 'risk factors' which are linked to criminality.[7]

---

[7] Ekblom and Pease (1995: 604) suggest that offender-oriented prevention also "has connections with the evaluation of 'correctional' treatment for offenders in prison or on probation". Thus criminality prevention deals with all theories connected to offenders and potential offenders.

Rutter and Giller (1983) provide a good summary of the risk factors associated with criminality, in particular for recidivist or persistent offenders. Persistent offenders are found to differ from occasional or non-offenders in background, life history, social behaviour and attitude, and their propensity for illegal exploits (West, 1982). Occasional offenders (also referred to as infrequent offenders) are those who commit one or two delinquent acts in their lifetime, typically during adolescence (Canadian Council on Social Development, 1989).

Persistent offenders differ from occasional offenders in many ways. Persistent offenders make up approximately 6% of the proportion of offenders in a cohort, yet account for over 50% of all officially recorded offences (Farrington, 1995: 934; Farrington, 1989a: 7). Persistent offenders start their criminal careers at an earlier age, continue longer, and engage in a wide variety of different types of crime (Farrington, 1995: 934; Waller, 1991: 16). The more commonly known risk factors have been confirmed through longitudinal research which has mostly been done with males. Research has found that the following factors are associated with criminality:

- criminal parents (Farrington, 1995: 940; 1989b: 11; McCord, 1979; West, 1982: 29-30);
- poor parental behaviour (Farrington, 1995: 941; Kolvin et al., 1990; Dishion, 1990: 148-149);
- lower intelligence at school (Farrington, 1995: 940; 1994: 216; Hirschi and Hindlelang, 1977; Wolfgang et al., 1972: 246);
- large family size (Farrington, 1995: 941; Wadsworth, 1979; West, 1982: 29-30; West and Farrington, 1973: 31, 190; 1977: 141, 157);
- economic deprivation or low income (West and Farrington, 1973: 157, 190; Kolvin et al., 1990);[8]
- A measure of 'troublesomeness' derived from observations by teachers and classmates at primary school, (West, 1982: 31, West and Farrington, 1977: 157).

---

[8] Rutter and Giller (1983: 162) caution that the association between social status and crime to a large extent "is a consequence of the problems that may accompany low status, rather than low status per se".

Although these factors could identify a minority of boys at risk of becoming delinquents, they cannot be considered as causes since some boys under these circumstances do not become delinquent and some without these adverse factors do still become delinquent. Therefore, these factors must be interpreted with caution. As West (1982: 119) states,

> The Cambridge study found delinquency most likely to occur where there was an agglomeration of interacting adversities, but no one item of adversity was in itself a necessary or sufficient cause and many delinquents, especially those with only brief conviction records, had no significant background adversities.[9]

One of the difficulties with offender-based theories is deciding what to do about them. For example, in discussing the role of parents in criminality prevention, Wilson (1975: 52) asked, "what agency do we create, what budget do we allocate, that will supply the missing 'parental affection' and restore to the child consistent discipline supported by a stable and loving family?"

Because of the controversies surrounding the consequences of risk factors, West (1982: 131) said that the question of whether research had any practical value to contribute to policy on prevention was less clear than it was a generation ago.

Defining Crime Prevention

Although the term crime prevention (or the prevention of crime) has been used throughout the history of the British Police, and even beforehand, it is a vague concept that has come to mean different things to different people. For some crime prevention might signify a programme such as Neighbourhood Watch, and for others it might signify one of the varying theories of what causes crime and therefore what would prevent it (e.g., getting rid of the causes).

Tuck (1988: 5), for example, stated that in its broadest form, crime prevention can include all formal criminal justice agencies, private

---

[9] See also Shaw and McKay (1969: 106) who argued that delinquency "is not an isolated phenomenon". They show how delinquency is associated with social problems and how these directly affect children.

actions, education and moral training, and social policy; or, in its simplest form, it could mean simply situational crime prevention. For others, crime prevention refers to conventional criminal justice policies. Harvey et al. (1989: 85) claim "there are effectively no boundaries to crime prevention work. Any 'good work' is arguably crime prevention". Similarly, Harris (1992: 67) states "crime prevention is a catch-all concept for a range of disparate activities".

Several attempts have been made at conceptualising crime prevention in some form or another but little success has been achieved in coming up with one definition which is understood by government officials, the public, academics and the police. In fact, even within one particular group, a single definition has not been agreed upon.

Brantingham and Faust (1976) classified crime prevention based on three points of intervention: primary, secondary and tertiary. These points of intervention are based on the public health model of prevention.[10] Primary prevention "identifies conditions of the physical and social environment that provide opportunities for or precipitate criminal acts"; secondary prevention "engages in early identification of potential offenders and seeks to intervene in their lives in such a way that they will never commit criminal violations" (Brantingham and Faust, 1976: 284, 290). As Lavrakas and Bennett (1988: 223) state, "the problem already exists and measures are taken to strengthen the 'resistance' of certain individuals or targets from falling victim". Tertiary prevention deals "with actual offenders and involves intervention in their lives in such a fashion that they will not commit further offences" (Brantingham and Faust, 1976: 290).

Van Dijk and de Waard (1991) crossed Brantingham and Faust's classification by situational, offender-oriented, and victim-oriented schemes to generate a 3 x 3 table.[11] Ekblom (1993: 7) states this classification is "not formal enough or sufficiently theory-based to be fully useful; and it confuses two functions of the victim; as a target of

---

[10] The public health model defines primary prevention as "<attempting> to ensure that problems do not arise"; secondary prevention as "requiring early identification and intervention" with existing problems; and tertiary prevention as "concerned with developing effective programs so that problems do not reoccur" (Wharf, 1989: 43).

[11] The situational, offender-oriented, and victim-oriented components were inspired by Cohen and Felson's (1979) routine-activity theory (van Dijk and de Waard, 1991: 484).

criminal activity, and as a channel for implementing preventive action in the rest of the situation". Van Dijk and de Waard's (1991) classification is not exhaustive since it excludes deterrent criminal justice procedures such as "investigation and prosecution of crimes, sentencing and the execution of conventional punishments" (van Dijk and de Waard, 1991: 483).

Graham (1990) grouped crime prevention into social crime prevention, situational crime prevention and community crime prevention. In 1995, his work was updated (in Graham and Bennett, 1995), and the term social prevention was modified to criminality prevention (Graham and Bennett, 1995: v). Although the importance of the criminal justice system and its agencies in the prevention of crime were acknowledged, they were excluded in the work.

Graham and Bennett (1995: 9) defined criminality prevention as "measures aimed at tackling the dispositions of individuals to offend". The approaches may be targeted either at the general population, at specific groups, or an individual at risk of offending. Criminality prevention tends to focus on six policy areas: urban, family, health, education, youth and employment (Graham and Bennett, 1995).

For situational crime prevention, Graham (1990: 12) stated that it was "primarily concerned with reducing opportunities to offend". As far as community crime prevention goes, Graham and Bennett stated, "there is as yet no clear agreement on a precise definition of community crime prevention" (Graham and Bennett, 1995: 71).

Ekblom's (1993) classification of prevention is based on proximal circumstances. He defines crime prevention as "the intervention in mechanisms that cause criminal events" (Ekblom, 1993: 9). The mechanisms include "anything that by its presence or absence or its particular state affects the probability of a criminal event occurring, whether alone or in conjunction with other such mechanisms. Mechanisms are linked together in chains of cause and effect" (Ekblom, 1993: 9).

Ekblom (1993) distinguishes between mechanisms that are proximal (e.g., those directly linked to the event in question, and generally close in time and space) and those that are distal (e.g., circumstances that are more remote such as an abused childhood, or social conditions). However, it is questionable whether all causal mechanisms have the same degree of effect. It does not appear that his 'paradigm' accounts for this.

One cannot assume that proximal circumstances have more causal effect than distal ones or vice versa.

To date, there has not been one universally accepted conceptualisation of crime prevention. Clarke (1980: 36) stated, "conventional wisdom holds that crime prevention needs to be based on a thorough understanding of the causes of crime". This, however, is difficult when one considers that (a)"<criminology> is not an exact science. It deals largely with probabilities and correlates rather than certainties and causes" (Graham 1990: 11) and (2) that "generally speaking, governmental agencies collect far more information on crime rates and criminals than on their causes" (Reiss, 1986: 26).

Because one of the aims of this research was to explore how crime prevention has come to be defined in policy terms at the national level, the definition of crime prevention was open to whatever the policy makers said and how their respective agency portrayed it in their publications. Definitions from all other sectors of society were ignored.

Outline of the Research

Chapter 2 examines the Home Office as a whole and Chapter 3 examines the specific departments connected to crime prevention policy. Chapter 2 examines the origins and structure of the Home Office, Home Office circulars, Home Office Annual Reports, Conservative party ideology and finally, the national committees organised through the Home Office.

Chapter 3 examines the directorates within the Home Office that have a responsibility for crime prevention policy. Within the Research and Statistics Directorate, the former Research and Planning Unit (now divided into three sections incorporating both statistics and research) and the Programme Development Unit are reviewed. Within the Criminal Policy Directorate, the Crime Prevention Agency (formerly known as the Crime Prevention Unit) and Crime Prevention College (formerly known as the Crime Prevention Centre) are examined. Within the Police Directorate the Police Research Group is examined. Where possible, publications from these departments were analysed to investigate any trends. The subject matter of the publications were, for example, found to be consistent with Conservative party ideology.

Chapter 4 examines the Police Service and various sources that demonstrate how the police tackle crime prevention. After having described how the police service is organised, the effects of the newly structured police authorities on crime prevention is reviewed. Sources such as Her Majesty's Chief Inspectorate of Constabulary Annual Reports, Police Papers from the Audit Commission, Minutes from the Association of Chief Police Officers (ACPO) sub-committee on Crime Prevention, the Operational Policing Review, the Police Probationer Training Foundation Course Manual, and responses on how police officers in Boroughville defined crime prevention are then analysed. All these sources confirmed suggestions that crime prevention for the police is predominantly about situational prevention.

Chapter 5 examines the role that the probation service has played in national crime prevention policy. It examines the work done by the probation service and how it is structured. It then examines how crime prevention fits into the service by examining national probation directives and the work of the Association of Chief Officers of Probation (ACOP) Crime Prevention Committee which has since been replaced by a system of lead officers. A commentary on how the probation service considers it can help to prevent crime, and on their position in national crime prevention policy in 1995 is also included. Analysis of how probation officers defined their crime prevention work confirmed that, at least in Boroughville, it is mostly through one to one supervisions with offenders. As with the police, most probation officers surveyed believed that they performed crime prevention work in their daily work related tasks.

Chapter 6 examines the role of both Crime Concern and NACRO in influencing national crime prevention policy. The purpose of each organisation is reviewed, followed by an analysis of their annual reports and other documents produced by them. A discussion examining their similarities and questioning the competitiveness of their work follows. This chapter shows that although NACRO are actively involved in crime prevention initiatives such as through the Safer Cities Projects, their influence in crime prevention policy making was minimal under the previous Home Secretary.

Chapter 7 examines the work done by the local government association and the previous associations. The growing capacity of both community safety officers and the national network which was formalised in 1996 are also reviewed.

Chapter 8 brings together all the findings of the issues raised in the research for an overall conclusion on how national crime prevention policy is structured, organised and determined in England and Wales.

2 The Home Office as a Whole

Introduction

The purpose of this chapter is to understand what the Home Office does as an organisation vis à vis crime prevention. This chapter examines the Home Office as a whole (as opposed to the individual departments which are examined in the following chapter). It does so by examining the responsibilities and structure of the Home Office, two key inter-ministerial circulars, Home Office Annual Reports, the crime prevention ideology within the Conservative government, and various Home Office committees connected to crime prevention. The committees examined include: the Ministerial Group on Crime Prevention, the Ministerial Group on Juvenile Crime and, the committees leading up to and including the National Crime Prevention Agency. Key issues that arise from this chapter are then highlighted in the conclusion.

This chapter shows that crime prevention policy materialised in the 1980s and its prominence generally increased ever since. As Heal (1992: 257) stated "Those seeking explanation of the change [in society's response to crime] must put the clock back to the early 1980s". Since 1984, the focus of crime prevention from the Home Office shifted from promoting multi-agency initiatives to promoting partnerships between the public and the police and CCTVs. The term 'partnership' also changed in meaning from one where agencies worked together to one where people and businesses help the police.

The significance of individual initiative and of relationships between individuals in affecting crime prevention policy is also highlighted. The political masters have their own ideas on what is needed to prevent crime which affects who they listen to for advice and who they invite to sit on their advisory committees.

One senior Home Office official stated that ideology plays a prominent part in policy. Crime prevention policy was described as being "more political and irrational" than one might suspect (Interview). "It is rarely based on research, but on what is thought by the individual minister to be popular to *The Sun* readers" (3 Interviews). This theme shall not only be addressed in this chapter but throughout the research.

Responsibilities and Structure of the Home Office

The department of the Home Office originated in 1782 (Tarling, 1993: 139). It is headed by the Home Secretary and three Ministers of State. The responsibilities of these three ministers are divided amongst them and change slightly over the years.

During the period of this research, Michael Howard was Home Secretary and David Maclean was responsible for policing matters, partnership and criminal policy, and crime prevention. Unless otherwise specified in this book, references to the Home Secretary means Michael Howard, and references to the Minister or minister for crime prevention means David Maclean. Under the new Labour government, Jack Straw is the Home Secretary and Alun Michael is responsible for crime prevention.
The Home Office overall deals with matters including "the administration of justice; criminal law; the treatment of offenders including probation and the prison service; the police; immigration and nationality; passport policy matters; community relations; certain public safety matters; fire and civil defence services" (Home Office 1995b: 406). In April 1996, the Home Office was restructured based on recommendations of the Senior Management Review. This 'new' overall structure for the Home Office is shown in Figure 2.1.

Within the domain of crime prevention, there are various Home Office sources with which one can firstly determine its 'definition', and secondly, its significance. These sources are analysed below.

Home Office Circulars 8/1984 and 44/1990

Although Home Office circulars are "in theory 'advisory' and the penalties (if any) for not complying with them often left vague, their heavily didactic tone is frequently indistinguishable from an instruction to conform to what they recommend" (Weatheritt, 1986: 103; Thomas, 1990: 584). Two circulars that have greatly affected crime prevention in England and Wales are Home Office circulars 8/1984 and 44/1990. The effects of the two circulars on crime prevention practice were also addressed in Jones, Newburn and Smith (1994: 97-99) and will become evident as this research evolves.

The Home Office as a Whole 29

Figure 2.1 Overall Home Office Structure, April 1996

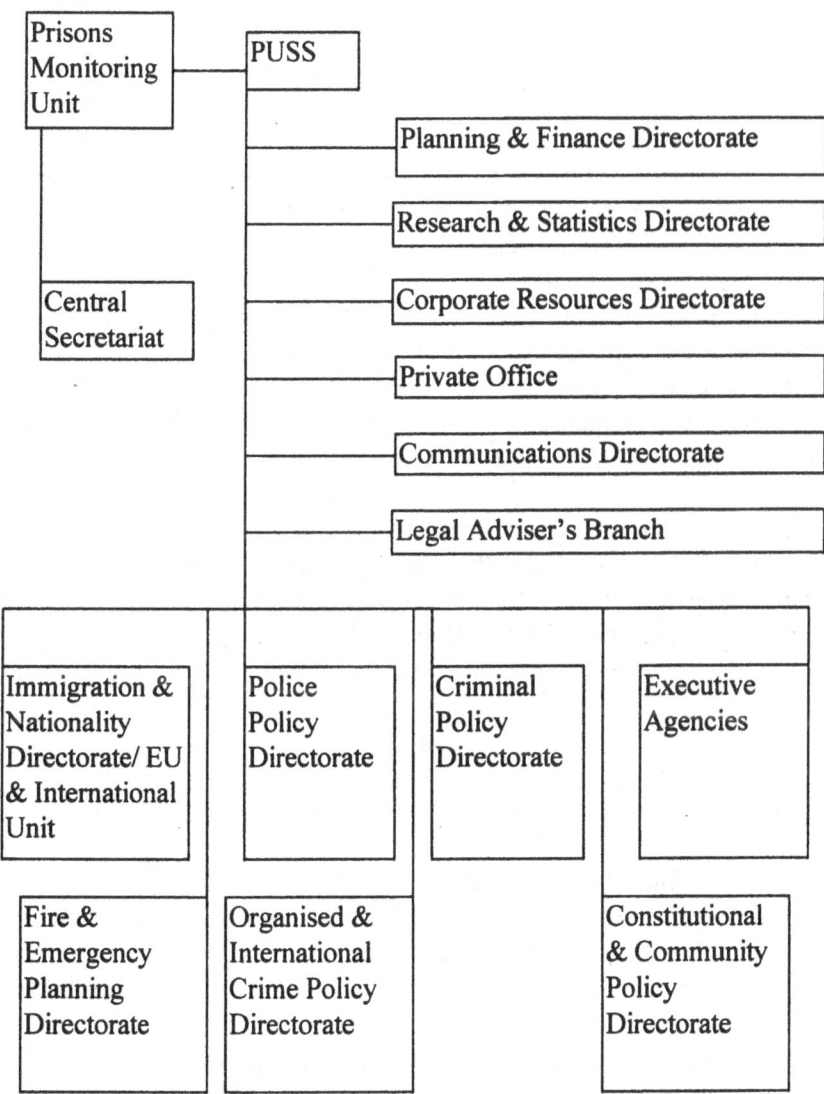

Source: Home Office (1995k: 2).

Home Office Circular 8/1984 has been described as "the most comprehensive statement of British policy on crime prevention" (Waller 1989: 25). The circular was signed by officials of the Home Office, the Departments of Education and Science, Environment, Health and Social Security, and the Welsh Office (Home Office, 1984a). The circular is acclaimed for recognising that some of the factors affecting crime lie outside the control of the police and it enjoins local authorities and other agencies to work together to develop strategies for crime prevention.

The circular also pointed to the necessity of monitoring and evaluating local multi-agency crime prevention activities, so that positive results could be applied in other similar areas.

Home Office Circular 44/1990 was also jointly produced by the members of the Ministerial Group on Crime Prevention. This circular invites "recipients to reconsider with others the contribution which their organisations are making to crime prevention" (Home Office, 1990b: 2). The circular also announces the setting up a working group for the purpose of producing the Morgan Report. The Morgan Report will be discussed later in this chapter.

The circular advocates the publication *Partnership in Crime Prevention* which confesses that "it does not explore specifically the separate question of how to prevent young people, in particular, from embarking on criminal careers" (Home Office, 1990c: 4). The focus of this publication is on the offence rather than the offender and is very general in nature.

Home Office Annual Reports

The Home Office Annual Reports were examined in order to determine how crime prevention policy developed over the years. In examining these documents the following issues were highlighted: the prominence of crime prevention over the years; the role of the Home Office in crime prevention; the role of the police in crime prevention; the role of probation in crime prevention; the role of the local authority in crime prevention; the notion of multi-agency crime prevention co-operation; and finally, the type of crime prevention advocated.

The Prominence of Crime Prevention Over the Years

The Home Office Annual Reports (or Government Expenditure Plans) made no mention of crime prevention or criminality prevention until 1985. The 1985 annual report is the first report since Home Office circular 8/1984 was released. In 1985 crime prevention was cited as an objective of the criminal justice system, a theme continued in future reports, and in relation to the police. Between 1986 and 1988 inclusively, crime prevention was only mentioned in relation to the goals and objectives of the Home Office as a whole.

The prominence given to crime prevention increased with the mentioning of the Safer Cities Initiative and Crime Concern in both 1989 and 1990. Mention was also made that the majority of publicity funding went to crime prevention.

As of 1991, the format of the reports changed so that an entire publication was dedicated to the Home Office and Charity Commission. As a consequence, more prominence was allocated to crime prevention. The one exception to this was in the 1993 annual report where only one article entitled "Car Crime Prevention Year" appeared (Home Office, 1993a: 26). Why crime prevention was overlooked in this annual report is unknown. It cannot be explained by a change of persons in office, since both the Home Secretary and Head of the Crime Prevention Unit (who would have had some say into what was written in the chapter) were the same as in 1992.

As of 1994, the prominence of crime prevention in the annual reports greatly increased. Two to three pages were dedicated to 'Crime Prevention' under the section of the Police Department in 1994 and 1995. In 1996 and 1997, an entire chapter was devoted to crime prevention! One interviewee stated that this was done to reflect the fact that the Crime Prevention Unit moved out of the police department of the Home Office and became the Crime Prevention Agency within the Criminal Policy Directorate (to be discussed in more detail in the next chapter).

The Role Of The Home Office In Crime Prevention

The role of the Home Office in crime prevention is an issue that is touched upon for the first time in the 1991 annual report. In 1996 the chapter devoted to crime prevention started by stating,

> The Home Office promotes and supports crime prevention in a number of ways, through funding, advice, encouragement, dissemination of good practice and research. ... The Home Office also contributes by identifying the best ways of reducing crime and encouraging their adoption through dissemination to the police and to the many organisations and individuals who work in partnership with them (Home Office, 1996a: 41).

The 1997 report goes on to mention "The parts of the Home Office principally concerned in crime prevention are the Crime Prevention Agency and within the agency, the Crime Prevention College" (Home Office, 1997a: 46). These parts of the Home Office are reviewed in the next chapter.

The Role Of The Police In Crime Prevention

The role of the police is also stressed in the annual reports. The 1985 annual report insinuates that crime prevention is associated with the police as the following statement illustrates:

> The recent increases in police and civilian strengths have enabled the police to devote more effort to foot patrols, the promotion of more effective crime prevention measures and close links with local communities while maintaining their ability to respond to calls for assistance from members of the public (Home Office, 1985a: 141).

As of 1991 crime prevention was always one of the issues discussed under the heading of the police department. In 1994 the idea that the police are key players in crime prevention was for the first time strongly suggested, as the following excerpt illustrates:

> The prevention of crime is one of the fundamental roles of the police ... A great many police officers are involved in crime prevention. For example, many home beat officers offer guidance on domestic security (Home Office, 1994a: 26).

The latter sentence could suggest that the police role in crime prevention is to give advice - a topic which is developed in the research. In 1995, the notion that the police are key players in crime prevention and that their role is to provide advice is repeated.

In 1995, the establishment of the Programme Development Unit was discussed under the heading of the Police Department when in reality it is located within the Research and Statistics Department. Therefore, this statement is misleading in that, on reading the annual report, one is not aware that this initiative is not within the domain of the police department.

The Role Of The Probation Service In Crime Prevention

In 1991, one of the main responsibilities of the probation service included "to contribute to wider work in the community to prevent crime and support victims" (Home Office, 1991a: 35) thus emphasising their role in crime prevention. No mention had been made in previous reports about probation's role in crime prevention, but then the format of the reports were different (i.e., less was said about the Home Office overall).

The responsibility of the probation service is restated in 1992, 1993 and 1994. It is not stated in 1995, 1996 or 1997. As will become clearer throughout the research, 1995 appears to have been a 'bad' year for the probation service in terms of recognising its role in crime prevention or criminality prevention.

The Role Of The Local Authority In Crime Prevention

The role of local authorities in crime prevention is addressed in both the 1996 and 1997 reports. In 1996, the report states, "Local authorities have an important role in helping to create safer communities. Some local authorities are producing their own crime prevention strategies in line with Government guidance; others have appointed crime prevention co-ordinators ..." (Home Office, 1996a: 45). The government guidance referred to probably includes Home Office Circulars 8/1984 and 44/1990, and the Morgan Report (even though the recommendations of this report were rejected by Michael Howard). The Morgan Report is discussed in more detail later in this chapter.

The 1997 report states "Local government also has a key role in crime prevention, through its support for the police and its responsibility for delivering other local services" (Home Office, 1997a).

It is suspected that these statements (in particular with reference to the important role of the local authority) reflect more the thinking of civil servants rather than of the Home Secretary. After all, these chapters were written by civil servants and not the Home Secretary or Minister. The fact that these chapters were not written by the Home Secretary would also explain why a paragraph was written about the need to strengthen families in 1996, and "to reduce the risk factors in early childhood that are now known to increase the likelihood of offending" (Home Office, 1996a: 49).

The Notion Of Multi-Agency Crime Prevention Co-operation

In 1991, the role of various agencies in crime prevention is acknowledged for the first time. The timing of this acknowledgement in the reports coincides with Home Office circular 44/1990. The 1991 report states that "The Home Office, other Government Departments, statutory and voluntary agencies and the public all have an important part to play in preventing crime" (Home Office, 1991a: 22).

In 1994, the term 'partnership' became a key phrase to refer to other agencies or bodies helping the police. The following paragraph illustrates the point:

> Partnership with members of the public and other agencies is central to the police crime prevention effort. There are a number of aspects to partnership, including individual members of the public giving their time in support of the police, local partnerships between the statutory agencies, and partnership between the public and private sector (Home Office, 1994a: 26).

This theme is repeated in the 1995 report in an article entitled 'Partnership against Crime' where initiatives such as Special Constables, Neighbourhood Constables, Neighbourhood Watch and Street Watch are mentioned. The need for the 'partnership' approach is repeated again in this report as illustrated in the following excerpt: "The Government's comprehensive strategy to tackle crime places particular emphasis on the need for a partnership between the police, communities and business in fighting crime ..." (Home Office, 1995a: 14). The notion of working in partnership is repeated in 1996 and throughout the chapter on crime prevention in 1997.

The Type Of Crime Prevention Advocated

The need for various approaches to crime prevention is recognised for the first time in the 1991 annual report. The 1991 report states,

There are many ways to prevent crime. It may be by reducing the opportunities with locks, bars, security lights, alarm systems and surveillance cameras but it can also be done by community regeneration, good parenting and a challenging education programme (Home Office, 1991a: 22).

This theme is repeated in 1992:

Fundamental to these policies is the aim of preventing people committing offences in the first place. Much can be achieved through work with families, in schools, by the youth service and by voluntary organisations. Experience so far suggests that the most successful action is taken locally, directed at local problems and supported by local statutory and voluntary agencies, working in partnership with each other and with local people (Home Office, 1992a: 11).

At the end of the 'crime prevention' sub-heading in 1992 the following was stated, "Much of this work <at the Crime Prevention Unit>... is concerned with reducing the opportunities for crime. Home Office policies are also directed at encouraging people not to offend, ..."(Home Office, 1992a: 19).

The 1996 annual report recognised that,

The susceptibility of some individuals to crime needs to be addressed by strengthening families, to reduce the risk factors in early childhood that are now known to increase the likelihood of offending, and by enhancing educational and recreational opportunities to motivate those most at risk (Home Office, 1996a: 49).

The 1996 report also mentions that only 15 out of 201 successful partnership bids in the first round of the Single Regeneration Budget Challenge fund were connected to initiatives aimed at diverting young people from crime. This illustrates that prevention aimed at diverting young people from crime or criminality prevention is not supported in the same way as other initiatives such as Safer Cities, Publicity Campaigns and now CCTVs.

Crime Prevention Ideology In The Home Office

Within the Home Office there is a political ideology which the Home

Secretary and Minister hold, and there are also the ideologies of individual civil servants. The role of civil servants is to act as advisors and information disseminators. Unfortunately this role is often dependent on the beliefs and individual character of the minister in power. This dependent relationship with the minister has in the past resulted in a few high level civil servants either retiring from the civil service or changing positions.

Within the civil service departments there are opposing views on how to tackle crime prevention. The main divide is between prevention based on offenders and that based on offences, or as those interviewed in the Home Office have said, between situational crime prevention and criminality prevention.

The ideology of the politicians is determined by analysing Conservative party manifestos and speeches, and publications put out by the Public Relations Branch of the Home Office. For the publications put out by the Public Relations Branch, only those distributed under Michael Howard are reviewed.

Political Ideology

The ideology of the former Home Secretary and Minister are thought to be based on political motives (in order to keep their individual positions and to re-elect their party) as opposed to being based on less populist research findings. The Home Secretary's views are most widely known to the general public and appeal to many individuals who think the criminal justice system is unreliable, and who know little about evaluative research or who do not work within the system (Interview). The philosophy of the Conservative party is revealed through their manifestos. The Conservatives were in power from 1979 until May 1997 and have therefore been able to make many changes related to criminality and criminal justice.

In 1979 the emphasis of the Conservative government was on "fighting crime" (Conservative Central Office, 1979: 19; 1987: 55) through detection and deterrence, "Surer detection means surer deterrence" (Conservative Central Office, 1979: 19). No mention is made of trying to divert those at risk of becoming involved in crime. The focus is on those already involved in criminal behaviour.

The 1983 manifesto stated that in their "war against crime" they have increased the number of police, they will build more courtrooms, they have provided the courts with tougher sentencing powers, and they will continue to build more prisons (Conservative Central Office, 1983: 33-34).

In 1987, when Douglas Hurd was Home Secretary, "the fight against crime and violence" was still important (Conservative Central Office, 1987: 55). In this manifesto, the government stated "The origins of crime lie deep in society: in families where parents do not support or control their children; in schools where discipline is poor, and in the wider world where violence is glamorised and traditional values are under attack" (Conservative Central Office, 1987: 55). This statement could be perceived as promising for those that tend towards offender-oriented crime prevention initiatives. It is the only such statement in the Conservative manifestos between 1979 and 1997. The fact that this paragraph was inserted in the manifesto could possibly be because Douglas Hurd was known to be one of the 'soft' Conservatives (Interview). However, the next paragraph reiterated the 'party line' and emphasised the police, tough legal sanctions, building more prisons, and detection:

> Government alone cannot tackle such deep-rooted problems easily or quickly. But Government must give a lead: by backing, not attacking the police; by providing a tough legal framework for sentencing; by building the prisons in which to place those who pose a threat to society - and by keeping out of prison those who do not; and by encouraging local communities to prevent crime and to help the police detect it (Conservative Central Office, 1987: 55).

In the 1992, the Conservative manifesto states, "we must tackle crime at its roots. Two-thirds of the offences dealt with by our courts are committed by only seven per cent of those convicted. Most of these constant offenders started down the path of crime while still of school age" (Conservative Central Office, 1992: 22). The manifesto does not, however, expand on this statement by possibly suggesting ways that potential offenders could be diverted from crime. Instead the focus is on attempting to stop further crimes once the individual has already been involved in the Criminal Justice System process. The emphasis of the party remains on the police, tougher sentencing and prisons.

Michael Howard had a reputation of being tough on crime. In fact in his first speech at the Conservative Party Conference, he stated, "I am going to take action. Tough action" (Conservative Central Office, 1993: 2). In his speech to the Conservative party in 1995 he stated six more prisons shall be built (Conservative Central Office, 1995: 12).

In piecing together the bits of information from various interviews, the author infers that the reputation of the last Conservative politicians was one that was tough on crime, pro-imprisonment, and very much wanting to give more power to the police including more autonomy from local government.

Both politicians were against giving local authorities more power, at least as far as crime and crime prevention go. According to one interviewee, one of the politicians stated that there was no need to endorse the Morgan Report because its recommendations were administered without legislation and funding from central government. The fact that most local authorities are not run by the Conservatives could also be a factor. Why would one party give another party more power?

The Home Secretary and Minister also promoted citizen involvement in crime prevention such as through Neighbourhood Watch, Street Watch and volunteering for the special constabulary. In 1995, Street-Watch was considered to be Howard's little project. By 1997, CCTV took over. One Home Office official stated that "Partnerships, Walking with Purpose, and CCTV were very popular with the ministers, especially CCTV". This popularity is without regard to what research shows.

When one article entitled "Cameras fail to beat street crime" (Ward, 1995: 4) was published, Michael Howard sent a quick reply (Howard, 1996: 47). Although Howard acknowledged "that there is a shortage of good quality research on CCTV" he felt that,

> CCTV is overwhelmingly popular. People want it in their town because it makes them feel safer, reduces the fear of crime and lets them use and enjoy their high streets again. The money we are putting into CCTV is partly a response to this public support, but it is also an indication of our confidence that it is worth it. ... When the evaluations of the schemes helped by the Home Office become available I am sure they will show the same.

After seeing this article, one Home Office official stated "Howard will clearly not take kindly to any 'bad news' about CCTV". A discussion about research within the Home Office will be addressed in more detail in the following chapter.

In reading through the documents, the author noted that although the word 'partnership' continued to be used while Michael Howard and David Maclean held their positions, the meaning appeared to have shifted from previous periods, from one which encouraged agencies to work together (for example in Home Office Circulars 8/84 and 44/90, and the Morgan Report) to one of individuals helping the police. The role of statutory agencies playing a part in crime prevention has very much been curtailed. This argument was confirmed in an interview early in 1996.

For example, the aims and role of the National Crime Prevention Agency includes, "encouraging the spread of partnerships such as Neighbourhood Watch, Street Watch, etc." (Home Office, 1995l); in *Your Practical Guide to Crime Prevention* (Home Office, 1994i: 44) it is stated, "You can take action by getting together with other people and working in partnership with the police to reduce crime in your area"; In *Partners Against Crime* (Home Office, 1994e: 3) it is stated,

> Many people will know about Neighbourhood Watch - or Home Watch, as it is called in some areas. Street Watch and Neighbourhood Constables are pioneering new ideas. These three partnerships, together with regular police patrolling, build up a spectrum of strong anti-crime protection for your neighbourhood.

David Maclean stated, "What they are experiencing is the force of unbeatable partnership of the best police force in the world working in a new partnership with the great British people" (Maclean, 1995a: 8); Howard's speech to the Conservative Party Conference in 1993 stated, "First, preventing crime. We can't leave it all to the Police. We must build a new partnership between the Police and the public" (Conservative Central Office, 1993: 4).

Under the former Home Secretary's and Minister's reign it would have been very unlikely that either Home Office Circular 8/84 or 44/90 would have been produced. Thus, within the history of the Conservative party (at least since 1979), one observes that the individuals appointed as Home Secretary and minister responsible for crime prevention can have much influence on crime prevention policy. In 1984 when Home Office Circular 8/84 was circulated, Douglas Hurd was Minister of State for the Home Office; in 1990 when Home Office Circular 44/1990 was circulated, John Patten was Minister of State for the Home Office which is also when the Morgan Report was commissioned; in 1990, the Home Office White Paper, stated,

> punishment in the community is likely to be better for the victim, the public, and the offender, than a custodial sentence. Imprisonment makes it more difficult for offenders to compensate their victims, and allows them to evade their responsibilities (Home Office, 1990a: 3).

In 1991 when the Programme Development Unit was set up John Patten was still Minister of State for the Home Office. These events could be regarded as demonstrating the 'soft' side of the Conservative party, as opposed to the hard, 'get tough on crime' approach of Michael Howard and David Maclean.

Publications from the Home Office Public Relations Branch

In September 1994, the Home Office Public Relations Branch circulated three booklets dealing with crime prevention: *Your Practical Guide to Crime Prevention* (Home Office, 1994i), *Partners Against Crime* (Home Office, 1994e), and *Guidelines for Street Watch Schemes* (Home Office, 1994b). Since 1979 they have also been publishing a periodical called *Crime Prevention News*.

In *Your Practical Guide to Crime Prevention* (Home Office, 1994i) the message is to lock up, get alarms, avoid isolated routes, stay in well lit areas, and to keep valuables out of sight or locked up. The prevention in this booklet is directed to the potential victim, not the offender. It does not for example tell you how to spend time with your children, nor does it indicate the risk of various crimes occurring. No mention is made of the odds of repeat victimisation.

The publication *Partners Against Crime* (Home Office, 1994e:2) states, "Securing your home is the first step against crime. Marking your property could be a second step. Joining a Neighbourhood Watch is adding a further layer of security".

The third publication *Guidelines for Street Watch Schemes* (Home Office, 1994b: 1) follows the trend that the public are the eyes and ears for the police: "The purpose of Street Watch is to assist the local police by being alert and observant when out and about in your neighbourhood - using your eyes and ears to help the police and your community". The pamphlet then sets out how Street Watch works.

These publications give the impression that the way to prevent crime is to use better locks, carry or install alarms, and to join Neighbourhood Watch or Street Watch schemes. The fact that research has not confirmed Neighbourhood Watch's potential for crime prevention (e.g., see Bennett, 1990) is not mentioned. This is an example where government policy can be said to proceed without regard for current research findings. It almost seems that if it does not work, the government does not want to know about it.

Crime Prevention News is targeted to those working in a practical sense in crime prevention or community safety. It is not targeted to the public in general as are the other publications above. It could be argued that it is just a promotional gimmick to try to win the hearts of its readers and to illustrate the Minister's support for crime prevention. However, it does inform the reader in a general sense about both national and local initiatives in crime prevention. They also describe what different groups and localities are doing, who was presented with awards, and about high profile individuals who have visited certain initiatives or handed out awards.

National Crime Prevention Committees Organised Through the Home Office

The Ministerial Group on Crime Prevention

The Ministerial Group On Crime Prevention started work in 1986 as a result of a seminar chaired by the Prime Minister at 10 Downing Street.[12] Its members included junior ministers and officials from 12 Government departments (Home Office, 1996a: 41). It was chaired by the crime prevention Minister.

The Ministerial Group on Crime Prevention "has been tasked with overseeing and co-ordinating crime prevention action at the national level and helping to ensure that Government departments pursue crime prevention objectives in the implementation of their own policies" (Home Office, 1993c; 1993f: 3; Wardle, 1993: 3).

Their main role was advisory but they acted more as an audit body on what was going on in crime prevention. One Home Office official stated in 1995 that they were "at a loss for an agenda because nobody had any money".

The Ministerial Group on Crime Prevention has not met since July 1994. According to one interviewee, the Ministerial Group on Crime Prevention was still on the list of committees as of July 1997. According to

---

[12] This seminar was held in January 1986 and was attended by the Home Secretary, the Secretaries of State for Scotland and for Wales and other ministries (Bottoms, 1990: 2; and Standing Conference on Crime Prevention, 1991: 38).

two interviewees the reason that the Group had not met was due to conflict amongst the various Conservative Ministers on what route crime prevention should follow. The newly elected Labour government still have to make a decision on the future of this group.

According to one interview with a Home Office official, instead of the Conservative government trying to revive the Ministerial Group on Crime Prevention, a Ministerial Group on Juvenile Crime was created.

The Ministerial Group on Juvenile Crime

The Ministerial Group on Juvenile Crime held its first meeting in January 1996. According to a Home Office official, the formation of this Group was a "pure example of Public Relations". The Group aims "to strengthen measures to intervene effectively with those children who are most at risk of offending" (Home Office, 1996c). The Group commissioned a consultation document called *Preventing Children Offending* (Home Office, 1997c). This paper recognised that "it would be better if young people did not offend in the first place" (Home Office 1997c: 3). It recommended the creation of Child Crime Teams to identify children at risk of offending and to refer these children and their parents if appropriate to suitable schemes that may reduce the likelihood of offending.

Membership of the Ministerial Group of Juvenile Crime included: Department for Education and Employment, Department of Health, Welsh Office, Department of the Environment, Law Officers' Department, Department of National Heritage, Scottish Office, Lord Chancellors' Department, Northern Ireland Office, Department for Social Security and of course the Home Office itself (Home Office, 1996c: 2).

According to one senior Home Office official this group has not existed since the new government came into power. Instead a Ministerial Group on Youth Justice was created by the Labour Government. It met for the first time in July 1997 (Home Office, 1997d). As one interviewee stated "with a new government the frameworks may stay the same but the names may change".

The Lead Up To The National Crime Prevention Agency

In 1965, the Cornish Committee on the Prevention and Detection of Crime (Home Office, 1965) recommended that a central advisory body be created. This body would have co-ordinating and declarative functions. This body, the Home Office Standing Committee on Crime Prevention was formed in 1967 and met twice a year (Weatheritt, 1986: 47).

In 1985 it was replaced by the Home Office Standing Conference on Crime Prevention which was replaced by the National Board for Crime Prevention in 1993. This body was then replaced by the National Crime Prevention Agency in 1995. The National Crime Prevention Agency is not to be confused with the Crime Prevention Agency. The first is a national committee similar to its predecessors. The second is a unit within the Home Office Criminal Policy Directorate.

This section will review the Home Office Standing Conference on Crime Prevention and the publication of the influential Morgan Report, the National Board for Crime Prevention and The National Crime Prevention Agency.

The Home Office Standing Conference On Crime Prevention The most significant document commissioned by this committee is known as the Morgan Report. As will be evident later in the research, it greatly influenced many local authorities and services such as Probation. This document has had a major affect on crime prevention policy. Now that the Labour government is in power, the Morgan report shall be endorsed. The Labour manifesto stated,

> We will place a new responsibility on local authorities to develop statutory partnerships to help prevent crime. Local councils will then be required to set targets for the reduction of crime and disorder in their area (Labour Party, 1997: 23).

The Morgan report examined the delivery of multi-agency crime prevention and provided nineteen recommendations based on its findings (Standing Conference on Crime Prevention, 1991: 6-7). Five of these recommendations that are relevant to this particular research are:

1) In the longer term local authorities, working in conjunction with the police, should have clear statutory responsibility for the development and stimulation of community safety and crime prevention programmes, and for progressing at a local level a multi-agency approach to community safety (recommendation v)
2) the development of a community safety strategy should take place at a level equivalent to the highest tier of local government (recommendation vi)

3) in the shorter term, the importance of local authorities playing their full part in multi-agency partnerships should be recognised and encouraged through the publication of a 'Code of Practice' (recommendation viii)
4) local multi-agency partnerships should give particular attention to the issue of young people and crime in preparing a portfolio of crime prevention activities (recommendation ix)
5) wherever possible a co-ordinator with administrative support should be appointed in each unitary or county level local authority. He or she should be at a level to command the confidence and support of senior management in local government and other agencies and have direct access to chief executives and the local police Commander (recommendation xiii) (Standing Conference on Crime Prevention, 1991: 6).

The working group also stated,

that the social aspects of crime prevention, which seek to reduce those influences which lead to offending behaviour, and the fear of crime, need to receive attention at least equal to the situational aspects of crime prevention, in which efforts are made to reduce opportunities and 'harden' potential targets for crime (Standing Conference on Crime Prevention, 1991: 13).

Many organisations have followed the recommendations made by the Morgan Report and have supported it even though Michael Howard had rejected the Report's recommendations.

The National Board for Crime Prevention The National Board for Crime Prevention was formed in 1993 and replaced the Standing Conference on Crime Prevention. The last time that the Standing Conference on Crime Prevention met was in 1990 (Interview). To quote one Home Office official "they ran out of steam and were re-constituted in a different form which was much smaller". In 1995, the National Board for Crime Prevention was replaced by the National Crime Prevention Agency (to be discussed below).

The National Board for Crime Prevention was made up of individuals who were personally asked by the Minister to join (Interviews). The minister at the time was Michael Jack who was replaced by Charles Wardle before the Board's first meeting. Charles Wardle was later replaced by David Maclean. Membership to the Board expired in May 1995 at which point, memberships were to be renewed and/or others invited.

The Home Office as a Whole   45

Because the Minister himself decided who should join the group some persons/organisations had been purposely omitted. Some people thought that Crime Concern, the Association of British Insurers and local authority associations should be represented. However, the Minister allegedly chose not to invite them to sit on the Board for personal or political reasons.

Since the membership expired for this Board, no further meeting were held. On 4 September 1995, it was leaked through an article in *The Times* (Ford, 1995: 6) that a National Crime Prevention Agency would be formed.

The National Crime Prevention Agency The National Crime Prevention Agency held its first meeting in January 1996. Members of this agency (in January 1996) included:

Jack Acton	Director, Home Office Crime Prevention Centre
Peter Batchelor	Chair, Vehicle Crime Prevention Group; formally Executive Director Sales and Marketing, Vauxhall Motors
Ken Pease	Professor of Criminology, University of Huddersfield
David Quarmby	Chair, Retail Action Group for Crime Prevention; Joint Managing Director, J Sainsbury Plc.
Nick Ross	Broadcaster and Journalist
John Stevens	Chief Constable, Northumbria Police; Chair, ACPO Crime Prevention Sub-Committee.
Anthony Tisdale	Councillor and Chair, Surrey Police Authority
Nigel Whiskin	Chief Executive, Crime Concern.

Their membership was for a two year term which started on 30 August 1995. A Director for the Crime Prevention Agency was not announced until September 1996. The director of this committee also heads the Crime Prevention Agency in the Criminal Policy Directorate of the Home Office. This board is chaired by the minister responsible for crime prevention which at its inception was David Maclean. One interviewee stated that it was basically like the National Board for Crime Prevention except with fewer members.

In setting up this committee, David Maclean wanted the director of this committee to head the Crime Prevention Agency at the Home Office. Prior to the director's appointment, it had been rumoured that David Maclean wanted the position to be filled by a high ranking police officer. Although the post of director was open to competition, it was known (by the author and others in the field since December 1995) that Richard Childs, an Assistant Chief Constable, was very likely to get the position. One Home Office official stated that the appointment of Richard Childs was "heavily Maclean's preference". In September 1996 it was announced that Richard Childs was the Director of the Crime Prevention Agency.

The detailed remit of the Agency is:

The Board is appointed by the Home Secretary and will:
- act as the managing body for the Home Office Crime Prevention Unit and the Home Office Crime Prevention Centre.
- co-ordinate the activities of all the key players in crime prevention by:
    - ensuring their representation on the Board
    - developing stronger links between each other; and
    - maintaining links with other organisations
- Initiate, develop and promote innovative ideas to help prevent crime and reduce the fear of crime by:
    - following up new research
    - identifying good practice; and
    - ensuring guidance and advice is available
- Work with the police, local authorities, business, industry, the voluntary sector, the community and others to target specific types of crime or crime situations by:
    - setting up groups to examine specific issues (such as the retail group and the vehicle crime group)
    - supporting other groups with similar aims
- Ensure that all sections of the community have the opportunity to be involved in crime prevention by:
    - encouraging the spread of partnerships such as Neighbourhood Watch, Street Watch etc.,
    - promoting youth involvement; and
    - publicising effective community activity
- Offer advice to Ministers on the major strategic and policy implications relating to these issues and on other effective crime prevention strategies (Home Office, 1995d).

In examining the remit critically, one might ask whether the agency is appropriate to act as the managing body for the Home Office Crime Prevention Unit and the Home Office Crime Prevention Centre. This is because the Board is politically driven in three ways:

1) the minister responsible for crime prevention chairs it. This fact is understandable since he is appointed by the Home Secretary who is responsible for the Home Office. Being part of, or the chair to a 'managing body' related to a Home Office Unit is therefore not unreasonable, but it does make it political;

2) those sitting on the Agency are personally selected by the minister responsible for crime prevention. The Minister chooses *persons* that he wants on the Agency. He does not ask the key organisations to nominate one ore more persons that he can select to sit on the Agency to represent their organisation. Thus the people on the Board do not necessarily represent the organisation's views in which they work. An example is with Anthony Tisdale, the councillor and chair, Surrey Police Authority. The Association of County Councils were not approached asking for a nominee to sit on the Board. Anthony Tisdale, therefore, does not technically represent the interests of all local authorities or of all police authorities. The fact that he even is a member of the Board could possibly be due to pressures that local government be represented nationally. It could be seen as a token gesture. One interviewee confirmed that the associations had not been approached because the Minister did not want a Labour party representative. The Minister allegedly searched for a Conservative elected member who would be suitable. Anthony Tisdale was that individual.

3) David Maclean essentially selected the director for the Crime Prevention Agency within the Home Office. This is connected to the point above. By having the Minister personally select the agency's members and the director of the Crime Prevention Agency, the Minister maintains control of the crime prevention policy-making process.

One interview held after the author had written this section confirmed these criticisms. The interviewee stated that due to the fact that the Agency was chaired by the Minister and that the members were personally selected by him, it was "not a management board in the true sense". As the individual stated "How can an advisory board be independent when it is chaired by the Minister?" According to this individual there is an "inner group within the Agency that runs it" thus suggesting that some people are on the group for 'display' purposes.

One consequence of the managing body for the Crime Prevention Unit and Crime Prevention Centre being 'political' is that the work carried out by these organisations could consequently become more 'politically' focused. Any assurance that these organisations, although being part of the Home Office, are independent in thinking could therefore be questioned. They could be seen as pawns of the Home Secretary and thus fall under the adjectives "political and irrational" or as "following populist 'The Sun' ideology", as one senior Home Office official suggested.

The remit is also interesting in that it states it will co-ordinate the activities of all key players in crime prevention by ensuring their representation on the Board. What is interesting with this is the organisations that are not represented on the Board. The message implied is that those agencies not represented are not key players in crime prevention. Examples include the Probation Service, Youth Service organisations such as the National Youth Agency, NACRO, organisations connected to family stability, education, health (in particular drug and alcohol abuse), Victim Support or other associations that have connections to what are considered to be factors leading to crime. The fact that the National Youth Agency and the Probation Service were not invited to sit on the Agency was, according to one interviewee, based solely on the organisation (as opposed to personal differences).

Based on the Agency's membership, the definition of crime prevention is very narrow. Three of the eight members are connected to the police, two specific types of crime are targeted (vehicle crime and retail crime). Knowing about other crimes of concern to communities, for example through the National Association of Victim Support Schemes, is therefore not readily available.

Another criticism about the Agency's remit is the point that the Agency and Home Secretary will work with the police, local authorities, business, industry, the voluntary sector, the community and others to target specific types of crime. This point can be taken with a grain of salt when for example local authorities (technically speaking), the voluntary sector, the community and others are not represented on the Agency. How can they effectively work together when some agencies are not represented on the Agency? Maybe the Agency's idea of working together consists of providing funding for CCTV's in local areas. After all, the Agency will determine how to distribute £15 million worth of funding for CCTVs (Maclean, 1995b).

Finally, the remit states that in working with these agencies, they will target specific types of crime or crime situations by 'setting up groups to examine specific issues (such as retail and vehicle crime) and by supporting other groups with *similar* aims'. By only dealing with groups with similar aims, this statement clashes with an earlier one that said the Agency shall try to initiate, develop and promote innovative ideas to help prevent crime and reduce the fear of crime. If innovative ideas were genuinely to be promoted, agencies would not be excluded from the Agency, and their manner in working with other organisations would not be so restricted. If the Agency is to only deal with retail crime and vehicle crime then its title should reflect this. Are Neighbourhood Watch and Street Watch only to 'keep an eye out' for these two crimes? Will the Crime Prevention Agency and Crime Prevention College only deal with retail and vehicle crime?

According to one interview, the Agency's first task was to distribute the £15 million pounds allocated to CCTVs under the auspices of the Challenge Competition (see Home Office, 1995l). One of the negative side effects of this competition and the one previously held in 1995 (for a total of £5 million) was according to one interviewee, that money that might normally have gone to other forms of prevention (in its broadest sense) was drawn in for CCTVs, thus limiting the approaches or techniques utilised to prevent crime. The reason for this is that one of the conditions of the competition was that 'outside' money also be utilised. The *Bidding Guidance* (Home Office, 1995c: 5) states,

> one of the main criteria for success for all bids will be the ability to attract private sector or other funding. The more additional money that can be raised, the more likely an award will be made, taking into account the size and nature of the bid and the local partners involved.

When one combines this information with Table 2.1 on Crime Prevention Expenditure then one comes to realise that at least for the next three years crime prevention will essentially mean CCTV schemes (since over 78% of the crime prevention budget will go towards this approach).[13] One could also go as far as saying that the role of the National Crime Prevention Agency therefore is to manage this £15 million for CCTV

---

[13] This was assuming the Conservative party remained in power. It still remains to be seen whether or not the Labour government will continue with the CCTV funding. Some interviewees believed the third phase would be abolished.

schemes which will be aimed at preventing/reducing retail and vehicle crime.

The role of the agency to "initiate, develop and promote innovative ideas to help prevent crime and reduce the fear of crime by: following up new research; identifying good practice; and ensuring guidance and advice is available" will obviously be minimal since only £200,000 is allocated to crime prevention research. This sum is equivalent to 1% of total crime prevention expenditures for each of 1996-97, 1997-98 and 1998-99.

One condition of the CCTV Challenge Competition is that the schemes be locally evaluated. No money has been put aside for the Home Office to evaluate the programme as a whole. One Home Office official is, as a consequence, worried about the quality of research evaluations that will be conducted. This official stated, "There are views that when you are

Table 2.1 Crime Prevention Expenditure (£m)

Year	Publicity	Safer Cities	CPC	CPU	Crime Concern	Crime Prevention Research	CCTV	Total
1990-91	6.2	6.6	0.6	0.9	0.5	0.2	0.0	15.0
1991-92	5.9	7.2	0.7	1.0	0.5	0.3	0.0	15.6
1992-93	6.1	7.7	0.8	0.7	0.5	0.6	0.0	16.4
1993-94	5.0	6.0	0.9	0.8	0.5	0.1	0.0	13.3
1994-95	8.2	2.1	0.8	0.9	0.6	0.2	5.0	17.8
1995-96	5.6	1.0	0.8	0.9	0.5	0.2	0.0	9.0
1996-97	1.5	0.3	0.8	0.9	0.5	0.2	15.0	19.2
1997-98	1.5	0.3	0.8	0.9	0.5	0.2	15.0	19.2
1998-99	1.4	0.3	0.8	0.9	0.5	0.2	15.0	19.1

Source: Home Office Crime Prevention Unit. 1996.

evaluating things for guiding national policy, you are shaping the decision making of loads and loads of future schemes across the country so it is quite important to invest a bit more time and a bit more sophistication'.

The author suspects that the role of the National Crime Prevention Agency to "encourage the spread of partnerships, such as Neighbourhood Watch, Street Watch, etc.; promoting youth involvement; and publicising effective community activity" will come from the budget set aside for publicity. This amount of £1.5 million for 1996-97 is equivalent to 7.8% of the total budget. Thus more is spent on publicity about issues whose effect on crime is questionable (for example, see Bennett, 1990 for an evaluation of Neighbourhood Watch) than on determining through research what does work and what ingredients actually make a particular programme successful.

One final point to make is that according to David Maclean, the National Crime Prevention Agency will be based at Easingwold College, North Yorkshire along with the Home Office Crime Prevention Centre and the Emergency Planning College of the Home Office (Maclean, 1995b). To say that a committee that only meets when it needs to is based in a particular location does not make much sense. The people sitting on the Agency all work elsewhere.

According to one interview, the political masters wanted people to believe that the agency is an agency in the true sense, but in reality it is a "National Board for Crime Prevention Phase II" and "it is not an agency in the true sense". The fact that the word 'agency' was used for this committee and for the unit within the Criminal Policy Directorate was a subject that was disputed between senior Home Office Officials and the Minister.

Based on this analysis one can conclude with confidence that very little will actually be spent on what has been termed by some as "criminality prevention" within the Home Office. To envision that both "situational prevention" and "criminality prevention" will have equal roles within the Crime Prevention Agency in the Criminal Policy Directorate of the Home Office is therefore 'wishful thinking'.

One can also conclude that these committees are very political, in that politicians make the final decisions. To believe that these committees are completely independent of politics is idealistic.

One member thought that this committee was 'dead' now that a new government was in power. At the end of June 1997, an informal meeting took place to decide on the board's future. Alun Michael decided not to make any decisions. The author noted that the membership for the board members expires in August 1997. This begs the conclusion that Alun Michael will just let this 'agency' expire. When questioning another member about the national crime prevention agency in 1997, s/he stated "it isn't an agency, it isn't a board, it isn't anything".

General Discussion

It seems that these agencies, boards or conferences are always changing. From the outside, one wonders what they actually do. The people on these committees tend to remain the same except that there are fewer of them. Apart from the Minister himself, most of the members tend to sit on the same crime prevention committees. That any new information is brought into the Agency is questionable. The only differences are that the minister chairs this committee and that with the National Crime Prevention Agency, funds will be 'donated' towards CCTV schemes.

If anything, the national agencies, boards or committees identified above are a good idea in that they have allowed the Minister to meet those influential in the field in one go (and vice versa). Information provided to him through other sources could also be confirmed in these meetings. One interviewee stated that the agency would act as a think tank for the Minister.

Each time that a new committee is announced, no mention is made by the Home Office or current government that a similar body had already existed and has been dissolved. For example, in a press release about the new Agency it is stated "The fight against crime will be sharpened and focused by a new agency unveiled by Home Secretary Michael Howard today" (Home Office, 1995l) or an article by David Maclean stated "We have announced the establishment of a Crime Prevention Agency to build on this partnership approach to cracking crime" (Maclean, 1995b: 26). Michael Howard's Speech at the Conservative Party Conference stated, "That is why I can announce today the creation of a brand new Crime Prevention Agency" (Conservative Central Office, 1995: 8).

The only 'public' hints that this Agency replaced the National Board for Crime Prevention were in (1) the article which appeared in *The Times* (Ford, 1995: 6) which stated, "The agency will largely take over the work of the existing National Board for Crime Prevention..." and (2) in the Appendices of the 1996 Home Office Annual Report, where it stated, "The National Crime Prevention Agency Board has replaced the National Board for Crime Prevention" (Home Office, 1996a: 177).

The purpose of the newly created committees differ only marginally to its predecessor. The newly formed Agency differs from the National Board for Crime Prevention in that they are to act as managing bodies for the Crime Prevention Centre and Crime Prevention Unit. Their purpose of "building on the partnership approach to cracking crime" is not dissimilar to the previous committees that it replaced.

One factor that does come out of the creation of this new Agency is that it illustrates how both the ACPO sub-committee on crime prevention and Crime Concern have come a long way in trying to influence/be involved in national crime prevention policy. The ACPO sub-committee on crime prevention and Crime Concern had not initially been invited to sit on the National Board for Crime Prevention but now they were involved in setting up the new agency.

Furthermore, both the ACPO sub committee on Crime Prevention and Crime Concern have proved themselves as prominent crime prevention players in the eyes of the Ministers. The Minister himself stated, "The Association of Chief Police Officers will be represented on the agency's board along with the Home Office and Crime Concern - the three main players in crime prevention" (Maclean, 1995b: 26). This will likely benefit them in their day to day activities, making them ever more influential. Unfortunately those groups not represented will likely suffer as a consequence. Their ideas shall not be as clearly heard.

One question raised was whether, in some cases, some groups were not represented due to personal differences between the Minister and the key person of the non-represented group. One interviewee confirmed that at least one individual had not been asked to sit on the Agency due to personal differences. If agencies were appointed rather than people, this could be avoided by nominating another person from the organisation. However, as stated earlier, this is not so simple for this Agency since the Minister preferred to have a non-Labour supporter.

One point that should be made is that the membership to the National Board for Crime Prevention was made by another Minister, who was described as one of the 'soft' Conservatives. The period of membership ended in May 1995, and so when Maclean got his position he could choose the people he personally wanted. This Agency is Maclean's making.

Under the new Labour government, the author is certain that when the current memberships expire, a 'new' body will be formed with a change of membership and probably a change of name. At the time of updating the information for this book, there was a debate on whether the new labour government would set up a National Crime Prevention Council.

Finally, one should acknowledge that the advisory/influencing capacity of these committees on policy making is dependent on the individual character of the minister. Some ministers already know what they want to do, regardless of the opinions of the 'advisory committees'. Others are much more open or dependent on the advice of others.

Conclusion

The Home Office has a major role to play in crime prevention policy since it actually determines the policy in conjunction with the Home Secretary and Minister. Its views are advocated through Home Office circulars, publicity campaigns, and publications. The difficulty with these instruments of information is knowing what is actually the consequence of a politician's own preferences (maybe for political reasons) and what is a result of informed advice derived from quality research.

This chapter examined the Home Office as a whole (as opposed to the individual departments within it) by analysing two circulars, the Home Office Annual Reports, and various crime prevention related committees that it chairs or has chaired. It also examined the ideology of the Conservative Government, Michael Howard and David Maclean.

The findings of this chapter, have been categorised into six issues discussed below.

1) The first issue has to do with the increase in prominence given to crime prevention over the years. The genesis of crime prevention occurred in the early 1980's with the setting up of the Crime Prevention Unit and with Home Office circular 8/1984. The first reference to crime prevention in the Home Office Annual Reports was in 1985, possibly as a result of Home Office Circular 8/1984.

By 1990, the significance of crime prevention had become stronger with the creation of the Inter-Ministerial Group on Crime Prevention in 1986, the launching of Safer Cities and Crime Concern, the production of the Morgan Report, and the release of Home Office circular 44/1990.

Since 1991, we have so far witnessed:

- Phase II of Safer Cities,
- The replacement of the Home Office Standing Conference on Crime Prevention with the National Board for Crime Prevention, which was subsequently replaced by the National Crime Prevention Agency,

- More money being invested in crime prevention (if one includes the budget to be spent on CCTV) than ever before! and,
- The promotion of the prevention of crime to the extent that in the 1996 and 1997 Home Office Annual Reviews it generated a chapter of its own.

2) The second issue has to do with the type of crime prevention advocated by the Home Office. When one examines the documentation that has come out of the Home Office over the years, one notes that crime prevention has shifted from one of promoting multi-agency initiatives to promoting partnerships between the public and the police, and installing CCTVs. Throughout the years very little attention has been given to preventing young people from embarking on criminal careers in comparison to opportunity reduction strategies such as Neighbourhood Watch, informing the public to lock up, and to walk in well lit areas.

In Home Office circulars 8/1984 and 44/1990, the notion of agencies working together to prevent crime was encouraged. The term multi-agency seems, however, to have been replaced by politicians with the word 'partnership'. This word originally had an expanded definition in that it not only encouraged agencies to work together, but also suggested that people at a local level should help in preventing crime. This is evidenced in the 1992 Home Office Annual Report when it stated "...by local statutory and voluntary agencies, working in partnership with each other and with local people" (Home Office, 1992a: 11).

With Michael Howard and David Maclean, the definition of partnership seems to have been narrowed down to individuals helping the police. For example, both the 1995 Home Office Annual Reports, and the publicity from the Home Office Public Relations Branch stress the importance of the public working with the police. No mention is made of 'agencies'. The 1995 annual report states, "... the need for a partnership between the police, communities and business in fighting crime" (Home Office, 1995a: 14) and the publications put out by the Public Relations Branch talk about a partnership with the police through Neighbourhood Watch, Street Watch and Neighbourhood Constable schemes.

The fact that the politicians seem to prefer the word 'partnership' does not mean that the word multi-agency is no longer used within the Home Office. Mike Sutton, for example, prepared a report entitled 'Implementing crime prevention schemes in a multi-agency setting' (Sutton, 1996). Now that the Labour government have been elected the word 'partnership' will likely take on a new context in the Crime and Disorder Bill.

The allocation of crime prevention funding also provides some indication of what types of crime prevention the Home Office advocates. The Morgan Report in 1991 admits that it does not explore how to prevent young people from embarking on criminal careers. The Crime Prevention Expenditure Table (Table 2.1) suggests that the Home Office plans to spend 78% of its crime prevention budget on CCTVs over the next three years (1996-97 until 1998-99 inclusively). Thus at the end of the Conservative reign, crime prevention could be equated with CCTV. Everything else received little funding in comparison.

3) The third issue is that until 1996 crime prevention fell under the domain of the Police Department in the Home Office Annual Reports. This, the author suggests, gives an impression that crime prevention is the responsibility of the police. Very little is said in other chapters about crime prevention. In discussing all crime prevention matters under the police section is in at least one case misleading. The example is when the Programme Development Unit was addressed under the police section when in fact it forms a part of the Research and Statistics Directorate.

In 1996, crime prevention was assigned a chapter of its own. This gives the impression that crime prevention is not the responsibility of any one particular department or agency. According to one senior Home Office official, this was a reflection of the fact that the Crime Prevention Unit was moved to the Criminal Policy Directorate. The Crime Prevention Unit and Criminal Policy Department will be discussed in the following chapter.

4) The fourth issue is the effect of individuals on policy making. The effect that certain people have on policy making is very much a question of personalities. Just because someone holds a certain position, it does not mean they have much influence. What matters is how that person interacts or gets along with others.

Thus, in 1995 the head of the Crime Prevention Unit got along well with the Chief Executive of Crime Concern who got along well with the chairman to the ACPO sub-committee on crime prevention. The later two got along well with David Maclean. Having these four individuals who all got along well with one another, not only led to non-police being represented on the sub-committee on crime prevention, but it also resulted in the three individuals being heavily consulted in setting up the National

Crime Prevention Agency. Within the Agency, there was according to one interviewee an inner-group that ran things. Decisions tended to be made informally out of meetings, and once a certain position was agreed it was put forward to the remainder of the committee.

The values and personality of the Minister and Home Secretary are also very important in policy making. Some ministers heavily rely on the advice of civil servants (whose own beliefs would come through in their advice), whereas others pretty much know which direction they want to follow. Thus, it is very unlikely that Home Office Circulars 8/84 and 44/90 would have been circulated under the reign of Howard and Maclean. Now that the Labour government is in power it is possible that CCTV or Street Watch will play a much less apparent role. The role of the Probation Service, for example, might once again be thought of as valuable in the prevention of crime, and local authorities will be given statutory responsibilities for community safety in conjunction with the police.

One interviewee within the Crime Prevention College (to be analysed in the next chapter), said that their policy role came about by sitting on various committees. If one considers that the National Crime Prevention Agency is an avenue for affecting crime prevention policy, then one can conclude that the ministers themselves determine the direction of policy making by selecting the committee's members. One interviewee stated that as ministers change so does the interest in crime prevention. This once again supports the views that individuals affect crime prevention policy and that policy making is political.

5) The fifth issue is connected to the role of ideology in policy making. To speak of one ideology would be somewhat unfair since ideology can be a personal issue. This however, does not mean that generalisations cannot be made. For example, although the Conservative party portrays a certain ideology, the individuals who take up posts such as those of the Home Secretary and his ministers have views of their own. The former Home Secretary and Minister responsible for crime prevention were very much to the right of the party, and not favourable to schemes aimed at diverting young people from becoming criminal in the first place. Their approach was one of individual responsibility and 'get tough on crime'. They were very much in favour of solutions based around prisons and police. This pro-police theme will be discussed again in the research.

Crime prevention policy has not necessarily been based on research findings, but rather on personal convictions. This is evidenced by the fact that Safer Cities Phase I was launched before the findings of the Five Towns Initiative; that Safer Cities Phase II was launched before the findings of Phase I; that the Crime Prevention Centre was moved to North Yorkshire before the recommendations of an inquiry into police training were known; and that £15 million was spent on CCTV's without conclusive research results. The politicians decided that the time was now and just went ahead without empirical information.

6) The author argues that the Home Office only supports certain forms of crime prevention and it does not necessarily encourage the best ways (proven through research) of reducing crime. Crime prevention for the Home Office appears to flow in trends that come and go.

For example, if one examines Table 2.1, one notices that from 1990-91 until 1993-94, Safer Cities appears to have been in favour. Publicity also appears to have been favoured until 1996-97 when its funding was severely decreased. The current fashion appears to be CCTVs. From 1996-97 until at least 1998-99, over 78% of the crime prevention budget went towards CCTV! In this area, the research is not clear-cut. It is not just the CCTV camera which prevents crime but rather where it is located and how it is utilised. For example, Brown (1995) illustrated how some cameras are placed in locations where their view is obscured by such things as trees or mailboxes, thus limiting their potential to reduce crime.

One also notices that the smallest portion of funding goes towards crime prevention research! With so little money spent on research, how can policy makers be certain that funds are being put to the best use? It is the personal conviction of Howard that has led to the push for CCTVs, not research findings. When so much of the crime prevention budget is to be used on one single initiative, one would ideally like there to be some concrete evaluations on whether this is the right area to focus upon.

Thus, the Home Office does not necessarily promote and support 'the best ways of reducing crime'. Good intentions prevailed over determining efficiency and effectiveness.

3 The Home Office Departments

Introduction

Although national crime prevention policy officially comes from the Home Office overall (as opposed to an individual department), the potential role of the individual departments in influencing policy through advice, the dissemination of information, and through funding research is equally as important.

The purpose of this chapter is to obtain a clearer image of how crime prevention within the Home Office works. Within the field, one often hears that the Home Office funded a particular programme, but when asked out of whose budget it came, few practitioners can answer. The Home Office does not act as a whole - it is the individual departments along with one of the three ministers that makes a decision. For example, in dealing with an individual immigration or nationality issue, it is very unlikely that the Police Research Group, or the Crime Prevention Agency are involved. Knowing who funds what provides insight into how a particular problem is viewed and, who has a professional interest in the subject matter.

This chapter examines those Home Office departments and the particular units connected to crime prevention policy and research by having crime/criminality prevention as a part of their remit. Three directorates were examined along with the various components responsible for crime prevention. They included 1) the Research and Statistics Directorate, 2) the Criminal Policy Directorate, and 3) the Police Directorate.

Where appropriate, publications of the particular department in question were analysed. One of the aims of this analysis was to determine whether disseminated information is consistent with the views of the Home Office as a whole and with political ideology, as discussed in the previous chapter. The conclusion reviews the key issues raised in this chapter.

The Research and Statistics Directorate

In 1989, the Statistics Departments merged with the Research and Planning Unit to form the Research and Statistics Directorate with Chris Nuttall as Director.[14] Research within this directorate is determined each year through a research programme. Croft (1978: 1) stated,

> In the Home Office the planning of the research programme is determined by the requirements of those who make policy. Constitutionally, Ministers make policy; they act on the advice of public servants and of various committees of independent persons established for the purpose.

The research programme is established by first consulting with the various policy divisions on their needs. Negotiations occur regarding their priorities and a draft programme is created. This draft then goes to the ministers and in the end a 'thinner final programme is produced'.

This section examines the Research and Statistics units and Programme Development Unit since they are the two units most directly involved in national crime prevention policy making in the Research and Statistics Directorate.

The Research and Statistics Units

In total, the three Research and Statistics Units have approximately 62 researchers and statisticians (Home Office, 1996f: iii). As with the former Research and Planning Unit, these three units comprise one of the main sources of funding for criminological research (Tarling, 1993: 139; Interview). The research produced by these units is intended to be policy-oriented.

In order to determine the research interests of the Research and Statistics units or in reality the interests of the Research and Planning Unit as it were, between 1979 and 1997, the publications instigated by the former Unit were analysed. The publications analysed included,

---

14 For information on how the Research (and Planning) Unit came into existence, the reader is referred to Lodge (1974); Clarke and Cornish (1983); Tuck (1987; 1989). For information on Chris Nuttall's appointment as Director of the Department, the reader is referred to Rock (1994).

The Home Office Departments 61

1) Studies in the Causes of Delinquency and the Treatment of Offenders
2) Home Office Research Studies
3) Home Office Research Bulletin
4) Programme of Research
5) Research and Planning Unit Papers
6) Research Findings
7) Home Office Occasional Papers.

Method Used to Classify Documents The author's classification of documents was based on the categorisation system of the *Home Office Research Bulletin* issue 19 and 29.

Since this subject index accounted for over half of the issues published and almost half of the articles, this categorisation was maintained, except for the fact that the category 'Drugs' was eliminated and the category 'Criminal Process From Prosecution to Sentencing' was renamed 'Courts and Sentencing'. The 'Drugs' classification was eliminated since so few articles fell under this category (11 articles out of 395). The category 'Courts and Sentencing' was named as such since in Issue 29, the subject index differed slightly.

By using the title 'Courts and Sentencing' the author was able to classify articles more easily. This category included all topics related to courts and sentencing, but excluded research about the criminal justice system process which was not specifically about courts or sentencing.

All articles in the remaining categories were similarly categorised. The articles that had been under 'Criminal Process from Prosecution to Sentencing' were either classified under Courts and Sentencing or another category. Those articles that had fallen under Drugs where classified in another category or 'Other'. The classification used for this research was therefore based on the following headings:

1) Crime Prevention
2) Police
3) Courts and Sentencing
4) Prisons
5) Probation and Non-Custodial Disposals
6) Patterns of Crime and Criminal Behaviour
7) Race, Immigration and Voluntary Services; and
8) Other.

By using this categorisation the author was able to classify all articles. The classification of *Home Office Research Bulletin* articles solely classified under probation, crime prevention, police, prisons, race relations or other were maintained. In all other instances the following system was utilised:

1) If the publication could be categorised by title alone, then the publication fell under that category (e.g., the publication entitled 'The attitudes of ethnic minorities' was classified under Race and Immigration; 'The Parish Special Constable Scheme' was classified under policing). Very few publications were classified in this manner.
2) If the title did not clearly indicate under which heading the publication should fall, or if by the title the publication could fall into either of two categories, then the author read the Foreword to the publication. For example, the publication entitled 'Young people, victimisation and the police' could be classified under Police or Patterns of Crime and Criminal Behaviour. The author read the Foreword, which indicated that the publication should be classified under Patterns of Crime and Criminal Behaviour: "The BCS <British Crime Survey> sample provides the first national picture in England and Wales of the extent and nature of young people's victimisation away from the home. In addition, the 12 to 15 year olds were also asked about their experiences with the police and about their attitudes towards a number of crime-related topics" (Tarling, 1995: i).
3) If the Foreword did not provide enough clarity then the publication itself was examined. In most cases, this method was utilised. For example, it was only after examining the actual publication that the author determined that the publication entitled 'Study of the Juvenile Liaison Scheme in West Ham 1961-1965' should fall under Crime Prevention (the scheme was aimed at both offenders and non-offenders).

When analysing the *Programme of Research* only the research under the categories of 'current' or 'in progress' were analysed. This is because research under the heading of 'under consideration' or 'in planning' had more potential of being dropped before they even started. Thinking of something was not considered to be as solid as actually doing it. The number of research projects and total external funding were examined in order to see whether the two indicators were consistent.

Unfortunately, research conducted in house by, for example, the Research and Planning Unit, or the Crime Prevention Unit, did not identify the total cost of the project. For this reason the author decided to separate research done internally by national government departments (of which the majority are done by the Research and Planning Unit) from research done externally (e.g., academic institutions).

One problem with analysing the cost of research was the fact that all research programmes between 1975 and 1983-84 inclusively did not identify research costs. As a consequence, the research from 1984-85 until 1994-95 inclusively were examined. No further *Research Programmes* were published after this date. According to one Home Office spokesperson, the series will not be continued. However, *Research Bulletin* issue 38 has a section on current research but this section was not analysed in this research.

Within the *Research Programmes* the same research was cited in more than one publication in some cases. For example, the research "Implementation and use of the combination order" in 1993-94 (Home Office, 1994g: 24) is also cited in 1994-95 (Home Office, 1994h: 27).

The problem with repeat projects was determining whether further funding had been provided to these programmes or whether the same research had just been accounted for twice. In the example cited above, one observes that in both instances the title of the research is the same, the research body is the same, the RPU contact is identical, the start date is identical, as is the description. In this case and others similar to it, only the first excerpt is counted. Repeat projects were identified by utilising the search key on the computer to find all identical words or phrases. The projects were examined more carefully by comparing the various publications before deciding whether they were the same project or a second or third phase with additional funding.

Before eliminating repeat projects, 640 projects were identified as being in progress during the period 1984-85 until 1994-95 inclusively. After eliminating repeated projects, there were a total of 451 projects (i.e., 189 projects were repeated).

In some cases the project was considered to be the same, but the total cost changed slightly in the different publications. For example research on the "The Youth Court" is identical in terms of title, research body, RPU contact, start date and description in both 1993-94 and 1994-95 (see Home Office, 1994g: 23; 1994h: 16). The cost of the project, however, is slightly different in the 2 publications. In 1993-94 the cost is cited as £162,000, however, in 1994-95, the cost is cited as £160,000. In cases where this occurred the most recent cost is used in calculating total funding for each category of research. All decisions made in analysing the publications from the Research and Planning Unit are available in Koch (1996).

Analysis of Publications Two series of publications began prior to 1980: the *Studies in the Causes of Delinquency and the Treatment of Offenders* and the *Home Office Research Studies*. Combined, these publications suggest that from 1955 until 1979, the priority of research was in the field of probation. Of the thirteen publications within the *Studies in the Causes of Delinquency and the Treatment of Offenders*, (1955-1969), seven dealt with probation/borstal training. Eighteen of the fifty-eight (31%) *Home Office and Research Study* papers prior to 1979 had to do with probation and non-custodial disposals. Lodge (1974: 20) stated that the justification for the establishment of the Research (and Planning) Unit "was the need to study the treatment of offenders, and it is this sequence of events that largely explains why for so long the Research Unit's own work, ... was confined to that subject".

An analysis of the Home Office Research Studies, the Home Office Research Bulletins, the Home Office Research Programme,[15] the Research and Planning Unit Papers, and the Home Office Occasional Papers,[16] between 1980 and 1995 shows that the largest proportion of research was dedicated to Policing issues (15.9%), followed by Courts and Sentencing (15.7%), and Prisons ([15.5%] see Table 3.1). The category 'Probation and Non-Custodial Disposals' received the least attention between 1980 and 1995 (9.1%). The number of reports relating to 'Patterns of Crime and Criminal Behaviour' is partly explained by results of the British Crime Survey which began in 1984. This category accounted for 12% of all documents analysed. These results suggest that research from the Home Office Research and Planning Unit is consistent with Conservative party ideology. Issues connected to Courts & Sentencing were always one of the top three priorities in all of the publications analysed in Table 3.1.

It is interesting to note that crime prevention and policing related publications within the *Home Office Research Studies* emerged for the first time in 1976. Until then the focus was mostly on probation and non-

---

[15] This series only consists of data from 1984/85 until 1994/95.

[16] These papers only consist of data from 1984.

custodial disposals. After 1979 the emphasis on the treatment of offenders greatly subsided. Between 1980 and June 1997, probation and non-

Table 3.1 Type of RPU series by subject matter for the period 1980-July 1997 (number and column percentages)

	HOR Series	HOR Bullet	HOR Prog.[a]	RPU Papers	HO Occas. Papers[b]	HOR Finding[c]	Total
Probation	11	30	40	7	6	3	97
	10.2%	9%	8.9%	7.5%	21.4%	5.8%	9.1%
Police	22	49	76	17	-	5	169
	20.4%	14.7%	16.9%	18.3%	-	9.6%	15.9%
Patterns of Crime	16	46	48	5	1	12	128
	14.8%	13.8%	10.6%	5.4%	3.6%	23.1%	12%
Courts & Sentencing	15	51	63	24	5	9	167
	13.9%	15.3%	14%	14%	17.9%	17.3%	15.7%
Prisons	11	49	79	8	12	6	165
	10.2%	14.7%	17.5%	8.6%	42.3%	11.5%	15.5%
Crime Prevention	14	42	56	4	-	5	121
	13%	12.6%	12.4%	12.4%	-	9.6%	11.4%
Race, I. & V.S.,	8	22	55	11	1	3	100
	7.4%	6.6%	12.2%	11.8%	3.6%	5.8%	9.4%
Other	11	44	34	17	3	9	118
	10.2%	13.2%	7.5%	18.3%	10.7%	17.3%	11.1%
Total	108	333	451	93	28	52	1065
	100%	100%	100%	100%	100%	100%	100%

a: This series only consists of data from 1984-85 until 1994/95.
b: This series only consists of data as of 1984.
c: This series only consists of data as of 1992.

custodial disposals received much less emphasis with only ten additional publications. It is at this time that policing and crime prevention matters received more attention in the series.

Table 3.2 illustrates the total funding provided externally for research based on the *Programme of Research.*. These findings are consistent with the number of projects per subject-matter as discussed above. The majority of funding went for prison research (£2,934,100+ spent between 1984-85 and 1994-95), followed by police research (£1,943,671+ spent between 1984-85 and 1994-95). Research done on crime prevention and courts and sentencing also received much funding (£1,824,621 and £1,707,532+ respectively).

In conclusion, most research is done on issues related to courts and sentencing, prisons, and policing. The total expenditure of external research is similar. All this is in line with the Conservative government philosophy. It will be interesting to see whether differences will occur under a Labour government. Will research on prisons decrease and will research on probation and other non-custodial issues receive more prominence? It is not

Table 3.2 Cost of External Current Research Projects in the Research Programme Publications by Subject Matter (1984/5-1994/5)

Subject Matter	Cost of External Research
Prisons [a]	£2,934,100
Police [b]	£1,943,671
Crime Prevention	£1,824,621
Courts & Sentencing [a]	£1,707,5322
Probation & Non-Custodial Disposals	£1,322,800
Race, Immigration & Voluntary Services	£1,189,616
Patterns of Crime & Criminal Behaviour	£821,710
Other	£1,583,463

a: excludes one project where no cost was stated.
b: excludes three projects where no cost was stated.

an unknown fact that the Conservative government attempted to provide an image of being very much pro-police and pro-prisons.

The Programme Development Unit

The Programme Development Unit (PDU) was the one apparent anomaly to Michael Howard's and David Maclean's ideology. The PDU was established in 1991 within the Research and Statistics Department, under the leadership of Kenneth Baker and John Patten (the Home Secretary and Home Office Minister at the time). Prior to this there was a smaller scale development fund within the Research and Planning Unit. The push for the creation of this Unit came from Chris Nuttall, the Director of the Research and Statistics Department. He was influenced by the development programme within the Solicitor General's Office in Canada. He had worked there before taking up his current position as head of the Research and Statistics Department.

Rock (1994) recounted how the Programme Development Unit was established. He described how the focus of the Unit was influenced by David Farrington's findings from the Cambridge Study in Delinquent Development (Rock 1994: 150). Not only was David Farrington invited to a luncheon with the Home Secretary at the time, but one of his articles "circulated about the Home Office at just that time" (Rock, 1994: 150). Three important predictors of offending were identified as (1) economic deprivation; (2) school failure; and (3) poor parental child-rearing behaviour (Rock, 1994).

Rock (1994: 151) also recounted how criminality prevention "was a break from the 'secondary' crime prevention of target hardening and opportunity reduction". The outlook of the PDU coincided with Conservative party thinking at the time.

> When they <Home Office ministers> talked about criminality prevention, they centred it in an evolving Conservative politics of the family that emphasised the importance of responsibility, discipline, and right conduct. They described the family as a moral institution whose members should not only become more strongly self-reliant and self-regulating, but also more obviously accountable for one another's delicts (Rock, 1994: 151-152).

The Programme Development Unit is responsible for the development, funding, monitoring and evaluation of innovative local projects, particularly in relation to crime and criminal justice issues (Tarling, 1993: 139). The remit of the PDU is "not to do research" but rather to "fund local innovative practical project work and have it evaluated ... within the broad area of crime and criminality. Criminality here is the magic word for what are the roots of crime, and what is the genesis of criminal behaviour, rather than what leads to specific crimes" (Interview). One document states,

> Its purpose is to encourage and develop innovative and experimental local projects in the areas of crime and criminal justice, to ensure that projects are properly monitored and independently evaluated; to disseminate the results and to help with the replication of similar programmes where appropriate (Home Office, 1995i).

The objective of the Unit is "to take forward the development of policy and practice through experimental initiatives from which general lessons can be drawn" (Home Office, 1995i). In 1992 the focus was on:

> domestic violence which in 1992 was an important priority of the criminal department of the Home Office and on reducing criminality which at the time was a preoccupation of ministers. They had moved from crime prevention which at the time here was essentially primary crime prevention or street lighting, car crime campaigns and so on, to secondary crime prevention and very much what are the roots of crime, why do children become criminal, why do people not become criminal, what are the causal factors and so on (Interview).

These first round projects are now finished and the evaluation reports will begin to be published in a series "a bit like the Police Research Group Series" (Interview). The reports will not be based on scientific research but rather on process and development of the projects. The reports are intended to be practical rather than academic. These reports will primarily inform policy development in the Home Office. They will also inform civil servants, local authorities and practitioners such as teachers and social workers. When addressing teachers and social workers, the reports will attempt to alert them to the role of how their work is interrelated with crime and at risk behaviour .

Of the 12 projects which were agreed upon in the first round six dealt with domestic violence and six dealt with young people. The programmes were aimed at people as opposed to physical targets.

Although the Unit had agreed to fund 12 projects in the first phase, only eight projects completed the three-year pilot phase. Two projects declined external evaluation and were not funded; one failed to agree objectives, and one project was wound up because of serious management difficulties.

The manner in which these projects were decided upon is similar to the method utilised to choose the second round of projects. In deciding which projects got funded, there were various stages. Bids were invited from a wide range of public and voluntary organisations. The first stage of selection involved a review and preliminary selection by the Programme Development Unit (which consists of a staff of 3 people, including 1 support staff). This generated a list of 40-50 projects for further consideration.

A review group was set up which consisted of representatives from relevant Home Office departments like the Crime Prevention Unit, the Criminal Department, and the Research and Statistics Department, together with people from other Departments such as Health or Education. The review group produced a short list of about 12-15 recommended projects for ministers to consider and agree a final short list.

The second phase of projects dealt solely with reducing criminality while working "with children and adolescents in the contexts of family, school and community" (Home Office, 1995i). Examples of projects provided for guidance purposes included:

- parenting projects directed at improving positive and consistent parenting;
- pre-school work with children and families;
- working with children identified as having problems at school (school failure, truanting, violence);
- helping families to deal with at-risk children;
- co-ordinating community involvement with young people;
- drawing together inter-agency approaches to children at risk (Home Office, 1995i).

Six projects were agreed upon in the second round of funding. However, the decision of the ministers to fund the second round of projects was only made after considerable hesitation. There was a clear perception, both inside the Home Office and among outside organisations, that the level of political interest in and commitment to the Programme Development Unit was low. The future of the Unit appeared to be in the balance for some months. However, perhaps because the Programme Development Unit was the only Unit within the Home Office involved in actively developing programmes for young people at risk of offending, ministers finally decided to maintain the Unit's programme. Again the perception both inside and outside the Department was that ministers were more concerned with high profile programmes such as CCTV.

After much contention, the six projects to receive funding were finally agreed upon by the end of 1995. Funding for these projects was formally announced in the summer of 1996, a decision that had been at least ten months overdue. During these ten months (if not longer) the future of the Unit was very much questioned. Although it was anticipated that £2.3 million would be provided over the next three years (Home Office, 1995i), their current budget is just under 2.1 million.

The projects funded by the PDU are very much focused on criminality/social prevention, as opposed to focusing on the offence. The focus of the unit's research was not consistent with Howard's and Maclean's thinking. This must have placed the Unit under considerable strain.

As a consequence, the PDU has to date kept a very low profile. One senior Home Official noted that it is very difficult for the Unit to have a high profile when they have relatively little funding in comparison to that available elsewhere for development work. This places them in an uncomfortable position since without a larger budget they are not taken very seriously. Since their current budget is so small they run the risk of being scrapped when cost-cutting procedures occur.

The bright side is that there is now a new government who are thought to be more research oriented. At a conference in Nottingham in June 1996, Alun Michael stated "we need more research" (Crime Concern, 1996b: 9) But as one civil servant stated "whether this means more money is still to be determined". The Unit anticipates that the evaluations of the first round of projects will be available by the end of 1997.

In discussing who the unit deals with most within the Home Office, one senior Home Office official stated in 1995 that it relates primarily to C1 division (Criminal Policy Division) who are responsible for this sort of discussion on the roots of crime and how it affects broader government policy which goes beyond the Home Office to the Department of Education and Department of Health. In 1997, this same official stated that now that the Home Office had be restructured, they deal primarily with the Juvenile Offenders Unit in the Criminal Policy Directorate. Although the Juvenile

Offenders Unit is not reviewed, the Crime Prevention Agency within the Criminal Policy Directorate is reviewed below.

The Criminal Policy Directorate

The Criminal Policy Directorate is responsible for various matters including "policy on reducing crime and criminality" (Home Office, 1995b: 407). Their role is to advise other government departments and Government on research and policy work. "We give advice to ministers on policy avenues based on research and hope that our suggestions are reflected in for example, social policy, sentencing policy and, prison policy" (Interview).

The criminal policy department does not carry out research. If research is needed to support policy decisions, it is done through the Research and Statistics units or the Programme Development Unit. The department is involved in the decision making process of both units in terms of what research should be carried out throughout the year. Once a short list is made, the final decision is up to the minister.

> Typically, what happens is the RPU <now Research and Statistics units> and PDU put up suggestions on research that they think should be done. They then discuss it with us and other policy divisions. We have ideas which also seem interesting in how to address the problem of criminality and why some people become criminal. No one factor on its own causes crime and we are looking for programmes that incorporate many of the known factors that can in combination contribute to criminality, such as poor parenting, unemployment, aggressiveness in school and so on ... We give them our input and then it goes to higher levels to decide upon the research (Interview).

In April 1996, the Criminal Policy Directorate was restructured to include 9 units. One of these units is the Crime Prevention Agency which is the result of merging the former Crime Prevention Unit and parts of the Policy Department. The Home Office Crime Prevention College (formerly known as the Crime Prevention Centre) is the responsibility of the Crime Prevention Agency. The Crime Prevention Agency pays the salaries of those seconded to teach there and of the administrators.

According to two sources the re-structuring of the Criminal Policy Directorate has not been very successful. This is for two reasons. The first is that people inside and outside of the Home Office no longer know who the contact people are for information. As a consequence it seems that the left arm doesn't always know what the right arm is doing. Secondly, the work of the Juvenile Offenders unit, the Crime Prevention Agency, and the Action Against Crime unit overlaps. Civil servants are unclear about who should be doing what within their units. In essence the boundaries of the units have not been clearly defined.

The Crime Prevention Agency is reviewed below.

The Crime Prevention Agency

History of the Crime Prevention Agency Around 1974, the Crime Policy Planning Unit was created. It was made up of senior Home Office administrators and operated somewhat like a 'think tank' (Croft, 1982: 5; Interview). This unit had a working group on crime prevention which consisted of four members, one being Dr. Ronald Clarke. Dr. Ronald Clarke believed at this time that there should be a Crime Prevention Unit. An attempt had been made to set up the Crime Prevention Unit which had failed due to lack of resources. In 1980 two major publications were released (Clarke, 1980; and Clarke and Mayhew, 1980) which strongly advocated situational approaches for crime prevention.

Tilley stated (1991: 6),

> the political ground for these criminological seeds to grow in was fertile. It offered an approach to crime prevention which did not entail 'softness' towards offenders, but was consistent with their responsibility for their acts; it was uncritical of aspects of the social order which might otherwise be seen to create criminality; and it removed responsibility for failure to control crime from the police force. These features were not uncongenial to a Conservative administration.

When Dr. Ronald Clarke became head of the RPU in 1982, "<he> saw it as <his> chance to get the <Crime Prevention Unit> going" because now he could provide the resources by seconding some of his staff (Interview).

> Now I was head of the Research and Planning Unit, I had a little bit more power than I had before, or a little bit more influence possibly and this was a chance to try and get it going and fortunately there was a receptive assistant secretary in charge of F3 who was also interested in the idea (Interview).

Dr. Ronald Clarke wanted the Crime Prevention Unit to "go into the Police Department mainly because <he> felt that the police really needed this to help change them from a sort of para-military organisation into a more service organisation" (Interview). He also felt that by being in the Police Department "it was more likely to do the kind of crime prevention <he> liked than if it were located in the Criminal Department" (Interview).

The Crime Prevention Unit started off as a three year experiment in 1983 with 4 researchers seconded from the Research and Planning Unit. "The philosophy of <the Crime Prevention Unit> came from <Ronald> Clarke" (Interview). Paul Rock later referred to the Unit as "the intellectual progeny of Ron Clarke" (Rock, 1990: 265). Thus Dr. Ronald Clarke was initially the major driving force behind the Crime Prevention Unit, although he states that once it was established both Dr. Gloria Laycock and Kevin Heal were "the moving forces who really did everything". When the Crime Prevention Unit was created, Kevin Heal was made head of the Unit and Dr. Gloria Laycock was made head of Research and Development within the Crime Prevention Unit.

The Crime Prevention Unit's task was to promote preventive action against crime. "Included in its remit <was> a particular responsibility for the dissemination of information on crime prevention topics" (Smith and Laycock, 1985: ii).

> The Crime Prevention Unit had quite a lot of things to do, one of which was research. A part of the underlying philosophy of it was that research influenced policy. It was a unique experiment in the Home Office in that you put researchers in a policy division in that way. They have not done it like that ever since (Interview).

The Crime Prevention Unit did not solely consist of the research and development group, it was also responsible for police training, advice to ministers, the Standing Conference and various working groups.

At the end of the three year period, Dr. Ronald Clarke had left and Mary Tuck was the head of the Research and Planning Unit. Mary Tuck asked that the researchers be returned to the Research and Planning Unit but the Police Department of the Home Office considered the Crime Prevention Unit to be

> an experiment which worked quite well and they wanted to keep the researchers in the policy division. The managerial line of the researchers in

the Crime Prevention Unit was changed from the Research and Planning Unit to the Police Department. Thus the Crime Prevention Unit Research and Development Group which <Dr. Gloria Laycock> headed was the only social science research group in the Home Office which was independent of the Research and Planning Unit (Interview).

Crime prevention became the responsibility of F3 division (known in 1995 as "Crime-Police Operations and International Affairs") and a framework for crime prevention was produced which unlike other policy areas, was articulated within a quasi-research framework (Tilley, 1991: 9).

The Crime Prevention Unit seemed to have an interest in criminality prevention but they did not push it (Interview). "At various stages the Crime Prevention Unit did try to get a bit further into offender-oriented work, as with Kirkholt phase II, where the probation service came in which ended up more in community development" (Interview).

In conducting the interviews, it appeared that Kirkholt Phase II, was considered a turning point for the Crime Prevention Unit, in that what they were trying to accomplish became "fuzzy" (2 Interviews). One interviewee stated "It rehabilitated itself. It went through a phase when it was trying to do things that I do not think it could do very well - you know trying to find a role for the probation service in prevention for instance. It is a nice idea <to include probation> but we do not know what they should do."

In 1992, the research arm of the crime prevention unit split from the Crime Prevention Unit to form the Police Research Group (PRG). The role of the PRG was to "carry out and manage research relevant to the work of the police service" (Hirst, 1993: ii). The reason for this split was said to be because the Crime Prevention Unit was becoming too large. The fact that the research component of the Crime Prevention Unit was transferred to the Police Research Group was considered by some as "a shame" and those people were a "bit worried about what will happen now" (3 Interviews).

In January 1993 a Crime Prevention Strategy was issued by the Crime Prevention Unit which to date has not been updated. The 1993 strategy stated that the most effective way of dealing with crime was to prevent it from happening in the first place and that on a narrow level, the Crime Prevention Unit was "concerned with activities specifically aimed at preventing crimes from occurring in the first place" (Home Office, 1993c: 1-2). It defined crime prevention as "any measure which seeks to enhance safety and reduce crime, incivilities and disorders, fear of crime and criminal behaviour" (Home Office, 1993c: 1).

Their policies were aimed at,

- enhancing the ability of the police to combat crime;
- strengthening the powers of the courts to deal with offenders;
- strengthening the probation service to reduce re-offending and support those likely to offend;
- providing a wide range of non-custodial penalties backed up by increased prison capacity;
- helping victims to cope with the consequences of crime and to avoid multiple victimisation;
- involving voluntary organisations in all aspects of crime prevention and work with offenders (Home Office, 1993c: 1-2).

The main mechanisms for the crime prevention strategy included:

- creating a new type of Safer Cities Project;
- the Ministerial Group on Crime Prevention;
- the National Board for Crime Prevention;
- the Home Office Crime Prevention Centre; and
- support for crime prevention through Crime Concern, publications and funding innovative projects (Home Office, 1993c: 2-3).

Since this document was published in 1993, changes have occurred, such as (a) Safer Cities Phase II getting its budget from the Single Regeneration Budget run by the Department of the Environment, (2) the Ministerial Group on Crime Prevention not having met since July 1994, (3) the National Board for Crime Prevention being replaced by the National Crime Prevention Agency, and (4) the Crime Prevention Unit merging with parts of the criminal policy department to form the Crime Prevention Agency in April 1996.

One senior Home Office Official stated that it made sense to merge the Crime Prevention Unit with parts of the Policy Department since "The work of the Crime Prevention Unit in diversionary schemes, such as the summer programmes for young people, meshes into the work of C1. This is one of the reasons why it makes sense to merge the two". With the newly formed Crime Prevention Agency, it is anticipated that research will continue to be done by both the Police Research Group in the Police Policy Directorate and the Research and Statistics Directorate.

What the author finds interesting is that the Crime Prevention Unit which had a reputation for the situational approach merged with C1 which was known for its social approaches. This point in itself is not astounding since many have argued that in order to tackle crime effectively, all approaches to crime prevention have to be considered together. However, although the unification of crime prevention policy now falls under one heading in the Criminal Policy Directorate, it is headed by a high ranking police officer. The police, generally speaking, have the reputation of being situational in their approaches.

Furthermore, a 'proactive team' has been set up within the CPA to raise the profile of the Agency and to highlight the role and value of crime prevention and community safety. This team is made up of five police officers. This reinforces once again the connection of the Home Office with the police and the notion that the CPA is situational in focus.

Thus, although the Crime Prevention Agency no longer falls within the Police Directorate, the police still have control in crime prevention policy making within the Home Office. This once again raises the issue that crime prevention within the Home Office is focused on situational techniques. Now that a new government is in power, things might shift more to criminality prevention, but this remains to be seen.

One interviewee stated that the four changes that have occurred (as cited above) were all due to political reasons. For example, the fact that the Department of the Environment runs the Single Regeneration Budget is not a complete surprise when one considers that Michael Howard's position before he became Home Secretary was with the Department of the Environment. The Home Office had been opposed to giving its 'crime prevention budget' to the Department of the Environment prior to Michael Howard's appointment as Home Secretary. However, when Michael Howard took his position as Home Secretary he had the final say. One responsibility that stayed with the Home Office was the budget for drug prevention. According to one civil servant, David Maclean regrets the decision of giving the Home Office crime prevention budget to the Single Regeneration Budget since it is mostly about 'target hardening stuff and designing out crime'.

The fact that the Ministerial Group on Crime Prevention has not met is also allegedly due to political conflict. It had become "a bit of a talking shop" (Interview). The third change of the National Board for Crime Prevention being replaced by the National Crime Prevention Agency was discussed in the previous chapter.

The set up the Crime Prevention Agency also appears to be very politically based since the formation of the Crime Prevention Agency is tied to the National Crime Prevention Agency. The latter is to act as a managing board for what was the Crime Prevention Unit and the Crime Prevention Centre. According to one senior Home Office official, the agency was created because the Home Secretary "did not want to lose control of the Crime Prevention Unit and Crime Prevention Centre". This same official stated that these Agencies are not agencies in the true sense: "The Crime Prevention Agency is a renaming of the Crime Prevention Unit and the Crime Prevention Centre" and "the National Crime Prevention Agency is not a management board in the true sense" (Interview).

As stated in the second chapter, the fact that Richard Childs was appointed as head of the Crime Prevention Agency was allegedly the desire of both David Maclean and Michael Howard.

The author questions how the agency will work in the long run, or even in the short run with a new Home Secretary. If in the future the police no longer headed the Crime Prevention Agency, and/or working relations were not as amicable as they were in 1995, then it is questionable what will become of crime prevention. In the author's opinion, trying to co-ordinate a balance between both situational and social approaches in which everyone is happy will be an extremely difficult and delicate task.

Furthermore, according to five interviews, the current head of the Crime Prevention Agency is "unhappy". Whether he lasts the year is questionable. If Richard Childs does leave, it will be interesting to see who replaces him. According to one interview the new government is in a very delicate position with regards to who should take the lead in crime prevention. The new government is supposedly committed to including a clause in the Crime and Disorder Bill which should come out at the end of 1997. The difficulty lies in who should take the lead in crime prevention. If crime prevention stays with the police, then it may continue along situational lines and give the message that what other agencies or local authorities are doing is not important. If local authorities take the lead in crime prevention, then the police are worried that local authorities might interfere with operational policing decisions which would consequently affect resources. In other words Chief Constables would loose their resources to local authorities. Furthermore by excluding the police from a legislated role in crime prevention, tensions might develop which would be uncondusive to reducing crime effectively. As one interviewee stated, "Police co-operation is required".

As a consequence the new government will make both the police and local authorities the leaders in crime prevention. The question then becomes who will head the Crime Prevention Agency, or will an entirely new structure be created which lies outside of both the Criminality Department and the Police Department.

The Crime Prevention Unit Series of Publications Issues 1-32 of the Crime Prevention Unit Series were the responsibility of the Crime Prevention Unit. When the Police Research Group was formed, the series went to them since they are responsible for research. The Crime Prevention Papers, are now organised through the Police Research Group and have changed in appearance and name over time.

Issues 33-54 (inclusive) were published through the Police Research Group as the front cover of the publications demonstrates.[17] As of issue 55 (Maynard, 1994), the 'series' changed its title to the "Crime Detection and Prevention Series". One of the reasons for changing the layout and title was "to try and bring prevention and detection closer together so that the police stop thinking of crime prevention as being over there somewhere, and start to think of crime management bringing the two things together" (Interview).

In this section, issues 1-54 shall be analysed to reflect the thinking of the Crime Prevention Unit. Although issues 33-54 were published through the Police Research Group, much of the research, if not all is considered to have been initiated/funded by the Crime Prevention Unit. Issue 55 is also when the title of the publication changed, and from this point on, the publication is considered to fall entirely under the wing of the Police Research Group. Thus issues 55 and above are analysed in the section on the Police Research Group.

Issues 1-54 generally focused on survey/questionnaire results, programme evaluations and general informative publications including reviews of the literature on a certain topic. The majority of the publications (53.7%) were based on research conducted at a single point in time.[18] They told a reader about the current state of affairs. They most often consisted of

---

[17] Issues 1-32 display the title of the article, the author and then states "Crime Prevention Unit, Paper <number>" Issues 33-54 display the title of the article, the author and then states "Police Research Group, Crime Prevention Unit Series, Paper <number>". The words "Police Research Group" are slightly larger than what follows.

[18] Included issue numbers: 1, 5, 6, 7, 14, 15, 16, 17, 18, 19, 20, 21, 24, 25, 26, 27, 32, 33, 34, 35, 36, 37, 40, 44, 45, 49, 52, 53, 54.

questionnaire or interview data. A few of the publications analysed data collected within certain organisations such as the police service.

Research based on a "before-and-after scenario" (e.g., an evaluative method) accounted for 31.5% of the series.[19] Most of this research was based on a programme evaluation which compared crime figures before and after implementation of a programme.

The final group of publications consisted of reviews of the literature, and informed the reader about various crime prevention strategies.[20] They were not considered to be a "results" paper in that they did not provide the reader with the results of an empirical investigation. This category accounted for eight (14.8%) of the publications.

The author also decided to analyse the 54 publications by subject-matter. The publications were categorised into one of the following subject-headings:

1) Situational Techniques: Includes publications where the twelve techniques of situational prevention (Clarke, 1992: 15) were solely utilised as a form of prevention. It also included publications about design and layout, and publicity about target hardening approaches. No mention was made about multi-agency approaches in the title of the publication. In the text, the fact that agencies worked together might have been mentioned but the focus of the text was considered to be on the situational technique rather than the fact that more than one agency worked on the project.
2) Multi-agency approaches: Includes publications where multi-agency or inter-agency work was mentioned in the title of the text, and publications where the focus was on how agencies worked together rather than on the technique itself.
3) Multiple Techniques: Includes publications where more than one technique was used to prevent crime. By more than one technique the author refers to two or more of the following methods of preventing crime: situational prevention, social prevention, detection or investigation, or community-type approaches.
4) Topic Inquiry: Includes publications where the focus was on the current state of affairs of the topic of the publication as per the title.

---

[19] Includes issue numbers: 3, 8, 9, 12, 13, 22, 23, 28, 29, 30, 31, 39, 41, 42, 43, 50, 51.
[20] Included issue numbers: 2, 4, 10, 11, 38, 46, 47, 48.

In some cases this category examined how resources can be better managed to reduce crime more effectively, and also how certain factors could help in predicting the likelihood of further crimes occurring.

5) Youth Targeted Techniques: Includes publications about programmes run for youths in the community.

Table 3.3 shows that based on this categorisation, of the 54 publications the majority fell under the heading of Situational Techniques (24). This was followed by Topic Inquiry (15), Multiple Techniques (7), Multi-Agency Approaches (6), and two reports focused solely on Youth Targeted Techniques. From this one can clearly discern that the focus of the unit was on situational approaches and providing information about various subjects. Criminality prevention received little attention in comparison.

The author also noted that one fifth of the publications were about Burglary, Robbery and Theft (20.4% of publications); and 13% were about car crime specifically. Prior to 1992, only one publication had been released about car security. In 1992, however, car crime received more prominence with the publication of 3 issues on the topic. The year 1992 was designated as 'Car Crime Prevention Year' which might explain why 3 issues were published. In 1994 the first publication was released concerning domestic violence against women. The fact that so many publications were specifically about 'burglary, robbery and theft' and 'car crime' can be explained by the fact that many of the crimes reported to the police fall into one of these categories.

The *Crime Prevention Unit* series appears to have a narrow and 'safe'

Table 3.3 Number of Publications in the Crime Prevention Unit Series by Subject Matter

Subject Matter	Number of Publications
Situational Techniques	24
Topic Inquiry	15
Multiple Techniques	7
Multi-Agency Approach	6
Youth Targeted Techniques	2

focus. It has not published anything about more complicated or controversial issues such as child abuse, truancy, immigration, drug and alcohol abuse or about social, economic or political factors that may influence crime. Social and economic generators to crime are only mentioned in relation to multi-agency co-operation. The publications dealt with the most common forms of crime, and did not examine why one commits crime to begin with. They were generally factual reports as opposed to philosophical debates.

The Home Office Crime Prevention College

"In 1960 a Home Office Committee was formed to enquire into and report upon the organisation and procedure of the police forces of England and Wales for the prevention and detection of crime" (Home Office, 1983a: 4). At the same time, the Home Office considered the establishment of a centre "where selected police officers could be given specialist training in crime prevention techniques" (Home Office, 1983a: 4). At the time it was considered that the centre should be "near a lock and safe manufacturing centre" (Home Office, 1983a: 4). The centre was located in Stafford until 1996 when it was moved to North Yorkshire.

The first course commenced in April 1963. Subjects on this four week course included: intruder alarms, safes and strongrooms; speaking in public, and juvenile liaison. The centre was named the Crime Prevention Centre until September 1996 when it was renamed the Crime Prevention College.

The Home Office Crime Prevention College offers crime prevention training not only to police officers, but to other agencies and companies/institutions. "The Centre also acts as an information and advice centre collecting and disseminating best practice in crime prevention" (Home Office, 1993c: 5). It is made up of four police officers seconded to the Home Office (i.e., the Crime Prevention Agency pays their wages); two civilian instructors (whose posts used to be filled by Chief Inspectors), a Deputy Director (who's post has also been civilianised) and 8 support staff. Of the four police officers seconded, one is the Director of the Centre, and the three remaining officers are called directing staff. They are basically the instructors to the courses. The police officers are generally seconded for two years with the possibility of an extension to three years.

The instructors to the courses hope that by the end of the training sessions, the students will have a "wider vision of crime prevention" and that they will have received training in the ability to communicate. As one interviewee stated, "ninety percent of crime prevention is about manipulating people and other departments into spending their money in other ways". The college advocates ten principles to crime prevention which they apply throughout their courses. These 10 principles conform to Clarke's (1992) twelve techniques of situational prevention. The 10 principles of Prevention advocated by the Centre are:

1) Target Hardening
2) Target Removal
3) Remove the means to commit crime
4) Reduce the payoff
5) Access Control
6) Surveillance (natural, formal, employees)
7) Environmental Design
8) Rule Setting
9) Increase the Chance of being caught
10) Deflecting Offenders (Home Office Crime Prevention Centre, 1995).

The current courses on offer by the centre include the Standard Course, the Architectural Liaison Officers' Course, the Senior Crime Prevention Officers' Course and, the Explosive Liaison Officers' Foundation Course. The Standard Course, which was reduced from a four week course to a three week course at the beginning of 1997 is the most common course.

The first week of the course is "very much about physical security" (Interview). Topics reviewed include: "situational preventive techniques", 'communication', 'Access control systems', 'PVCU doors and windows', 'Locking devices - principles and practice', a practical survey exercise, etc.

The second week is still very much about physical approaches to crime prevention although they do go into the social side. On the physical side, topics discussed include, CCTVs, CPTED, intruder alarms, security of public buildings and hotels, auto crime, Sold Secure Police Against Car Theft (SSPACT), vehicle protection, and Tracker. On the social and inter-agency/partnership side the following are discussed: Home Office Circulars and the partnership approach, the local authority and government schemes, youth action groups, the watch concept and crime prevention panels. Other topics include media training and interview techniques.

The third week is about "Marketing, Campaign Management and evaluation both internally and externally" (Interview). Crime Management is also emphasised during this final week.

In addition to the training aspect of the college, there are two other roles it plays. It has a policy role and an information role. The policy aspect of the college is mostly fulfilled by having its staff sit on various committees as a Home Office representative (e.g., various ACPO committees and sub-committees, the British Standards Institute [BSI], the Security Industry Training Organisation [SITO], etc.). Their final role as an information centre is by disseminating best practice. The questions the college receives come mostly via the police.

In conclusion, the Home Office Crime Prevention College is very much about situational or physical approaches to preventing crime. One interviewee stated that in the future, the college will most likely provide more information than it currently does on "community affairs type prevention". When asked what was meant by this, the reply was that community affairs prevention was about social aspects to prevention such as the school liaison officer and partnerships. The prominence of the situational approaches would, however, remain dominant, as would the importance of communication skills.

At the time of writing up this section in the summer of 1997, the college had commissioned a consultant to examine the core competencies required within the field. It is expected that when these results come in, the course syllabus will be modified. The modifications will not only reflect the findings of the 'core competencies' but it will also reflect the position of the labour government. One individual from the college stated that the scope of crime prevention would widen and that the social side would be looked at. Once the Labour government legislates the role of local authorities and the police in crime prevention, courses will have to be tailored to the individuals holding the respective positions. It is uncertain at this point in time whether the college will take on that role.

It is also uncertain whether the college shall remain in North Yorkshire. Her Majesty's Chief Inspectorate of Constabulary are currently reviewing the role of crime prevention within the police service which amongst other things will make recommendations on whether the college should be situated in Bramshill where other police training occurs.

According to one senior Home Office Official the move of the college to North Yorkshire once again showed a disregard for policy from the Conservative Government. At the time, there was a review of police training that was being carried out. Instead of waiting for the results of this evaluation, on for example seeing whether crime prevention training should be conducted at Bramshill with the rest of police training, the Conservative government decided that now was the time to announce the move of the College. When asked why this location was selected, the same senior Home Official stated that there was much space for expansion which would ideally give the College a higher profile due to the fact that there is more accommodation. Civil defence which was severely cut back was a main industry there before, and so empty government buildings are available for the College. It is therefore a cost effective move to re-use government buildings.

The Police Directorate

The Police Research Group

The Police Research Group formed in 1992. This section describes how it was formed. Although this section is descriptive in nature, it illustrates how the Group is very much geared towards the police. Not only is the research done for the police but it also encourages the police to take on research of their own. The influence of the Home Secretary and Minister on police research is also addressed in this section.

The Formation of the Police Research Group When Mark Cunliffe was head of the Crime Prevention Unit, Gloria Laycock argued,

> that there should be a police research group established which should not only take responsibility for crime prevention for the police but all other police research related matters, detection and everything else (Interview).

At the same time that the Police Research Group was formed, the Police Requirements Support Unit (PRSU),[21] formerly a section under the

---

[21] Weatheritt (1986) referred to this group as the Police Research Services Unit, but one Home Office official, pointed out that the unit was actually called the Police Requirements Support Unit.

The Scientific Research and Development Branch (SRDB) also discussed by Weatheritt (1986) were "wiped out in around 1990" (Interview).

Science and Technology Group of the Police Department, split up. Staff in the PRSU were placed around the Police Department of the Home Office. Some of the PRSU went to the Police Research Group, including the Superintendent's post. This post is vital in that the Superintendent can help the Group to get its "ideas across better to the divisional commanders, particularly on developing strategic approaches to crime management. This will necessarily mean they will have to think about crime prevention" (Interview).

While still in the Crime Prevention Unit, the Research and Development Group (RDG) started off with three researchers. When SRDB split up a few more researchers joined the RDG and they were allocated a budget of £150,000 for external research. With the break up of the PRSU, the Police Research Group received more staff and money which gave them a budget of one million pounds. Thus, upon leaving the Crime Prevention Unit, the 'research group' "expanded quite considerably" (Interview).

Prior to the formation of the Police Research Group nobody was doing research for the police on social science and management issues other than crime prevention. "The reason of the Police Research Group was to fill in this central gap" (Interview). The creation of the Police Research Group brought with it "a much broader remit to do anything to do with the police" (Interview). Its main customers are the Police Policy Directorate, the Criminal Policy Directorate and the Organised and International Crime Policy Directorate.

The Police Research Group do crime prevention research where it solely involves the police. If the research were to involve the police and another agency such as local authorities, probation, or the views of the public, the work would be done through the Research and Statistics units. Thus, the Police Research Group is solely interested in matters affecting the police, whether it be crime prevention, detection or something else.

PRG in Focus (Oldfield, 1995: 4) states, "one of PRG's key objectives in 1993 was to establish a programme of research into detection and police operations to balance its existing work on crime prevention. Greater urgency was placed on this objective when the findings of the Audit Commission's study of crime management began to emerge." [22]

---

22 Audit Commission (1993).

When asked whether the Police Research Group works closely with ACPO, an interviewee replied "we try to. We are trying to get the police to see that research is something that can help them with their inquiries. ... It really is about trying to help them to develop and do their job better and you can't do that if you do not work with them. ... Most of the work we are doing is with the crime committee or their subgroups". The head of the Police Research Group is a member of the ACPO crime prevention sub-committee. More will be said about the ACPO crime prevention sub-committee in the next chapter.

Unlike the Research and Statistics Directorate, the Police Research Group budget was not cut in April 1996. Some people within the Home Office have interpreted this as,

> They come under this holy umbrella of the police, so 'oh we must not cut the police'. It is quite tricky, and I think it is more that the Police Research Group are doing much more of a service role, rather than, a questioning role (Interview).

There is currently some debate on whether the Police Research Group should remain within the Police Directorate. Although the Police Research Group would like to remain within the Police Directorate, others are arguing that they should be a part of the Research and Statistics Directorate since they do research. If the Police Research Group were to move to the Research and Statistics Directorate, it would be somewhat ironic. Before the Crime Prevention Unit was set up, prevention was the responsibility of the Criminality Department (as the Crime Prevention Agency is now) and research was conducted within the Research and Planning Unit. In some ways if the Police Research Group were moved to the Research and Statistics Directorate, organisationally things will be similar to the way they were twenty years ago.

Research Within the Police Research Group In an interview, it was stated that the research within the Police Research Group is decided by three groups. The first priority is the Minister or Home Secretary (who commissioned the Sheehy Inquiry and the research on paperwork).

The second group to have priority is the Policy division (also driven by the Home Secretary). Examples of work requested by this group include the research on CS gas and Batons. The third group is the police themselves who say they would like some research done in a certain area (e.g., personnel training).

The Police Research Group has structured three formal schemes into their organisation in an attempt to "encourage innovation" (Oldfield, 1995: 4). They consist of (a) the Police Operations Against Crime Programme; (b) the Home Office Police Research Award; and (c) the Home Office Award For Equal Opportunity Achievement in the Police Service (the reader is referred to Oldfield, 1995: 4-8 for more information about these schemes).

Police Research Group Publications Since the Crime Prevention Unit series of publications changed its name to the *Crime Detection and Prevention Series*, twenty-five publications have been released.

The author had attempted to compare this series to the Crime Prevention Unit Series, however, the series is in the author's opinion not comparable. Over time this series has become very much aimed at the police and not crime prevention practitioners at large. Trying to stop individuals from becoming involved in crime in the first place is not of relevance to this series.

A second publication regularly published by the Police Research Group is the *Police Research Series*. This series started with the instigation of the PRG (as opposed to the *Crime Detection and Prevention Series* which is a continuation of the CPU series). By July 1997 there were twenty papers. These publications are essentially for the police. They deal with policing issues such as investigative interviewing courses, management and supervision of police interviews, and court attendance by police officers. The varied subject-matter of the publications all fall within the police service. The publications are said to be about "research and development work in non-crime prevention and detection areas. It shares the same objectives [as the Crime Detection and Prevention series] in presenting the main issues and lessons from the work rather than expanding at length on technical aspects" (Oldfield, 1995: 21).

The Police Research Group also puts out a *Special Interest Series*. By June 1997 nine were published. These have more to do with policing issues and trying to catch offenders than with preventing crime in the first place. For example, some of the issues addressed in this series include: seconded police officers, the police initial recruitment test, and resettlement support for police officers.

The final regular publication is *Focus*. By June 1997 there were eight issues. This publication is like a magazine for the Police, as opposed to an academic journal. It provides the police with information on Award Schemes, and provides short summaries of research done by the Police Research Group and through the Home Office Police Research Award Scheme. It includes a few articles on crime prevention but also on many other aspects of policing. Each article is about 1-2 page(s) long.

Conclusion

This chapter examined various units within the Home Office that have responsibility for the prevention of crime. These units included the Research and Statistics units, the Programme Development Unit, the Crime Prevention Agency and Crime Prevention College, and the Police Research Group. The chapter also described how the Home Secretary and Minister have priority and the final say in research conducted by the research units.

This chapter suggested that since 1979, less research was done which involved probation and non-custodial disposals. Publications released by the various Home Office Units parallel Conservative party ideology. More focus was given to courts and sentencing, prisons and, policing. The allocation of external funding from the Research and Planning Unit was also consistent with these findings.

The one apparent anomaly with Conservative ideology was the creation of the Programme Development Unit in 1991. At the time, the Minister was John Patten who "was quite a liberal sort of thinker; he was interested in the family" (Interview).

From this chapter four issues arise.

1) Although inter-ministerial committees have been created within the realm of crime prevention, the Home Office itself does not have an inter-departmental committee that discusses crime prevention issues. This is somewhat ironic since, at least in the past, the Home Office encouraged groups to work together at the local level (e.g., through the inter-ministerial circulars and the Morgan Report). Much of the co-ordination that does go on within the Home Office is done informally. The notion that decisions get made 'behind the scenes' is compatible with an earlier statement that even where committees do exist, much of the decisions get made by an inner group outside of the meetings themselves.

Knowing the above, one cannot help but wonder whether the consequence of all this informal decision making is that personalities count when trying to influence policy. Furthermore, when decisions get made informally, there is less likelihood of any particular group or person being accountable for the decisions.

2) Within this chapter, the role of the individual in making things happen is evident once again. The three people who have made the greatest difference in crime prevention thinking (at least within the Home Office) are Dr. Ronald Clarke, Chris Nuttall and Dr. Gloria Laycock.

Dr. Ronald Clarke was the catalyst in forming the Crime Prevention Unit, which has been an extremely important unit in developing both crime prevention policy and research in England and Wales, if not around the world. Dr. Ronald Clarke was very committed to situational crime prevention and strongly believed there was a need for the Crime Prevention Unit. When the opportunity arose, he seized it.

Chris Nuttall, the director of the Research and Statistics Directorate, pushed for the formation of the Programme Development Unit, and was able to get it started. Although its future was uncertain for ten months, its funding was confirmed by the Conservative government for another three years.

Dr. Gloria Laycock, the head of the PRG, managed to get this group up and running. Not only did she succeed in getting it established, she managed to gain more resources and to be unaffected by the last round of budget cuts under the Conservative government.

3) The third issue is the relationship between research and Conservative party ideology. The finding in this chapter is that since the 1980s there has been a move away from probation and treatment research, and a move towards much more policing research. The decline in probation research is especially evident in the Home Office Research Studies and in the Home Office Research Bulletins.

Within the Research Programme, the largest portion of both research projects and funding went to prisons and policing research. The funding for probation research was less than one half that for prisons. Within the Research and Planning Unit Papers, the largest portion of publications fell under the subject headings of Courts and Sentencing, and Police. Probation and Non-Custodial Disposals accounted for less than one third that of Courts and Sentencing, and less than one half that of Policing.

These findings are all very consistent with Conservative party ideology. Since the 1980's, the prominence given to the police has increased dramatically. Like Conservative party ideology, the emphasis for research within the Home Office has been on prisons, policing, courts and sentencing. One gets the impression that the function of the probation service has been seen as less relevant.

4) The fourth issue examines the type of crime prevention advocated by the Home Office Departments. Within the Home Office, the type of prevention that dominates is situational prevention. Criminality or social prevention has a very low priority. One senior Home Office official stated, "It is all very well to say that the Home Office has moved towards social crime prevention but I have yet to see any products from any of that. I don't know where they are". Other interviewees have suggested that when the Crime Prevention Unit tried to include the probation service as part of crime prevention, their direction became, to use one interviewee's adjective, "fuzzy".

Almost one half of the publications published through the *Crime Prevention Series* dealt solely with situational approaches. Only two focused on youth targeted approaches. The focus of the Home Office Crime Prevention College is also predominantly situational. Their aims and objectives stated their emphasis was "on special security problems" (Home Office, 1995h); their ten principles are all connected to the situational approach and; the first and second week of their Standard course was to quote one interviewee "very much about physical security". Although the Crime Prevention Agency and Crime Prevention College fall within the Criminal Policy Directorate, the head of the Agency is a former high ranking police officer.

According to four interviews, the head of the Crime Prevention Agency is very much 'a police officer'. According to these interviewees he is not as supportive towards research as some had hoped which has strained a few relationships. Until someone replaces him that is a little more keen on broadening the scope of crime prevention, crime prevention will in the author's opinion remain very much situationally focused within the Home Office.

4 The Police Service

Introduction

The role of the police in crime prevention has been instilled in the police since their inception in 1829 through Sir Robert Peel's *Principles of Policing*. One of the principles stated that the police must "prevent crime and disorder as an alternative to their repression by military force and by severity of legal punishment" (cited in Normandeau and Leighton, 1990: 140). Rowan and Mayne, the first commissioners of the Metropolitan Police, declared in 1829: "The principal object to be attained is the prevention of crime. To this great end every effort of the police is to be directed" (cited in Audit Commission, 1993: 11). The responsibility of the police to prevent crime is still agreed upon today, although they are not considered as the only ones responsible for the prevention of crime.

The chapter begins by examining the structure of the police service and police authorities. It then examines several sources in an attempt to determine how the police define crime prevention. The sources examined include works from Her Majesty's Chief Inspectorate of Constabulary, the Audit Commission, the Representative Associations for the police and the work of the ACPO sub-committee on crime prevention, the *Operational Policing Review*, and the manual for the Police Probationer Training Foundation Course. The results of how the police in Boroughville defined crime prevention are analysed with the aim of indicating whether national and local definitions coincide. A conclusion is then drawn from these sources illustrating that crime prevention for the police is very much targeted to opportunity reduction, or in other words, situational approaches. The role of the police in crime prevention also seems to be about giving advice.

The Structure of the Police Service

In England and Wales there are 43 police forces. The *Police Act* 1964 states the police are politically accountable through a tripartite structure consisting of the Chief Constable, the police authority and the Home Secretary. Chief constables are appointed by, and are accountable to, their local police authorities. The role of the police authority is discussed in the next section.

> The Home Secretary ... has various powers to influence practice nationally, for example by participating in senior appointments and by issuing circulars, which forces are expected to comply with, on the general direction of policing policy (NACRO, 1993).

The Home Secretary is also empowered to set key police objectives (which are discussed under the heading of the police authorities). "The Home Secretary also influences policy through the Inspectorate of Constabulary" (NACRO, 1993).

> The Inspectorate's role is to inspect and report to the Home Secretary on the efficiency and effectiveness of forces. Inspectors also report informally to the police authority (ACC/AMA, 1994: 11; Home Office, 1995f: 104).

The Police Authority

As stated above, the police are partly accountable to the local police authority. Until April 1st 1995 the police authority was closely connected to the politics of local government. The budget of the local police authority had to be approved by the county council and they could advise on matters such as "law enforcement, policing priorities and the allocation and deployment of police resources" (NACRO, 1993: 1). This body was made up of two thirds local councillors and one third magistrates, all appointed by the local authority. The number of persons appointed to represent the local police authority was based on the population of the area.

With the *Police and Magistrates Courts Act 1994*, local police authorities have become more detached from local government. "They have their own budget for policing and now have statutory responsibilities which they exercise themselves" (Interview). According to one interviewee, the reason for the new structure for local police authorities was to remove politics and focus more on policing. This is supported by a statement made by David Maclean at the time: "The new authorities are leaner, meaner and more interested in policing than politics" (Maclean,

1995a: 8). The Act also gives police authorities better defined responsibilities than it had in the past.

One way of separating politics from policing was to reduce the number of local councillors that sit on the committee. Under the previous structure 2/3 of the local police authority were local councillors. Also, the number of persons on the committee was not fixed but was based on the population of the area. Under the current system, local police authorities are all the same size regardless of population.[23]

Under the new system there are 9 local councillors, 3 magistrates and 5 'independent' people. In selecting the 5 independent persons, a panel is set up consisting of three people. One is chosen by the councillors and magistrates in the local authority; one is nominated by the Home Secretary and the third is chosen by the previous two. The vacancies for the five independent representatives must be advertised in two newspapers circulating in the area (ACC/AMA, 1994: 4). The panel of three generates a short list of 20 people and then forwards their details to the Home Secretary. He and his officials return a maximum of 10 names to the local police authority. The local police authority in turn selects the five members to sit on the police authority.

One requirement of the newly structured local police authorities is that every year they produce a Policing Plan which some might argue is a conceptually shorter and more easily understood operational plan. In drawing up this plan, the police authority is legally required to consult the public about policing their area and seeking their help in preventing crime. Every local police authority is also required to have regard to the key policing objectives set by the Home Secretary. For 1995-96, the following key objectives were identified as needing to be incorporated into the policing plans:

1) To maintain and if possible increase the number of detections for violent crimes.
2) To increase the number of detections for burglaries of people's homes.

---

23 Although in exceptional circumstances, "the Home Secretary may, by statutory order specify that the members of a police authority can be an odd number greater than 17" (ACC/AMA, 1994: 4-5). For example, the Home Secretary has increased the size of three police authorities to 19: Devon and Cornwall; Greater Manchester and Dyfed Powys. The proportions are 10 councillors, 6 independent members and 3 magistrates.

3) To target and prevent crimes which are a particular local problem, including drug-related criminality, in partnership with the public and local agencies.
4) To provide high visibility policing so as to reassure the public.
5) To respond promptly to emergency calls from the public (Home Office, 1996b: 72).

According to one interviewee, the new police authority is more likely to consider crime prevention as a key objective (as 3 of the police key objectives illustrates) which consequently means that crime prevention will probably gain more recognition.

On a more negative note, one interviewee stated that the new structure "has not helped with ... the communications issue. At the end of the day when we are talking about working together... to get organisations to mesh into each other, then in a small way the creation of the new police authorities has not really helped with that process".

Although the 'new' police authority structure was partly set up to remove local politics, one could question whether this move in itself was not political (see for example Loveday, 1994a, 1994b). In the interviews for this research there was a consensus that the Conservative government was against local authority control (most local governments are not run by the Conservative party). The 'new' police authorities withdraw some of the control of the local authority over policing. More control is provided to the police service in areas such as staffing and decisions on expenditure and to the Home Secretary (see for example Loveday, 1994a, 1994b; 1996). One interviewee stated, "the main gainers are the new police authorities and the Government".

Her Majesty's Chief Inspectorate of Constabulary

The Inspectorate is "the principal, but not sole, source of professional advice to the Home Secretary and Home Office on all aspects of policing" (Home Office, 1995f: 105). For example, the Inspectorate is expected to contribute advice on the selection of key objectives, performance indicators and targets; and policing plans. The Inspectorate is also expected to collaborate with the Home Office and other interested agencies such as the Audit Commission, "to develop good practice guidance and to provide co-ordinated advice and support to forces on implementation of key policies"

(Home Office, 1995f: 106). At the time of writing this book, the Inspectorate was reviewing the role of crime prevention and detection in police forces with the aim of bringing these two themes closer together. Given that the Inspectorate has such duties and responsibilities, the author decided to examine the role of crime prevention in the Inspectorate's Annual Reports from 1979 until 1996.

Over the years, the format of the reports changed. By grouping the reports into categories based on the varying annual report formats, one comes up with four periods in which the significance of crime prevention can be analysed. These four periods are: 1979-1981, 1982-1989, 1990-1993, and 1994/5 -1995/6. In doing so, one finds that crime prevention is not a new concept and the term itself has been used in every report.

From 1979-1981, crime prevention received little attention in comparison to the 1994/95 and 1995/96 reports. During this time period crime prevention was only included in the seventh chapter on policing and community relations.

From 1982-1989, crime prevention was given more prominence by the fact that it was included as a sub-section of the first chapter 'Review of the Year', and again in the seventh chapter on policing and community relations.

Between 1990-1993, crime prevention's prominence seemed to subside. The reports from 1990 until 1992 were all written by the same Chief Inspector of Constabulary thus *possibly* reflecting his own views of crime prevention (i.e., it is not an issue which requires much attention). In 1993, there is no section on crime prevention but there is one on 'crime management'. One possible explanation is that this phrase was chosen to reflect the thinking of the Police Research Group which is attempting to bring prevention and detection under the heading of crime management.

As of 1994/5 crime prevention and tackling/preventing crime was given more prominence under the chapter entitled "The Policing Task". In analysing all the reports, the author noted 11 themes that were repeated. They included:

1) The need to co-operate with other agencies
2) The opportunistic/situational approach to crime prevention
3) The role of the police in crime prevention being about giving advice
4) The importance of 'publicity' in crime prevention
5) The 'social' causes to crime

6) Neighbourhood Watch
7) Crime prevention through deterrence
8) Crime pattern analysis
9) Crime prevention as being a cost effective approach to controlling crime
10) Repeat victimisation and CCTV
11) Crime prevention as a key objective for policing.

The first theme is evident in 1979 when the report states,

> if the police are to succeed in preventing or reducing juvenile crime, it is essential that they should work in close co-operation at the local level with all the various agencies concerned with juvenile crime and its consequences (Home Office, 1980: 42).[24]

In 1988 and 1989, "the importance of the Service, other statutory bodies and, in particular local authorities" was emphasised (Home Office, 1989: 6; 1990d: 8). The report stated, this approach was commended in Home Office Circular 8/84. The theme is repeated again in the 1994/95 report (Home Office, 1995f: 28; see also Home Office, 1996b: 31).

The second theme (on the opportunistic nature of crime), is evident in the following statements:

- "police files hold many thousands of cases which illustrate the extent to which carelessness over security invites theft, and it is unfortunately true that too few companies pay adequate attention to this aspect of their profitability" (Home Office, 1980: 46).
- a publicity campaign "aimed at stressing the need for householders to take sensible precautions against burglary, and in particular to secure windows at the rear of the house, a common means of access for burglars" (Home Office, 1982: 50).
- "property offences are often opportunist acts and many would be prevented if only more care and forethought were exercised ... equally, building security can be best effected during construction ..." (Home Office, 1991b: 24, 25).

---

24 The theme is repeated in 1982, 1988, 1989, 1993 and 1994/95 (Home Office, 1983b: 5; 1989: 6, 61-62; 1990d: 8; 1994c: 19; 1995f: 28).

These statements not only imply that crime is opportunistic and that the solution is perhaps through situational methods such as better locks and bolts, but they also have an element of victim-blaming.

The third theme (on the role of the police in crime prevention being about giving advice), is evident in 1980 when the report stated, "shops can do a lot to protect themselves in this field by sensible preventive action, on which they can always obtain advice from crime prevention officers" (Home Office, 1981: 48).

The fourth theme, on publicity, is evident in 1983 when the report stated, "publicity is an essential feature of measures to prevent crime" (Home Office, 1984d: 49). This emphasis on publicity is reiterated in 1986 (Home Office, 1987: 53), and publicity campaigns are mentioned in almost every publication (Home Office, 1980: 46; 1981: 47; 1982: 50; 1983b: 44; 1985b: 49; 1986: 56; 1988: 55; 1989: 64; 1990d: 65; 1993d: 33).

The fifth theme on the 'social' causes to crime is unique to the 1983 report which stated,

> The upsurge in crime in this country, and indeed elsewhere, is due to a combination of many factors. We are all aware of significant changes in society; the erosion of the family unit; the development of a less authoritarian system of education; the growth in unemployment; changes in moral values often leading to a more tolerant attitude towards anti-social behaviour and the lack in urban areas of a sense of community engendering a lack of civic pride and responsibility. The media have affected people's perceptions ... (Home Office, 1984d: 5).

This statement might have been a reflection of the Chief Inspector of Constabulary at the time, demonstrating a wider sphere for crime prevention than just dealing with 'locks and bolts'.

Neighbourhood Watch is also a theme that comes up in almost every publication since 1983, with comments such as,

> By the end of 1984, 29 police forces in England and Wales implemented a total of 3,537 Neighbourhood Watch schemes, and others have indicated their intention of following suit (Home Office, 1985b: 6, see also 1984d: 48; 1985b: 48; 1986: 7, 54-55; 1987: 5, 52; 1988: 54; 1996b: 35).

Crime prevention through deterrence (the seventh theme), is evident in the following comment:

- When considering the general police involvement in community relations and crime prevention, the basic principles have not changed greatly in the past century. A major part of the philosophy is to deploy the maximum possible number of police onto the streets (Home Office, 1984d: 46).

This comment suggests that crime could be prevented through deterrence by having more police officers. This would act as a visual deterrent.

The eighth theme on crime pattern analysis and other information technology was reported as having an effect on the efficiency and effectiveness of operations against crime in 1987 and in 1989 (Home Office, 1988: 5; 1990d: 7).

The ninth theme states that crime prevention potentially results in savings elsewhere. In 1986, it was stated,

Any substantial achievements in <crime prevention> will produce benefits in reducing the level of resources committed to investigation and also help to minimise the fear of crime (Home Office, 1987: 52).

The tenth issue on repeat victimisation and closed circuit televisions (CCTV) is addressed in 1994/1995 and 1995/96 (Home Office, 1995f: 29; 1996b: 33, 34).

Finally, the key performance indicators for the Home Secretary's Key Objectives for Policing (the eleventh theme) are provided in the 1994-95 and 1995/96 reports. The third objective in both years is,

to target and prevent crimes which are a particular local problem in partnership with the public and other local authorities (Home Office, 1995f: 72; see also Home Office 1996b: 72 where the wording is almost identical).

Although the 1994/95 report was not certain on how to devise an indicator for crime prevention, the 1995/96 report states,

Tackling repeat victimisation looks to be the most fruitful area, since reduction in repeat victimisation can lead to significant reduction in crime generally. Work will continue on developing a performance indicator for repeat victimisation aimed at reducing its incidence (Home Office, 1996b: 72).

These eleven issues show how crime prevention has come to be understood within policing circles. Publicity campaigns and

Neighbourhood Watch are the most common topics discussed over the years, with the notion of repeat victimisation and CCTVs appearing for the first time in the 1994/95 report. The latter two topics are very likely to be repeated in future reports.

The Audit Commission

The Audit Commission was established in 1983 (Audit Commission, 1994: 6). The aim of the Audit Commission is to,

> be a driving force in the improvement of public services. It promotes proper stewardship of public finances and helps those responsible for public services to achieve economy, efficiency and effectiveness (Audit Commission, 1995: 5).

One way of achieving this aim is that the Audit Commission,

> undertakes national studies of value for money in public services. Published studies explain best practice and have a direct influence on public service policy and management (Audit Commission, 1995: 5).

The Audit Commission produced its first police paper in 1988. By the end of July 1997, the Audit Commission had produced 16 police papers. Of these papers, three of them mention crime prevention. In *Effective Policing* the section on crime prevention stated, "Crime detection identifies criminals, but is only one factor in crime prevention" (Audit Commission, 1990: 20). This section infers that detection is a component of crime prevention. The paragraph then continued to say,

> Proactive work, such as encouraging households to participate in Neighbourhood Watch Schemes and visits by officers to schools, also forms part of the police response to crime. But research over a number of years shows that such activity in isolation has a limited impact on the overall crime rate. There is now widespread acceptance that the police must work more closely with other agencies (Audit Commission, 1990: 20).

In 1993, the paper on 'Tackling Crime Effectively' was published. According to Boroughville's Force Crime Reduction Officer, this was a source document "by which we changed from crime prevention under community services to crime reduction under crime management".

The document advocated the multi-agency approach by saying "... the fight against crime is the responsibility not just of the police but also of government, business and each individual citizen" (Audit Commission, 1993: I). The non-acceptance of the Morgan Report recommendations by the Conservative government was considered an "impediment" (Audit Commission, 1993: 13). In 1996 the Audit Commission stated,

> Because the police cannot do it all there is an increasing need for co-ordinated action by the police and other agencies. To secure this, it may be necessary for the Government to clarify the responsibilities of various agencies, notably but not solely local authorities, and set these within a statutory framework (Audit Commission, 1996b: 48).

Three further themes were noted. They included:
1) The theme of victim-blaming which is evident in the following two instances,

- the police cannot be held responsible if cars are manufactured with poor security or if individual citizens do not in the words of the 1993 White Paper on Police Reform, 'do all that can be reasonably expected of them to protect their own property' (Audit Commission, 1993: 7).

- The public should ensure that all reasonable steps are taken to seek crime prevention advice and put this into effect, particularly in respect of securing homes and vehicles and joining neighbourhood watch schemes (Audit Commission, 1993: 43).

2) The theme of prevention and detection where the report states that "the police emphasise the detection of crime rather than its prevention" and that "prevention and detection are often perceived as separate strands of activity when they should be inextricably linked" (Audit Commission, 1993: 14, 15). This is consistent with the philosophy of the Home Office Police Research Group.

3) The role of the police which encompasses "not just personal and domestic security measures but also advice on 'designing out' crime on housing estates and in car parks" (Audit Commission, 1993: 13).

Until the National Report, *Misspent Youth* was published in 1996 it appeared that the Audit Commission's approach to crime prevention was narrowly focused and 'situational' in nature. In *Tackling Crime Effectively*, any role that the police might have in informing agencies about issues that need to be addressed (e.g., informing the local authority that a footpath should be closed because it is used as an escape route in some high crime estate) is not mentioned. The Audit Commission suggests that cars are manufactured with poor security. However, without information from the police about what needs changing, how do car manufacturers know what to change?

Although not a police paper, *Misspent Youth* strongly advocated the work of David Farrington with respect to preventing crime. The report stated,

> Offending by young people is associated with a range of risk factors including inadequate parental supervision; aggressive or hyperactive behaviour in early childhood; truancy and exclusion to offend; unstable living conditions; lack of training and employment; and drug and alcohol abuse.
>
> These factors can be used to help target measures to prevent crime by identifying areas where young people are at risk (Audit Commission, 1996a; 57).

The report also strongly urges that programmes in these areas be properly monitored and evaluated (Audit Commission, 1996a: 59).

Representative Associations For the Police

Within the police organisation there are three representative associations whose two principal functions include,

1) to protect and further members' interests and
2) to establish bodies within and through which matters of professional interest and efficiency can be developed and discussed (Committee of Inquiry on the Police, 1979: 3).[25]

The three representative associations are The Police Federation of England and Wales; The Police Superintendents Association of England and Wales; and The Association of Chief Police Officers.

---

25 Although this reference might seem dated, a spokesperson from the Police Federation informed me that this document still applied today.

The Police Federation of England and Wales is the largest of the staff associations within the police service. They are a trade union established by the Police Act 1919. "All members of a police force below the rank of superintendent and all police cadets are automatically members of the Federation" (Committee of Inquiry on the Police, 1979: 13).

The Superintendents' Association of England and Wales came into being in 1952 following both the Oaksey Committee report in 1949 and the report of the Committee of the Police Council in 1952 (Committee of Inquiry on the Police, 1979: 8).

The Association of Chief Police Officers (ACPO) was formed in 1948. Membership is open to all officers above the rank of Chief Superintendent. Within ACPO there are nine principal committees, each addressing a particular issue. The committee on crime has a sub-committee on crime prevention. This sub-committee is the subject of the following section.

The ACPO Sub-Committee On Crime Prevention

The subcommittee on crime prevention was established in 1986. The chair for this committee sits for a three-year term at which point the Secretary is then appointed as the new chairperson. A new secretary is then found. Both the chairperson and secretary are Chief Constables. Figure 4.1 illustrates the strategy developed for this committee. One interviewee stated that this strategy was accepted by all Chief Constables to be the way forward and showed the importance of crime prevention within the British police service. The strategy states that the goal is to promote crime prevention and to make it a priority for everyone in the Police Service and outside.

The subcommittee on crime prevention currently has four working groups. These four groups are:

1) The Project and Design Group. This group essentially deals with issues related to 'designing out crime' through architectural design. It examines how car parks and buildings can be made safer from crime before they are built.
2) Vehicle Tracking Group. This group works on tracking systems in vehicles.
3) Intruder Alarm Group - this group examines issues connected with alarms. They create police policy on, for example, how to address false alarms and when to respond. The group also

Figure 4.1 Crime Committee: ACPO Crime Strategy

CRIME PREVENTION	
GOAL: To make crime prevention a priority and promote it by influencing those within the Police Service and outside to see it as a responsibility of each individual.	
OBJECTIVES	**ACTIONS**
Change of culture	Seek to change the culture of the Police Service so that crime prevention enjoys a higher status and is accepted as a responsibility of all officers.
Partnership	To identify and work in partnership with agencies who can assist in the achievement of our aims.
Public responsibility	To seek to encourage the public to take responsibility for crime prevention in areas within their control.
Identification of causes	To identify the causes of crime and to assist in definition of crime reduction strategies.
Improving the information base	To improve the information base for crime prevention by integrating the technology and expertise on a local, national and international basis.
Developing the situational approach	To continue to develop the situational approach to crime prevention, including target hardening through architectural liaison, design and technology.
Communications and marketing	To create an effective communications/marketing strategy for crime prevention issues.

Source: ACPO (1995).

attempts to assess resource implications due to call outs to false alarms.
4) Intruder Alarm Liaison Committee: This committee liaises with the members in the alarm industry on matters related to alarms and police response.

The crime prevention sub-committee meets about 4 times per year. The inaugural minutes state that ACPO had not been sufficiently energetic and progressive in the crime prevention field. Therefore the sub-committee would attempt to enhance their image by producing position papers and providing ACPO viewpoints on relevant matters.

In reading through the ACPO sub-committee on crime prevention minutes from September 1986 until May 1995, several themes were apparent. These themes included: (i) The maintenance of the police as leaders in crime prevention; (ii) Promoting the sub-committee as an energetic and progressive organisation; (iii) Providing the ACPO viewpoint; (iv) The push for 'good practice' guidelines/standards; (v) The type of crime prevention addressed by the sub-committee; (vi) Forming an ACPO-ACOP relationship.

The Maintenance of the Police as Leaders in Crime Prevention On two occasions, the minutes from the sub-committee on crime prevention mentioned the fear and danger of the police losing their primacy in crime prevention. The first mention of this was in a meeting in 1987 where the police questioned whether they could maintain their primacy due to the increase in workload placed on crime prevention officers without financial compensation.

The second occasion was at the beginning of 1991 when the outgoing chairperson stated that by not elevating the status of this subcommittee to one of committee the primacy of the police service in crime prevention could be endangered. This was due to the fact that other agencies were seeking to take on a crime prevention role.

Two ways of maintaining their primacy, included 1) being represented on key crime prevention committees/groups; and 2) being consulted regarding any initiatives, television programmes etc., that were tied to crime prevention. The sub-committee felt it was important that their view be heard. Before the formation of the Crime Prevention Agency, the sub-committee had to struggle to be represented on government committees or working groups.

For example, in discussing the Home Office Standing Conference on Crime Prevention, one member felt that the involvement of the police was being diminished in the meetings. When the Working Group chaired by James Morgan was initially created, ACPO was not represented. Members of the sub-committee expressed their concern and in the end an ACPO representative became a member of Morgan's working group. When the National Board for Crime Prevention was created the sub-committee was concerned since (a) the police were not initially represented, and (b) they were not consulted before the official launch. It also appears that the Ministerial Group on Crime Prevention showed some reluctance in having the sub-committee represented. The ministerial group were only prepared to invite an observer.

The fact that the sub-committee were not fully consulted about Crime Concern also seems to have caused some tensions. In October 1987, Steven Norris gave the subcommittee a presentation about the proposed National Crime Prevention Association (now known as Crime Concern). Chief constables were supposed to have received a letter from Mr. Steven Norris explaining the aims and constitution of Crime Concern, however, members of the subcommittee reported they had not received this letter when Crime Concern was officially launched.

The ACPO sub-committee on crime prevention appeared to be very wary of Crime Concern. The fact that Crime Concern was viewed as a commercial organisation is reiterated in five of the ACPO sub-committee on crime prevention minutes between 1989 and 1991. Crime Concern was mentioned as a separate item in every meeting from January 1989 until April 1992 inclusively (13 meetings). It appeared that at first ACPO was annoyed with Crime Concern because they were not consulted before going ahead with various initiatives.

A change of attitude seems to have occurred around the first quarter of 1993 when it was agreed that the chairperson would chair a session at a Crime Concern Conference and that Crime Concern invited a representative of the sub-committee to sit on Crime Concern's board.

In June 1994, a new chair and secretary were appointed. This is of major significance since at the chairperson's first meeting it was decided that membership to the board would be extended to include non-police members such as Ian Chisholm (the head of the Home Office Crime Prevention Unit), Dr. Gloria Laycock (the head of the Home Office Police Research Group), an executive member of the Home Office PSDB (Police Scientific Development Branch), and a chief officer representative from the

British Transport Police. This is of major significance since it is the first time that non-police members are represented on the Board.

Prior to this, the sub-committee remained closed and somewhat secretive. For example, in 1992 the Home Office Crime Prevention Unit asked for receipt of the sub-committee minutes. However, the subcommittee replied that the minutes were only intended for internal circulation. By being a closed committee, as they were in the past, could make them appear unapproachable. It is no wonder that the sub-committee members were not invited onto committees, or approached for their opinions. One cannot always get without giving a little. Now that the Crime Prevention Unit is actually represented on the committee, the fact of it being a closed sub-committee is a non-issue. The committee now appears to have become more open.

According to the minutes, after the new chairperson and secretary were appointed, Crime Concern was no longer a point of discussion. In 1995 Nigel Whiskin of Crime Concern accepted an invitation by the sub-committee to represent Crime Concern. No mention was made in earlier minutes about this. According to one interviewee, the representation of Crime Concern on the committee was mostly the doing of the chairperson and of the head of the Crime Prevention Unit at the time.

The author's own interpretation of events is that the chairperson in 1995 had a good understanding of the 'game' of crime prevention. If the police want to be seen as leaders in crime prevention, they cannot do so by remaining closed to the rest of the world. If people do not know what the police do in the crime prevention sub-committee (assuming they even know the committee exists), then how can they be expected to be approached for advice? In order to raise the profile of the sub-committee, the police need to be represented on high profile committees/boards/agencies which they had been attempting to do. However in order to remain as equal partners, equal exchanges have to occur (e.g., an 'if you sit on my committee, I'll sit on yours' kind of approach). If the police are always asking to sit on other committees without ever reciprocating, alienation occurs which is exactly the opposite of what the police want. Unfortunately, the result of this is that the same people sit on all the different committees.

The fact that the former Home Secretary and Minister repeatedly reinforced the leading role of the police in crime prevention also helped the sub-committee in maintaining their role as (at least one of the) leaders in crime prevention. The status, however, has remained one of sub-committee as opposed to a mainstream committee.

Promoting the Sub-Committee as an Energetic and Progressive Organisation At the inaugural meeting it was stated that the subcommittee would attempt to make ACPO more energetic and progressive within the domain of crime prevention. The author argues that until the appointment of the chairperson in June 1994, little progress had been made in promoting the sub-committee as energetic and progressive.

The author believes that having invited 'outsiders' into the committee was a sign of progress. It follows the thinking that the police are (a) not solely responsible for crime prevention; and (b) that they alone cannot reduce crime. These three outsiders are 'big players' when it comes to crime prevention research, policy and advice. Duplication of initiatives has already been avoided which leads to efficiency and cost savings.

The 'energy' of the Board seems to come from individuals who are very committed to crime prevention and want to see its importance elevated. While discussing the set up of the new National Crime Prevention Agency, it was stated that the crime prevention sub-committee chairperson was actively involved. This is quite an accomplishment when one considers that in the past, it seemed that ACPO had to formally ask to be represented on these committees. Now that outsiders have been invited as members, the committee cannot go back.

One possible consequence of this, is that the sub-committee could become more 'political'. However, as of yet no evidence of this is apparent in the minutes. The sub-committee now seems to be a forum where the police can keep up to date on current events and research relevant to crime prevention, which leads to more informed practical decisions.

Providing the ACPO Viewpoint Providing the ACPO viewpoint was one of the aims stated in the sub-committee's first meeting. This was to be done by producing position papers.

In reading through the minutes, the type of research done for the position papers was by contacting all police forces to ask their opinion on a certain matter. The author does not believe the research conducted by the sub-committee would pass academic scrutiny. It could be that for this reason their views were not eagerly sought. The sub-committee itself is not in a position to do or commission 'academic' research. Now that they have joined with the Home Office and Crime Concern, by having them represented on their sub-committee, more informed views can be provided. However, these views are not necessarily representative of the police service. They are the views of managers, as opposed to practitioners.

The Push For 'Good Practice' Guidelines When the sub-committee was first formed, there seemed to be a push for producing good practice guidelines which basically meant that ACPO endorsed the document. For example, guidelines on cash carrying by small businesses were established and then endorsed by ACPO. The sub-committee also approached the British Standards Institute (BSI) to produce a gun-cabinet standard which was agreed upon in 1989.

The Type of Crime Prevention Addressed By the Sub-Committee One of the objectives of the ACPO Crime Strategy is "Developing the Situational Approach" (see Figure 4.1). The minutes of the crime prevention sub-committee definitely focus on situational approaches. Alarm-related issues are discussed in 25 of the 35 minutes, (excluding references to the alarm-related working groups). Neighbourhood Watch or similar programmes, (e.g., Horse Watch, or Street Watch), are mentioned in 28 of the 35 minutes. When one takes into account that the sub-committee has two working groups related to alarms, one can come to the conclusion that the issue of ongoing concern was alarms. Of particular interest was the notion of charging for false alarms.

The other two working groups focus on tracking devices for stolen cars, and architectural design. Programmes such as SPLASH or other offender-oriented activities are not mentioned in the minutes. This sub-committee most definitely is about situational, target hardening prevention.

Forming an ACPO-ACOP Relationship In August 1989 mention is made that a letter was received from ACOP to discuss possible links between the two organisations. At the beginning of 1993, the minutes state that a briefing paper would be produced on the agreement between ACPO and ACOP. In 1994 a meeting had taken place and further meetings were planned.

In an interview, the content of this meeting was uncovered. The probation service and the police are working on "the theme of utilising information for crime prevention purposes" (Interview). This essentially means developing an information system within the criminal justice system that could contribute to crime prevention planning. This project is viewed as being very long term (e.g., 20 years from now) since "it is a very complicated issue" (Interview). The meeting "was very complex with heavy stuff on the problems of drawing different departments more into alignment for more effective information exchange, and a whole range of other things. It is not just getting the concepts clear of what you are talking about" (Interview). The Home Office is also involved in these discussions.

This section demonstrates that there is a crime prevention relationship between the police and probation. Thus, the police and probation do acknowledge that both organisations contribute to crime prevention. The divide between offence-oriented approaches and offender-oriented approaches detected within the Home Office does not seem to be so strong once you withdraw yourself from the Home Office.

The Operational Policing Review

In 1989, the three staff associations worked together and produced the *Operational Policing Review* (Joint Consultative Committee, 1990). Although not a policy document, it was an effort to advance "the policy making process of the police service" (Joint Consultative Committee, 1990: 1). Two sections of this report are relevant to this research. One section on efficiency and effectiveness examined 'the community and crime prevention'. Another section consisted of a police survey in which questions connected to crime prevention were asked. These two sections provide some insight on how crime prevention was perceived by the police service at the time.

In the section on efficiency and effectiveness, the report states that crime prevention,

> is not just about reducing the level of reported crime as published by the police on a regular basis in their returns of criminal statistics ... it has to reflect the level of fear about crime that might exist in a particular community (Joint Consultative Committee 1990: section 2: 48).

The report defined crime prevention using the terms primary, secondary and tertiary. However, the author would argue that their definitions are contrary to those utilised by criminologists (who often use Brantingham and Faust's 1976 definition) and those from the medical profession (see Chapter 1). Here is what the Joint Consultative Committee (1990: section 2, page 48) said:

> Primary crime prevention can best be described as the workings of the mainstream criminal justice system. The patrolling police constable is a crime prevention source. The court which incarcerates an offender for a period of time is fulfilling a crime prevention function - bluntly by incapacitation. The probation officer who counsels and advises an offender to divert him away from further offending is preventing crime... .
>
> Secondary crime prevention can be described as steps taken to reduce the risk of crime occurring. Sometimes known as situational crime prevention this includes steps such as improvements to physical security (locks, bolts and alarm systems) as well as more comprehensive measures such as close circuit television, surveillance systems and property marking. Initiatives taken in response to this development are directed at specific forms of crime which involve the management, design or manipulation of the immediate environment in which crimes occur.
>
> Tertiary or social crime prevention is the subject at its widest. Rather than look at the offence in isolation it concerns itself with the social conditions in which the offence takes place.

What the Consultative Committee defined as primary prevention could be defined as tertiary prevention since one is dealing with the offender. However, the deterrent aspect of the criminal justice system could arguably be considered as primary prevention since general deterrence is aimed at the entire population. What the Consultative Committee considered as secondary prevention, could be considered as primary prevention since the initiatives are developed to discourage the public at large. What the Consultative Committee defined as tertiary prevention, could be defined as primary prevention since once again it affects the entire population and not solely offenders.

This section of the Police Consultative Committee illustrates that even the classifications of 'crime prevention' are misunderstood. Therefore if someone says "I work mainly in tertiary crime prevention", one doesn't really know what s/he does. Do they work in a treatment programme (e.g., drug or alcohol) or do they work with, for example, housing issues (e.g., social conditions in which offences take place). When one official from the police department of the Home Office said they focused on primary and secondary prevention ... what did he really mean? One cannot assume that one knows what the other is talking about.

In fact, Duplock (1993: 45-46) found this problem with his research:

> It arguably reflects the influence of an assumption on the part of both parties that each 'knew' what the other was talking about and on the part of the researcher that others reading the paper would be similarly informed.

The Review also states, "the role of the police in the area of situational prevention has been one of initiating and co-ordinating the development of initiatives. The actual measures that have been implemented to reduce crime through the reduction in opportunities are often beyond the scope of the police" (Joint Consultative Committee, 1990: section 2: 48). As with the annual reports of Her Majesty's Chief Inspectorate of Constabulary, the section then goes on to describe crime prevention initiatives such as the Kirkholt Burglary Prevention Project, Property Marking, Neighbourhood Watch, and the Five Towns Initiative. The role of the police in these initiatives is not addressed in detail.

Within the police survey, one question asked officers to indicate whether they thought certain tasks were 'very important', 'fairly important', or 'not very important'. One of the tasks listed was 'give advice to public on how to prevent crime'. Thirty-one per cent of police officers considered this task to be very important (Joint Consultative Committee, 1990: section 6: 8).[26]

Based on the findings of this review, it appears that the police have not clearly defined their role in crime prevention. In the section on efficiency and effectiveness, the police do not state their role in crime prevention generally, nor what their role was in the initiatives described. The police survey also leaves the concept of crime prevention open. The findings however do suggest that crime prevention is considered a low priority in terms of resources.

At around the same time as the *Operational Policing Review* (Joint Consultative Committee, 1990), ACPO produced *The Police Service*

---

26 The task with the highest percentage of police officers stating it was 'very important' was 'responding immediately to emergencies' with a response of 97%. The tasks with the least number of officers classifying them as 'very important' were 'control and supervise road traffic' and 'work with local council departments' each with a response of 13%.

Statement of Common Purpose and Values (ACPO, 1990). This Statement is at the beginning of the *Police Probationer Training Foundation Course* (Home Office Central Planning Unit, 1991) which is the current police training manual for all police in England and Wales today (see also Home Office, 1994c). According to *The Police Service Statement of Common Purpose and Values* (ACPO, 1990), the second purpose of the police is "to prevent crime". An elaboration on what is meant by "preventing crime" is not provided, but the contents of the training manual include a section on crime prevention which indicates how crime prevention is to be construed.

The Police Probationer Training Foundation Course

The *Police Probationer Training Foundation Course* manual is very much focused on approaches aimed at the offence rather than the offender. This section shall examine the parts of the manual that refer to crime prevention to illustrate the point.

The section "Crime Prevention" in the Police Training manual is divided into seven parts:

1) introduction;
2) what is meant by "crime prevention"?;
3) crimes other than burglary;
4) acting after a crime;
5) specialist knowledge;
6) community participation; and
7) local knowledge.

In addition to this section there are further references to crime prevention in the manual which will be examined.

Introduction

The introduction states "that crime prevention is a primary responsibility of all police officers". Further on it states,

> The majority of people who commit crime are opportunists ... a preventive strategy can cut down the opportunities for crime and benefit both the police

and the public ... . Crime can only be prevented through co-ordinated action by the police, other agencies and the community (2/9/1).

Based on the introduction, one could conclude that crime is based on opportunity. In this sense the police would consequently focus on situational prevention.

What is Meant by 'Crime Prevention'?

The meaning of crime prevention in the second part of the crime prevention section states that crime prevention "involves the *anticipation, recognition* and *appraisal* of a crime risk and the initiation of *action* to remove or reduce it" (2/9/2). Further down the page it states "often the action required will be straight-forward and may simply consist of giving tactful advice to members of the public" (2/9/2). In other paragraphs, it suggests that crime may be deterred by police presence (although "other duties will often prevent, <the police officer> from doing this), or through more long term solutions such as approaching the Council for improved street lighting' (2/9/2). The words 'approaching the council' could imply that the police alone cannot prevent crime and, therefore, are not completely responsible for the prevention of crime. Using 'street lighting' as an example demonstrates once again a 'situational approach' to crime prevention.

The crime prevention section then goes on to state,

> There are various measures which can be used to make a building and its contents less attractive targets for burglars. Good quality locks on doors and windows make the building harder to enter ... widespread use of physical security measures cuts down the criminal's opportunities, and increases the risk of being caught. They should therefore be less willing to go out looking for the chance to commit crime. Steps can be taken to make criminals more conspicuous. For example, street and house lighting can be improved. Barriers like tall hedges make a property private for its occupier, but they also provide cover for the potential thief. The criminal will also be put off if premises are overlooked by windows from which inquisitive neighbours could see him (2/9/3).

This approach follows the philosophies of Neighbourhood Watch and once again is situational in approach. The last 2 paragraphs of the section state,

> People are encouraged to mark movable property. Their post-code, followed by the house number gives a unique reference. It can be applied to household or office articles, cycles, car windows and other property. This makes property harder to dispose of and, therefore, less desirable to the thief. The criminal will only be deterred if it is clear that the property is marked, so owners should advertise the fact by the use of stickers or posters.
>
> Also when marked property is recovered from criminals, the owner can be traced easily. Owners of valuable antiques should be encouraged to photograph such items (2/9/4).

These two paragraphs are about property marking - once again situational. The emphasis is most definitely on 'the crime' and not risk factors associated with 'offending'. The potential offender is not described in any manner.

Crimes Other Than Burglary

This part states,

> Crime Prevention is not only aimed at reducing burglaries. Many other crimes can be prevented. Cycles without locks, cars with the keys left in and purses resting on shopping bags are all gifts to the opportunist. Children left unsupervised in parks and other public areas could be at risk (2/9/4).

Crime prevention relating to continuous crimes (e.g., assault, domestic violence) is not mentioned. Crime prevention thus appears to be associated with vehicles, homes/businesses, and theft in general.

Acting After A Crime

This part states,

> When you attend the scene of a crime that has already happened, you are there to investigate it, but you can also THINK PREVENTION. Ask yourself some basic questions:
>
> a) How did this crime happen? What did the criminal do to the victim, or to the property.
> b) Why did the criminal pick this victim, this house, or this car?
> c) Could this crime have been prevented and if so, how?
> d) What can I do to stop it happening again here, or some-where else?

> e) How do I persuade a potential victim to remove the crime risk that I have identified?
> f) What help can I get from colleagues and from other agencies? (2/9/4).

No mention is made on what can be done with the answers to these questions.

Specialist Knowledge

This part states,

> Every force has specialist Crime Prevention Officers (CPOs). CPO's are able to advise members of the public about the security of their homes or businesses ... if you feel you need expert help - ASK YOUR CPO (2/9/5).

According to ACPO sub-committee on crime prevention minutes in 1993, the CPOs role is only to act as a facilitator of advice for the public to make their own decisions. This part emphasises once again that the role of the police is to provide advice regarding crime prevention.

Community Participation

This part states,

> the community must be involved in crime prevention if it is to be effective. Schemes like 'Neighbourhood Watch' make people more aware of crime in their area. Residents are encouraged to help the police in preventing and detecting crime by:
>
> 1) improving the security of their own homes;
> 2) watching out for suspicious incidents and reporting them to the police. Close co-operation between residents and the police helps to build good relationships (2/9/6).

This ties into the concepts of 'community policing' and Neighbourhood Watch. The emphasis is again on the offence rather than the offender.

Local Knowledge

Finally the last part of the section on crime prevention states,

> By building your local knowledge you will work your beat more effectively and be better equipped to prevent crime. ... You will build up much of your knowledge through observation and talking to members of the community ... Crime prevention is constantly promoted by public bodies, voluntary organisations and, of course, the police ... by adopting a professional approach to the prevention of crime, you will enhance your own job satisfaction and be able to provide the public with accurate and practical advice (2/9/7).

This section once again touches upon the philosophies of community policing (e.g., by talking to members of the community) and it brings out once again the notion of giving advice.

Other References to Crime Prevention In the Manual

Section 2/37/1 of the police training manual states,

> The primary object of an efficient police service is the PREVENTION of crime ... It would be poor police duty, then, to stand by and wait until criminals commit the crime they obviously intend to commit.

Later, under the heading of conveyance, there is a subsection on crime prevention. It discusses ways of securing cars and motorbikes from theft. Once again the emphasis is on closing windows, locking doors and boots, parking in a well lit area at night (or preferably in a garage), and not leaving keys in the ignition or valuable items on display (2/49/4, 2/49/5).

Summary on the Police Probationer Training Foundation Course Manual

According to the manual, the role of the police in the area of crime prevention is situational. The focus is the prevention of a crime (the action), not the criminal (the actor). This, it appears, is mostly done through advice-giving. It should be pointed out that by 'advice-giving' one does not mean telling someone to lock their doors, or keep lights on while away. Advice-giving goes further than this to initiating actions to prevent crime, as an earlier example illustrated: 'approaching the Council for improved street lighting'(2/9/2). This role of theirs is under emphasised, especially when one considers that the means of reducing opportunities for crime are often beyond the realm of the police.

How The Police In Boroughville Defined 'Crime Prevention'

In the questionnaires distributed to both police and probation officers the first two questions were:

1) Do you consider that you perform any crime prevention work as part of your day-to-day activities?
2) If you answered YES could you please provide some examples of what you do.

Of the 150 police officers who returned a completed questionnaire, 137 officers replied 'yes' to the first question (91.3%), thus indicating that crime prevention is considered by most police officers to be a part of their day-to-day activities.

Twelve police officers considered that they did not perform any crime prevention tasks as part of their day-to-day activities.[27] Neither age nor years of service was a factor in the different responses. The only meaningful information was that five of the twelve respondents were constables, six were sergeants, and one was an inspector. The five constables accounted for 4.8% of all constables, the 6 sergeants for 19.4% of that rank, and the 1 inspector accounted for 11.1% of that rank. Thus the largest proportion of officers who considered that they did not perform crime prevention work as part of their day to day activities were sergeants.

For the second question, 82 different combinations of answers were categorised. The author then categorised these answers under the following headings:

1) No answer
2) Advice to victims
3) Other Advice
4) Patrol
5) Neighbourhood Watch
6) Arrest
7) Stop-checks
8) Through Schools

---

[27] 137 officers said they did perform crime prevention work, 12 stated they did not, and one did not answer the question. This adds up to 150 (the number of returned completed questionnaires).

9) Giving information to colleagues
10) Talking to members of the Public and Groups
11) Surveys
12) Inter-Agency Schemes
13) Security, Checks
14) Facilitating crime prevention
15) Press releases
16) Warnings and cautions
17) Collecting information/observation
18) Setting Policies
19) Managing Resources
20) Other.

The number of responses for each category is available in Table 4.1. Appendix I provides the 'code book' utilised for categorising the replies. If an officer stated that they prevented crime by "preventative patrol" and through "liaison with schools" then they were included both in the category of 'patrol' and the category of 'schools'. Thus double counting was admitted in this question.

By using this categorisation, the majority of responses fell under Patrol with 58 out of 137 (42.3%) stating that this was at least one way in which they prevented crime. Fifty-seven police officers (41.6%) identified advice to victims as a method of preventing crime; and 49 respondents (35.8%) were classified under 'other advice'. In all other cases less than 9% of police officers were accounted for in each category.

If one combined 'advice to victims' with 'other advice' (and eliminating double-counting within these two categories), 94 out of 137 (68.6%) police officers mentioned 'advice' as part of their day-to-day work. If one considers the responses of patrol, arrest, stop-checks, giving information to colleagues, warnings and cautions, and collecting information/observation to represent traditional policing then 69 of the 137 (50.4%) police officers considered traditional policing activities to be crime prevention work in their day-to-day activities.

The findings from this questionnaire suggest that crime prevention is thought of by the majority of police officers as a part of their own policing task. The findings also suggest that the method/technique by which crime prevention is most often perceived as being delivered is through police patrols or police presence and, by giving advice to others. One could therefore speculate that when the government announces that a certain number of police officers will be recruited, that the police believe their presence will help in preventing crime.

Table 4.1 Number of Police Officers by Percentage of Police Officers by Type of Crime Prevention done as part of their day-to-day activities

	Number of Police Officers	Percentage of Police Officers
Advice to victims	57	41.6
Other Advice	49	35.8
Patrol	58	42.3
Neighbourhood watch	9	6.6
Arrest	7	5.1
Stop checks	12	8.8
Through schools	8	5.8
Giving information to colleagues	3	2.2
Talking to members of the Public and Groups	4	2.9
Surveys	4	2.9
Inter-Agency Schemes	1	0.7
Security, Checks	4	2.9
Facilitating crime prevention	3	2.2
Press releases	1	0.7
Warnings & cautions	1	0.7
Collecting information/ observation	4	2.9
Setting Policies	1	0.7
Managing Resources	2	1.5
Other	5	3.6

Conclusion

Although the responsibility for crime prevention by the police is still recognised today, they are not considered to be the only agency responsible for the prevention of crime. The police service is informed about crime prevention through many sources some of which have been examined in this chapter. The sources examined include Her Majesty's Chief Inspector of Constabulary, the Audit Commission, the staff associations, in particular ACPO and the sub-committee on crime prevention, the *Operational Policing Review*, and the probationer training manual for new recruits.

The actual views of police officers in one city were also examined. The results confirmed that (a) police officers believe they do crime prevention as part of their day-to-day work and (b) that the main mechanisms for crime prevention are by giving advice and by patrolling the streets or being seen.

In this chapter, six issues were pulled out.

1) The first issue is that like the organisations to be described in the next chapters, the police service through the Audit Commission supported the recommendations made in the Morgan Report. However, according to 4 interviews in 1997, the police strongly objected to local authorities having a sole responsibility for community safety. As a consequence both the police and local authorities will be given a statutory responsibility for community safety in the upcoming Crime and Disorder Bill. Within this chapter there was a consistent view among the various sources that the police cannot work in isolation from other agencies if they want to be effective in tackling crime. The multi-agency approach was strongly advocated. This was evidenced (1) in Her Majesty's Chief Inspector of Constabulary Annual Reports through the theme of needing to co-operate with other agencies; (2) in the Audit Commission paper (1990: 20); (3) through ACOP and ACPO working together to come up with a national information base that could be used within the criminal justice system; (4) in the fact that many ACPO members sit on other agency committees; and finally (5) in the *Police Probationer Training Foundation Course* manual which states that "crime can only be prevented through co-ordinated action by the police, other agencies and the community" (Home Office Central Planning Unit, 1991: 2/9/1).

2) The second issue is that crime prevention is definitely incorporated as a policing task. This is evidenced in the fact that 91.3% of police officers in Boroughville stated that they did perform crime prevention work as part of their day-to-day activities. It is also evidenced in all sources reviewed, where crime prevention was separately listed as a policing task for all officers. Unfortunately, a few questions still remain: What exactly is crime prevention for the police? Is it deterrence through patrol or crime

prevention advice? In what way would the public consider police to perform a crime prevention function?

One fact remains, and that is the police are considered to be the crime fighters, and the agency that brings an individual to a criminal court. Foucault (1969: 50-51) suggested that some individuals are accorded a status of competence and knowledge and have through their profession the presumption that what they say is true. The author suggests that this is true of the police. As a consequence, having a police officer tell you that your property is at risk of theft is likely to be more meaningful than the information coming through any other agency.

The role for the police in crime prevention policy making is also a debatable issue. The extent to which the police are prominent in this capacity is dependent on the individual in charge, the next issue to be discussed.

3) Within the Police Service, the prominence received for crime prevention is very much dependent on who is in charge. This is evidenced both through the Annual Reports of Her Majesty's Chief Inspector of Constabulary and through the ACPO sub-committee on crime prevention.

In Her Majesty's Chief Inspector of Constabulary Annual Reports, one notes that from 1 April 1990 until June 1993 John Woodcock was Her Majesty's Chief Inspector of Constabulary (Home Office, 1993d and Home Office, 1994c). During the years that investigations were done under his reign, the reports included very little on crime prevention. This, one could suspect, might be due to his own views on the definition and degree of importance of crime prevention within the police service.

Within the ACPO sub-committee on crime prevention, one finds that the chairperson from 1994-1996 drastically changed working relationships between the Home Office, Crime Concern and the Police (at least at high levels). Prior to his appointment as chairperson, the subcommittee had to ask to be represented on working groups and committees.

Eight years later in 1995, the chair to the crime prevention sub-committee was one of the key people in forming the National Crime Prevention Agency. Under this chairmanship the sub-committee decided to invite non-police members to sit on the sub-committee. This is very significant in that the chairperson has direct access to the Minister and can therefore have much more of an impact in crime prevention policy making. In two interviews, the chairperson to this committee was described as "approachable" and both agreed that personalities mattered in the sphere of crime prevention policy making.

Furthermore, the director of the Crime Prevention Agency was an Assistant Chief Constable and member of the ACPO sub-committee on crime prevention.

4) The fourth issue relates to the definition of crime prevention within the sources examined. Two issues come out under this heading. One is that the definition of crime prevention is not very clear and not consistent amongst various publications. The second is that the only consistencies that do come out of all the sources is that crime prevention within the police service seems to be about multi-agency crime prevention with other agencies, partnerships with the community, and situational approaches to crime prevention.

The lack of a clear definition for crime prevention is evident in the *Operational Policing Review* (Joint Consultative Committee, 1990) when the definitions for primary, secondary and tertiary prevention are contrary to those used both in medical circles and to those of Brantingham and Faust (1976) who adapted the medical model into criminological terms. Why the Joint Consultative Committee used the definitions that it did is unknown, but this sort of contradiction in terminology is one factor that leads to confusion within crime prevention circles.

Within Her Majesty's Chief Inspector of Constabulary Reports, 11 themes were brought out that appeared under the crime prevention heading. These eleven themes were not found in the Audit Commission Reports nor in the ACPO sub-committee on crime prevention meetings. Within the Annual Reports the most consistent themes within crime prevention were Neighbourhood Watch and publicity campaigns. Is this what crime prevention is about for the police? According to the police in Boroughville, the answer would be 'no'. Only 9 out of 137 police officers (6.6%) of police officers stated that Neighbourhood Watch was a method by which they prevented crime in their day-to-day activities. No police officers stated they were involved in publicity campaigns. This is consistent with findings from Her Majesty's Chief Inspectorate of Constabulary annual reports which indicate that publicity campaigns are sponsored by the Home Office and not by police forces themselves.

More recently the notion of repeat victimisation, pattern analysis and CCTVs have come to dominate examples of crime prevention work in the literature. In fact the focus of the National Board for Crime Prevention and

National Crime Prevention Agency appears to be in repeat victimisation and CCTVs.

Finally, the view of the Audit Commission seems to be that the role of the police in tackling crime is to 'investigate and apprehend' which one could interpret as being about catching the offender after the offence was committed rather than stopping the crime before it actually occurred. This is a common perspective on what the police do (e.g., through television programmes such as '*The Bill*'), as opposed to what their role should be in actually stopping crimes before they occur (e.g., in preventing crime).

The second issue that crime prevention within the police service seems to be about multi-agency crime prevention with other agencies, partnerships with the community, and situational approaches to crime prevention was partly discussed above. The fact that the police advocate situational approaches is evident in Her Majesty's Chief Inspector of Constabulary Annual Reports where the philosophy that crime is opportunistic was implied.

The ACPO sub-committee on crime prevention actually states that one of their objectives is to "develop the situational approach". In 25 of the 35 sub-committee minutes analysed, the issue of alarms was raised. In addition two of the four working groups in the sub-committee are about alarms. The police probationer training manual also states that crime is opportunistic (Home Office Central Planning Unit, 1991: 2/9/1).

In addition to this, if one brings in the findings from the previous chapter that the Standard Course on Crime Prevention is very much oriented to situational approaches and advice giving, then one can clearly see that the notion that police crime prevention is about situational prevention is justified based on the sources analysed in this research.

5) The fifth issue is that the findings from the Questionnaires in Boroughville are consistent with findings of the literature at the national level. In particular, the finding that crime prevention for the police is about giving advice is strongly supported. 94 out of 137 (68.6%) police officers mentioned giving advice as a method in which they prevented crime. The third theme raised under Her Majesty's Chief Inspector of Constabulary Annual Reports suggests that giving advice is one task of police officers; the Audit Commission Report on Tackling Crime Effectively (1993: 13) also mentions the role of the police in giving advice. Finally, the advice giving role of the police is also mentioned in the police probationer training manual which states that "often the action required will be straight forward

and may simply consist of giving tactful advice to members of the public' (Home Office Central Planning Unit, 1991: 2/9/2).

6) The sixth issue is whether detection and prevention are 'inextricably linked' as the Audit Commission suggested they should be (Audit Commission, 1993: 15). Within the Home Office Police Research Group, the once entitled 'Crime Prevention Series' was renamed the 'Crime Detection and Prevention Series'. This it was stated, was done "to try and bring prevention and detection closer together so that the police stop thinking of crime prevention as being over there somewhere, and start to think of crime management bringing the two things together" (Interview). The 1992 annual report from Her Majesty's Chief Inspector of Constabulary also combined crime prevention and detection (Home Office, 1993d: 30). In the 1993 Annual Report under 'Management of Crime' both detection and prevention are reviewed (Home Office, 1994c: 26-28).

However, the minutes from one ACPO crime prevention sub-committee meeting in 1994 inferred that criminal investigation training and crime prevention training should remain separate. The author questions whether this is an indication that the two should not be seen as one and the same.

Furthermore, the Key Objectives for Policing set out by the Home Secretary separate detection from prevention. The first two objectives deal with increasing the number of detections and the third deals with targeting and preventing crimes. Thus although attempts are being made to link detection and prevention, evidence exists that the two are not uniformly linked across the police service.

5 The Probation Service

Introduction

The probation service's role in crime prevention is evidenced in four ways. The first is that the probation service was represented on the National Board for Crime Prevention, which was reviewed in Chapter 2.

The second is that the Home Office (1984c) Statement of National Objectives and Priorities for the Probation Service states that crime prevention is a task of probation officers. This task of theirs is supported in other reports and research (e.g., the Central Council of Probation Committees, 1987: 4; Home Office 1994f; Geraghty, 1991).

A third method in which the probation service has a role to play in the field of crime prevention is that some probation service areas continue to second officers to act as crime prevention co-ordinators in their community. According to one community safety officer, current and past probation experience are the commonest backgrounds amongst them.

Finally, the role of probation is acknowledged by the fact that they were involved in teaching one module of the Standard Crime Prevention Course at the Home Office Crime Prevention Centre in Stafford.

This chapter examines the probation service in general, the overall structure of the probation service, national directives influencing the work of the probation service, the Association of Chief Officers of Probation committee on crime prevention, how the probation service in general can help to prevent crime, and how probation officers of all ranks in Boroughville said they performed crime prevention in their day-to-day activities.

The issues of how the probation service can contribute to crime prevention, and what type of prevention they are involved in (e.g., crime versus criminality prevention) is also addressed.

The Probation Service

Like the police, the courts, prisons and the Crown Prosecution Service, the probation service is a criminal justice agency. The concept of probation work was influenced from experiences and practices in the United States and in 1907 was legislated in England and Wales under the 1907 Probation of Offenders Act (NACRO, 1988: 1). Eighty percent of their funding comes through the Home Office and 20% from the relevant local government (Interview and NACRO, 1988).

The main areas of work for probation officers include: providing services to the criminal courts such as seeking accommodation for the defendant, giving oral reports, providing information and practical advice to defendants' families; preparing social enquiry reports for the courts which consists of detailed background reports of offenders and their circumstances; supervising offenders in the community; providing community service schemes; running probation and bail hostels and day centres; providing social work service in prisons; providing after-care for prisoners; providing a range of constructive schemes in the community which is often related to preventing crime and family breakdown by supporting offenders, young persons at risk, victims, mediation and reparation schemes, housing and treatment programmes; and finally, providing social work service to the civil courts dealing for example in matters of divorce or separation when children are involved (NACRO, 1988: 2-4; see also Central Council of Probation Committees, 1990: 11).

The Overall Structure of The Probation Service

In England and Wales there are 54 probation areas. Each of these areas is governed by an independent probation committee which establishes an overall policy for its area, in consultation with its Chief Probation Officer (NACRO, 1988:1). The structure of the probation committee is defined in law and "is primarily composed of magistrates and a representative of the judiciary" (Interview). The local courts elect the people to sit on the probation committee. These 54 probation committees are all represented on the Central Council of Probation Committees.

Management within the probation service are represented by the Association of Chief Officers of Probation (ACOP) who in 1988 created a crime prevention committee which will be examined further in this chapter. In 1996, the Association "replaced the existing Committee structure with a new system of Lead Officers. Each Lead Officer is responsible for a subject area and progresses issues in conjunction with the Elected Officers.

Lead Officers may establish network and support groups to facilitate the work"(ACOP, 1996: 13).

For non-management personnel there is the National Association of Probation Officers which is a trade union. There is also a Probation Inspectorate which provides advice to Ministers and the Home Office.

National Probation Directives

In April 1984 the Home Office's Probation Service Division published a 'Statement of Objectives and Priorities' for the probation service. The document set out the nature and job of the probation service. Under the heading 'Other Work in the Community', it stated that crime prevention was formally considered as one of the probation service's tasks. The statement said that the Service should seek to attain the following specific objectives which included: "developing the service to the wider public by contributing to initiatives concerned with the prevention of crime and the support of victims, and playing a part in the activities of local statutory and voluntary organisations" (Home Office, 1984c: 5). The author suspects that this statement was included as a result of Home Office Circular 8/1984.

Later that year, the Central Council of Probation Committees established a working party on crime prevention. The terms of reference were "to examine the specific role which might be played by the probation service in the prevention and/or reduction of crime and in due course to publish a report containing recommendations to probation committees concerning national and local policy" (Central Council of Probation Committees, 1987: 4).

Probation Rules which was also published in 1984 stated under the heading 'other duties': "It shall be part of the duties of a probation officer to participate in such arrangements concerned with the prevention of crime or with the relationship between offenders and their victims or the community at large as may be approved by the probation committee on the advice of the Chief Probation Officer" (Home Office, 1984b: paragraph 37).

In 1990, the Home Office (1990e: 6) stated "the probation service must gear its work more and more towards crime prevention in its broadest sense. This involves firm and constructive work with offenders ... it also involves joining together with the police, local authorities and the rest of the community in initiatives to prevent crime".

After the implementation of the Criminal Justice Act 1991, three annual publications were produced: (1) Annual Reports (which until 1 January 1993 had not been openly published or available to the press);[28] (2) three year plans for the probation service (which supersedes the 1984 Statement of National Objectives and Priorities [Home Office, 1992d: 1]), and (3) the annual production of National Standards for the Supervision of Offenders in the Community.

Within the Annual Reports produced by Her Majesty's Inspectorate of Probation, the prevention of crime is only mentioned superficially in the section entitled 'Overview'. In 1992-93, the report states, "It will mean giving precedence to courts and demonstrating that the probation service is in business to attack crime, its overwhelming objective being that of preventing, reducing, containing and controlling offending" (Home Office, 1993e: 9).

In 1993-94, the Annual Report states "The most significant event for me over the past year or two, has been the discovery and observation of how effective probation services can be in reducing offending. It is also fair to say that I have been disappointed at how difficult it has been to get this message across to the wider community" (Home Office, 1994d: 9). When one considers that the Annual Reports from Her Majesty's Inspectorate of Probation do not address 'reducing offending', one could say that they themselves are guilty of not getting the message across.

The 1995 annual report stated, "The task is for the probation service to make the maximum possible difference in terms of preventing crime and protecting the public" (Home Office 1995g: 7).

The 1996 Annual Report mentions crime prevention with respect to offenders attempting to redress some of the damage to victims' and their property in community service projects (Home Office, 1997b: 29). Furthermore, the Statement of Purpose for the Inspectorate states that probation areas should make sure to "reduce offending, pay regard to victims and protect the public through the rigorous supervision of dangerous, serious and/or persistent offenders" (Home Office, 1997b: 43).

Within the four publicly available annual reports to date, the above

---

[28] Her Majesty's Inspectorate of Probation first annual report stated, "Until the end of 1992, circulation of reports was restricted to the probation committee, chief probation officer and relevant local authority or authorities. From 1993, all efficiency and effectiveness reports have openly published and are available to anyone interested in seeing them" (Home Office, 1993e: 24).

quotations have been the only references to preventing crime. This would suggest that prevention is not a principal concern of the Inspectorate.

Within the three year plans, more attention is provided to preventing crime. The plans for 1993-1996 and 1994-1997 are basically identical as far as what is said with regards to crime prevention. However, the plans for 1995-1998, 1996-1999 and 1997-2000 provide key performance indicators which suggest that the meaning of crime prevention shifted from one of participating in Safer City type schemes to reducing re-offending while under supervision.

The plans for 1993-1996 and 1994-1997 state that the probation service's main responsibilities include "to help communities prevent crime and reduce its effect on victims" and "to work in partnership with other bodies and services in using the most constructive methods of dealing with offenders and defendants" (Home Office, 1992d: ii; 1994f: 2). One of the operational goals of the probation service is "crime reduction - reducing and preventing crime, and the fear of crime, by working in partnership with others" (Home Office, 1992d: iv; 1994f: 4). Later in the document this goal is expanded upon and the following is stated,

> The probation service has a particular role to play in advising on and generating ideas for suitable local projects, and in running schemes such as those funded under Safer Cities which involve offenders. This is in addition to its prime task of working to reduce re-offending (Home Office, 1992d: 12; 1994f: 16).

The Plan for 1995-1998 states that one of the main responsibilities of the probation service is to "help communities prevent crime and reduce its effects on victims" (Home Office, 1995m: 4; see also Home Office, 1996d: 1; 1997e: 7). The Home Secretary's priorities for the work of the service over the planning period includes "contribute towards the reduction of offending behaviour" (Home Office, 1995m: 24; see also Home Office, 1996d: 8). Six goals are set out for the service including, "reducing crime and supervising offenders effectively" (Home Office, 1995m; 1996d, 1997e: 9).

The means by which this goal is to be achieved include:

I. developing local bail support provision
II. implementing community sentences
III. providing effective throughcare and post-release supervision

IV. providing or securing accommodation for offenders requiring supervision or support
V. partnership in inter-agency crime prevention (Home Office, 1995m: 25).

Interestingly, three key performance indicators have been created to measure the success of this goal. They include:

1) To maintain at a rate lower than predicted the percentage of offenders subject to community sentences subsequently reconvicted;
2) To increase the proportion of approved hostel residents completing their period of residence to 60 per cent in 1995-96, 65 per cent in 1996-97 and 70 per cent in 1997-98;
3) To achieve national standards relating to commencement of orders, frequency of contact and breach in 85 per cent of cases in 1995-96 and 90 per cent thereafter (Home Office, 1995m: 26).

No indicator is cited for measuring 'partnerships in inter-agency crime prevention'. Based on the information provided in this three year plan, one can conclude that the term preventing crime is used to refer to preventing re-offending while under supervision. Therefore, this means that preventing crime is based on tertiary prevention. This coincides with a statement made in the 1992-93 Annual Review (Home Office, 1993e: 44) which states, "<the probation service> will need to address a range of public relations issues in order to transmit effectively its image as the primary agency delivering community penalties and reformative efforts to the courts and communities it serves".

In the 1996-1999 three year plan, the goal of "reducing crime and supervising offenders effectively" remained (Home Office, 1996d: 9-15). The performance indicators for 1996-99 and 1997-2000 were also similar to those of 1995-98.

The third document to come out since the Criminal Justice Act 1991 is the National Standards for the Supervision of Offenders in the Community published annually. None of these publications mention the role of probation in crime prevention (e.g., Home Office 1992c, 1995j). This series is, as the title states, about supervision of offenders and not about all the roles and responsibilities of probation officers other than supervision duties. The words 'partnership' and 'liaison' do feature under 'The role of chief officers'. However, the context is in relation to the re-integration of offenders, and promoting effective and efficient supervision. No mention is made, for example, about doing this effectively in order to reduce the likelihood of re-offending.

In order to indicate the importance of the probation service in crime prevention, it would have been useful at least to have a footnote somewhere in the publication that stated there are other duties of a probation officer apart from the ones listed, or that, one should attempt to lower re-offending or re-conviction rates.

The ACOP Crime Prevention Committee

In 1987, ACOP set up a crime prevention committee "as a result of recognition of the relevance of the 1984 joint government interdepartmental circular <Home Office Circular 8/1984>" (Geraghty, 1991: 2; Interview). There had been "a continuing and growing awareness of the need to look outwards from beyond the <probation> services' immediate statutory responsibilities from supervising offenders to broader issues of crime and social problems and crime prevention" (Interview).

This committee consisted of a chairperson who could hold the position for as long as s/he liked (i.e., it was not for a fixed term as with ACPO's sub-committee on crime prevention) and of "about 10-11 people who have management responsibilities in one of the probation services in England and Wales and who have particular responsibilities or interests in promoting crime prevention work" (Interview).

However, in 1996, the committee structure within ACOP changed. Instead community safety was allocated to a lead officer (who happened to be the chairperson of the committee). In order to provide some idea on what work might be undertaken by the lead officer, the tasks that the committee worked on in 1995 are described. They included for example,

1) Producing "a fairly influential paper which unpacked the research <on repeat victimisation> and posed questions as to what the relevance was for probation, what the implications were" (Interview).

The idea of repeat victimisation was partly picked up by the fact that the chair of this committee sat on the National Board for Crime Prevention. The fact that probation transferred knowledge from the National Board for Crime Prevention to their own organisation is a good example of the benefits that can be achieved from agencies/people working together. If probation were not involved in the Board it is difficult to know whether they would have picked up on the notion of repeat victimisation.

Unfortunately, the probation service was not a member of the National Crime Prevention Agency, which the author shall discuss in more detail later in this chapter.

2) Commissioning work on car crime. The work examined "different approaches that were being adopted to working with auto offenders and to highlight how that work can then be networked with a wider range of agencies such as schools, youth and community service, and so on" (Interview).

3) Commissioning a sub-group to examine the various examples of probation service documentation on internal inspection and evaluation reports. The aim is to be able to provide some advice to area services about best approaches to evaluation of crime prevention engagement (Interview).

4) Looking at domestic violence issues and contributing to a broader ACOP initiative on highlighting domestic violence and the role probation can play in terms of its contact with victims and perpetrators and make contributions to that policy development (Interview).

5) Preliminary discussions with ACPO have been held concerning the exchange of information to inform agency crime prevention strategies (ACOP, 1995: 9; Interview).

6) The committee has also actively addressed the down-playing of crime prevention in the Home Office draft Three Year Plan; intervened to correct erroneous advice regarding the application of rule 41a and briefed C6 about Probation Service crime prevention for inclusion in an inter-ministerial report on the Home Office contribution to crime prevention (ACOP, 1995: 9).

The role of the committee is very much promotional and a lot of their work is about "informing, keeping information flowing" and running seminars for areas (Interview).

How The Probation Service Can Help To Prevent Crime

The Central Council of Probation Committees, (1990: 16) state, "The prevention of crime, or its containment, is a major preoccupation of the probation service". However, the probation service "would never claim <to be> central to crime prevention in the way in which the police would frequently claim to be, and to which local government should be ... The basic probation position has always been, in a nutshell, to very much support the Morgan Report sort of view" (Interview).

In 1990, the Central Council of Probation Committees (1990: 11) stated, "The main purpose of the probation service is to reduce re-offending". However, "various things grow from that in terms of the knowledge base to inform secondary and primary strategies" (Interview).

> If you have a knowledge and information base based on the offenders you are supervising, the reports that you provide for the courts on the motivation and on causation of offending then that gives the service a certain authority and credibility to make statements about why crime is happening which can inform secondary and primary strategies (Interview).

The probation service's contribution to crime prevention is said to occur through the following mechanisms: (1) through supervisory activities such as social enquiry reports which are designed to assist sentencers to explore the risk of future offending; (2) by appointing their own staff to run special crime prevention programmes (e.g., seconding a member of their staff to co-ordinate a multi-agency crime prevention committee); and (3) by participating in committees and providing information based on their experiences (Central Council of Probation Committees, 1987).

In addition to this, the probation service can contribute to crime prevention and works that are of community value through supervising offenders on community service orders. Offenders on community service can for example post car crime prevention warning posters, do graffiti clean up work, vandalism repair work, and so on. "If a local community is wanting to develop some adventure play area then community service may be a source of free labour to do some of these things" (Interview).

The probation service also contributed to the Standard Course on Crime Prevention at the Crime Prevention Centre in Stafford for over five years. In the course, the probation officer did not only say "something about the role of probation but more significantly tried to get the crime prevention officers who are heavily rooted in physical and situational responses, security measures and so on to think about what consideration they may need to give in their job to social factors' (Interview).

The crime prevention centre has now been re-located to North Yorkshire and supposedly the probation service no longer contributes to the course syllabus.

The Probation Service's Position In National Crime Prevention Policy

The potential influence that the probation service can have in crime prevention policy was diminished by the fact that they were not represented on the National Crime Prevention Agency. Although ACOP had requested that they be represented, their request had been denied. One member of the Agency stated that excluding the probation service was "a purely political decision", the Conservative government's ideology is not supportive of probation work (Interview).

The fact that the probation service's role in crime prevention was not supported by the previous Conservative political masters due to political reasons was known to them:

> from my observations within the Home Office in terms of the ministerial disposition that seems to have been displayed from the chair of the National Board for Crime Prevention as it was, but also from discussions that I have with people from the Home Office Crime Prevention Unit and elsewhere, the current complexion of the thing is very much to cite police and private sector as being the key players and I think a rather stronger orientation towards physical and situational approaches to crime prevention, rather than social, because in crude political terms social approaches equate with softness. I am slightly overstating this I know, but the only appropriate social approaches are criminal justice sentencing approaches, get tough on offenders and make it tougher for them to commit crime by property being better protected and better lit and so on (Interview).

The move to detach the probation service from crime prevention policy making, affected the morale of the probation committee on crime prevention. This is evidenced by the following two comments:

- "in the not so distant past we were in a relatively strong position in that politically, there was strong recognition within the Home Office that probation is a key player ..." (Interview).
- As far a policy influencing goes now, "it is a disappointing time compared with a few years ago when there was quite a lot of governmental support for probation to engage in a wider ranging way with a range of crime prevention initiatives. I mean this as a matter of degree" (Interview).

The lack of support by the previous political masters for the probation service has also affected their budget. This means that funding for full-time 'crime prevention' posts have had to be cut or greatly reduced. As one interviewee stated,

<now> at a time when resources are very tight indeed and the probation service is being pressurised very much to hold on to its core responsibilities, some of these wider multi-agency engagements such as crime prevention, I won't say are being ditched, but are clearly proving difficult to maintain at whatever relatively modest level they have been at previously (Interview).

The constraints of funding on the probation service and its effect on crime prevention were mentioned in the Morgan Report: "Other Probation Service employees, interviewed by Working Group members, suggested that constraints on resources prevented them fully deploying in crime prevention the knowledge and skills to which we have referred" (Standing Conference on Crime Prevention, 1991: 17).

Now that a new government is in power things look brighter for the probation service. The lead officer sits on various 'community safety' committees and their role in crime prevention might increase if local authorities are given a statutory responsibility for crime prevention (in that local authorities would probably have to consult the probation service in producing their community safety strategy).

How the Probation Service in Boroughville Defined Crime Prevention

Of the 31 probation staff that returned their questionnaire, 28 (90.3%) replied 'yes' to the question "Do you consider that you perform any crime prevention work as part of your day-to-day activities". The replies to the following question, "If you answered YES could you please provide some examples of what you do" were grouped into 6 categories. They were:

1) Detention
2) Supervisions
3) Multi-Agency Involvement
4) Welfare Assistance
5) Management
6) Other.

The 'code book' for these replies is available in Appendix II. Based on this categorisation and allowing for double-counting, 19 probation staff (67.9%) stated that they performed crime prevention work through supervisions, and 8 (28.6%) stated welfare assistance as an example. The replies of three respondents were grouped under each multi-agency involvement and management; two replies were grouped under detention and 6 replies were grouped under 'other'.

The finding that supervisions were the most often cited mechanism for preventing crime is consistent with the report by the Central Council of Probation Committees (1987: 4-5) that states that the probation service's contribution to crime prevention is through supervisory activities.

The categories of 'supervisions' and 'welfare assistance' could be considered as a form of criminality prevention - trying to stop the offender from offending again. One can therefore suggest that probation staff (at least in Boroughville) see their preventative role in terms of helping offenders.

As stated in the methods chapter, the results of the questionnaires in Boroughville are only to be used as an exploratory tool. To suggest that these findings would be similar across the county or country would not be justifiable in this instance. They are however useful as an exploratory tool, and it is interesting to note that the findings from Boroughville are consistent with the literature from the Central Council of Probation Committees (1987: 4-5).

Conclusion

This chapter examined the structure of the probation service and its role in crime prevention. The structure of the probation service is similar to the police in that there is a trade union for non-management personnel, an Association of Chief Officers of Probation and an Inspectorate which provides advice to the Home Office and Home Secretary.

In 1984, after Home Office Circular 8/84 was released, a 'Statement of Objectives and Priorities' for the probation service was published stating that the service should contribute to initiatives concerned with the prevention of crime. Since then other documents for the probation service have continued to include their role in crime prevention. It is also recognised that crime prevention is not a core statutory responsibility for the probation service.

In 1988, the Association of Chief Officers of Probation set up a committee on crime prevention as a result of Home Office Circular 8/84. The notion of committees within ACOP has been replaced by a system of lead officers. There is now a lead officer on 'community safety'.

Their potential for affecting Home Office policy in crime prevention was hindered since they were no longer members of the National Crime Prevention Agency. However now that a new government is in power things look a little more hopeful.

Five issues need to be accentuated from this chapter.

1) The finding in the Morgan report that "crime prevention is a peripheral concern for all agencies involved and a truly core activity for none of them" (Standing Conference On Crime Prevention, 1991: 3) holds true within the probation service. This statement is supported by the fact that crime prevention is included under 'Other work in the community' in the Statement of Objectives and Priorities and under 'other duties' in the Probation Rules. It is not considered to be a core activity.

Although crime prevention is not considered to be a core activity in the above directives, "reducing and preventing crime" was an operational goal of the probation service in the Home Office three year plan for 1993-1996 and 1994-1997 (Home Office, 1992d: iv; 1994f: 4). 'Crime prevention' has also been the focus of one ACOP committee since 1988 and is now under the direction of a lead officer. The ACOP 1995 Annual Review mentions the work of the crime prevention committee, thus giving recognition to crime prevention work being done.

Despite the fact that crime prevention is not a core responsibility of the probation service, it does receive recognition, and is considered to be an important aspect in which the service can contribute. The findings from Boroughville suggest that the majority of probation officers (90.3%) do consider that they prevent crime in their day-to-day activities demonstrating that crime prevention work is recognised by probation staff (at least in Boroughville). The question raised, however, is what is meant by crime prevention?

2) The definition of crime prevention within the probation service is not uniform. Although references about the probation service's role in crime prevention do exist, the meaning of this term is, in the majority of instances, not stated. Where definitions were available (e.g., through the three year plan, the ACOP crime prevention committee and through the questionnaire distributed), they are not similar.

Within the 1995-1998, 1996-1999, and 1997-2000 three year plans, the meaning of crime prevention appears to be one of reducing re-offending while under supervision. Within the ACOP crime prevention committee, the meaning appeared to be directed towards primary and secondary prevention by using information obtained through their dealings with offenders. The definition of crime prevention by probation officers in Boroughville was centred around work on a one-to-one basis which, although not stated, could imply an aim to reduce the likelihood of re-offending as with the three year plan.

Thus on a practical level, probation officers aim to prevent re-offending, but at the managerial level there appears to be two views: (1) maintaining the role of attempting to prevent re-offending and; (2) taking the role of the service further and using information from offenders on why they committed crimes, to try to divert others from becoming criminals. It is not surprising that individuals outside of the probation service have differing opinions on the probation service's role in crime prevention. It seems the probation service itself does not have one opinion.

3) The politics of the previous central government affected the contributions that the probation service could make to crime prevention policy. This was most obvious in the fact that the probation service was not a member of the National Crime Prevention Agency.

Research within the Home Office was also less for probation and other non-custodial disposals than, for example, the police, courts and sentencing, prisons, crime prevention and patterns of crime and criminal behaviour (e.g., in terms of number of Research Bulletin articles, Home Office Research Studies Publications, and in terms of number of research projects in the Research Programme Publication between 1984-85 and July

1997 [see Table 3.1]). Furthermore, less funding for external research is provided in subjects related to probation and non-custodial disposals than for prisons, policing, crime prevention and courts and sentencing (see Table 3.2).

It appears from the above information and from interviews that the previous central government was alienating the probation service in crime prevention policy. This was despite the fact that

- the probation service can contribute to crime prevention as discussed in this chapter;
- the Morgan Report recommended they be a principal agency "involved in the multi-agency approach to community safety" (Standing Conference on Crime Prevention, 1991: 16);
- many probation areas are involved in crime prevention initiatives by seconding staff to hold co-ordinating roles, or in other ways; and
- in attempting to create a national database within the criminal justice system that could be used for preventing crime, ACPO, ACOP and the Home Office are working together. This suggests that the probation service should not be completely ignored within the field of crime prevention.

4) Although the probation service's funding has been tightened (2 Interviews), the probation service is still involved in crime prevention to varying degrees within different regions across the country. Thus, the statement by one Home Office official, "agencies use lack of finance as a reason for not being able to give crime prevention more priority instead of incorporating it into their current budgets", is true in part within the probation service. The probation service did use finance as an excuse for not giving crime prevention more priority. However, the statement by the Home Office official errs in the fact that crime prevention is being incorporated into current budgets even though they complain about lack of resources.

5) The final issue is should the probation service be involved in crime prevention? The answer to this is very much a question of degree which is dependent on what type of crime prevention one is talking about, and what one hopes to achieve with a certain initiative.

At least two interviewees stated that "crime prevention activity is about good communication between agencies and people working together". The impact of how much an agency can contribute to crime prevention, is more dependent on the individual than on the agency. So for example, even though it is recognised that the police have a role to play in general, the 'usefulness' of the police is very much dependent on who is representing the police. This is true of all agencies.

The wealth of information that the probation service holds is through their social enquiry reports which consist of detailed background reports of offenders and their circumstances. The probation service is also in a position where they can obtain offenders' perspectives on issues such as CCTVs (what do offenders think about CCTV?) or why certain properties get repeatedly burgled. This information could be very enlightening alongside police data.

The information that the probation service holds is very much social in nature by, for example, knowing about problems at school, within the family and within the community. The problem with the information they hold is what to do about it. If a house gets burgled and had poor locks, then replacing the locks is an uncontroversial solution.

Trying to change a school system, or methods of parenting are very controversial since these are not only based on culture but also on an individual's own values. However, this does not mean that the information should be ignored.

Many people have stated that situational prevention alone is not the solution to preventing crime - it must be combined with social approaches (Bottoms, 1990; Home Office, 1993b). If one accepts this view, then the probation services do have a role to play in crime prevention since they are the agency that holds a great deal of 'social' information.

6 Crime Concern & NACRO

Introduction

In England and Wales there are several voluntary organisations which are either directly or indirectly affiliated with crime prevention. At a local level, some of these organisations can help disadvantaged people or alienated groups in a way unlike statutory agencies. This chapter shall examine the two organisations which are considered the most influential organisations affecting both crime prevention policy and practice. NACRO and Crime Concern are two organisations that have played a major role in community regeneration and community safety. NACRO is considered to be the first organisation interested in crime prevention outside of the police. Crime Concern, launched in 1988 by the Conservative Government was considered by David Maclean as one of "three main players in crime prevention" (Maclean, 1995b: 26).

Both these organisations work closely with local authorities across the country in trying to prevent crime. Although their work in the field of crime prevention may appear quite similar, their influence in national crime prevention policy making was quite different under the previous Conservative government. This chapter examines the work of both organisations and their position with respect to influencing crime prevention policy at the national level.

Crime Concern

The Creation of Crime Concern

Crime Concern is a charity launched by the Home Office in 1988 as a result of the Conservative election manifesto from the year before. The manifesto stated "We will build on the support of the public by establishing a national organisation to promote the best practices in local crime prevention initiatives" (Conservative Central Office, 1987: 58).

Before the Conservative manifesto came out however, various Home Office and ministerial representatives had contacted NACRO about crime prevention. NACRO was probably consulted because they were the first big organisation to get interested in crime prevention outside of the police.

After the election, a "high powered dinner" of about twenty people was held by Douglas Hurd, the then Home Secretary (Interview). At this dinner, Douglas Hurd stated that he wanted an organisation to act as a catalyst in bringing together all the players in crime prevention so that they could "float in the same way" (Interview).

Shortly after the dinner, two people were appointed as formateurs of Crime Concern. One was Steven Norris who had just lost his seat in the election and the other was David Birley who was a former NACRO employee and consultant to the Home Office Crime Prevention Unit. NACRO was once again consulted on many occasions regarding the setting up of Crime Concern.

"NACRO was basically a Labour organisation ... <and> when asked why another organisation needed to be created, the answer was basically political - the Conservative government wanted an organisation they could control - hence Steven Norris was the first chairman" (Interview). Interestingly however, the chairman's replacement in 1992 was Tim Clement-Jones who is not a Conservative party member.

In May 1988, Crime Concern was launched as a national crime prevention organisation to stipulate, develop and promote effective local crime prevention across the country. It was intended that Crime Concern would be partly funded through the Home Office Crime Prevention Unit for the first three years, and through contributions from businesses and other sources. After three years they would have to live off the latter. However, funding from the Home Office Crime Prevention Unit has continued to this day.

Although Crime Concern was launched in May 1988, the Chief Executive (Nigel Whiskin) did not take up his position until September 1988. This is of significance because it meant that questions about the organisation could not easily be answered after the launch was announced. For several months nobody really knew what Crime Concern was about. This put an added strain on Crime Concern once it was established and might at least partly explain why the ACPO crime committee sub-committee on crime prevention was at first hesitant when dealing with Crime Concern.

The impression of one interviewee was that when Crime Concern was first launched, chief constables thought that Crime Concern was part of a hidden government agenda to privatise crime prevention. Chief Constables were very suspicious of this because of the growth of the private security/crime prevention industry. Furthermore, the fact that Crime Concern had a political chairman was seen as a negative by some.

In the first few months of his post, Nigel Whiskin had to hire other staff and find an office for Crime Concern. By March 1989 an office was found in Swindon and most of the staff were in their posts. The five key areas of work were identified as,

1) Neighbourhood Watch,
2) Crime Prevention Panels,
3) Area Crime Reduction Programmes,
4) Youth Initiatives, and
5) Business and Crime (Crime Concern, 1989: 8; See also Crime Concern, 1990; Crime Concern, no date).

The Work of Crime Concern

By late 1991 the role of Crime Concern vis à vis the Crime Prevention Panels was questioned. A survey was done about crime prevention panels in which a poor response was achieved. Crime Concern tried the survey again and failed again. Although a select few were active, most of the panels were not. Crime Concern took a decision not to be involved in crime prevention panels early in 1992.

In 1991 Crime Concern set up a consultancy service directed towards "locally based community safety partnerships" (Crime Concern, 1992: 7). This service consisted of:

- helping set up partnerships;
- undertaking crime and community safety audits;
- conducting consultations with young people and preparing preventative strategies;
- assisting with the development of corporate community safety plans;
- developing comprehensive programmes in high crime residential areas;
- supporting town centre management programmes;
- developing and sustaining multi-agency partnerships;
- designing and implementing social crime prevention programmes aimed at the family, school and community" (Crime Concern, 1992: 7).

Until 1992, the Annual Reviews described in general terms what Crime Concern had done under the five areas of work mentioned in 1989 (see above) which can all be considered to be community type programmes. From 1992, the Annual Reports began to highlight families as a target for crime prevention. From 1992 onwards one notices a shift towards criminality/social crime prevention. The 1992 *Annual Report* states, "... Support for parents in high crime areas, designed to limit family breakdown; improve parenting skills; develop pre-school provision in vulnerable areas" (Crime Concern, 1992: 8).

Hamilton-Smith (1994) suggests that the focus on social and youth crime prevention was a result of Jon Bright's year in the United States in 1990-1991.[29] In addition, "youth crime prevention was given an extra boost after the 1989 Children Act, with the Criminal Justice Act 1991" (Hamilton-Smith, 1994: 45).

The back covers of the 1993 and 1994 *Annual Review* Reports state,

> Crime Concern is the national crime prevention organization working with local partners to reduce crime and create safer communities by:
> - developing new approaches to crime reduction and community safety
> - providing consultancy and developmental services to local government and other public service organizations
> - promoting crime prevention through publications, conferences and tried and tested programmes (Crime Concern, 1993b, 1994: back cover).

By 1993, Crime Concern could definitely be said to be advocating social crime prevention. Not only did it assist in the production of *Crime and the Family: Improving child-rearing and preventing delinquency* which "called for an innovative range of social crime prevention policies and to tackle the root causes of criminal behaviour" (Utting, Bright and Henricson, 1993: 12), but they also produced an information pamphlet which stated that Crime Concern "promotes social crime prevention through projects, publications, conferences and campaigns" (Crime Concern, 1993a). It is interesting that this differs slightly in comparison to what the back cover of the 1993 and 1994 Annual Reports state (i.e., this information pamphlet specifies social crime prevention rather than just crime prevention). In 1995 a briefing paper was produced on the prevention of criminality. This briefing paper stated,

---

[29] Jon Bright is the Director of Fieldwork at Crime Concern.

Crime Concern believes that both approaches are essential, particularly in high crime areas. The prevention of criminality has, however, received relatively little attention. This briefing paper therefore discusses its main features and suggests how they might be implemented by local partnerships. It recognises, however, that the effectiveness of local partnerships to prevent criminality is influenced by matters outside of their control. Changes in the labour market, for example, and the policies of central government, create the context in which local efforts will be more or less successful (Crime Concern, 1995b: 1).

The 1995 Annual Review states that Crime Concern aims to "develop new approaches to crime prevention, in particular through measures which address the risk factors associated with offending by young people" (Crime Concern, 1995a: 2). The Foreword in this Review, states "Whilst we know a great deal about the risk factors associated with youth crime, this diagnostic knowledge has not so far been widely translated into practical programmes" (Crime Concern, 1995a: 3).

The community safety aspect of Crime Concern is done through initiatives such as Kickstart (a youth activity club for 7-15 year olds in high crime estates); Cascade (a peer-led drug education project) Crucial Crew (for 10-11 year olds and teaches them about personal safety); SPLASH (summer holiday activity scheme); and Neighbourhood Watch (Crime Concern, 1993a). In October 1995 a National Neighbourhood Watch Association was set up making the schemes more independent of Crime Concern and the police.

In 1996, Crime Concern started providing courses on various aspects of crime prevention which is an aspect that they hope to expand. Crime Concern seems to have discovered two niches in the market. One being that there is a need for information by practitioners in the field, especially considering that more and more local authorities are hiring community safety officers and secondly that one way of selling crime prevention is by informing clients on the costs of crime. Thus in theory, prevention would cost less than the cure.

The cover of the 1996 annual review has a quotation from Nigel Whiskin which states "Our vital challenge is to demonstrate to policy makers, decision takers and the public that crime prevention is a cost-effective answer to the crime problem - that crime prevention both works and pays"(Crime Concern, 1996a).

Crime Concern seems to have picked up on the notion that crime costs money, and that by preventing crime, money can be spent more efficiently and effectively. HRH The Princess Royal for example states "the costs of dealing with the aftermath of criminal activity, through the criminal justice system and in repairing and replacing property are enormous" (Crime Concern, 1996a: 1). While working on various projects, it seems that Crime Concern is trying to determine how much can be saved (in pounds sterling) by instigating a certain programme. This it would appear would appeal to those that have to fork out the bill which is often businesses and local authorities. In the end, however, the money comes from the taxpayer/consumer and the author believes that Crime Concern is trying to emphasis this point when advising on prevention programmes.

A brochure in 1997 states,

- Last year alone public agencies spent £1 billion dealing with young offenders.
- It is estimated that the cost of crime to retailers is over £2 billion a year (Crime Concern, 1997b).

Another brochure states,

- Burglaries were the most expensive crimes affecting all sectors: the average cost of each burglary was over £1,100.
- The average cost of known crime borne by the typical business (including victims of crime and those not victimised) was £1390. This rose to £1998 for those who had been victims of crime. Adding in unexplained losses attributed to crime by the business (but not witnessed), the average cost to the typical business was £1,542 (Crime Concern, 1997a: 2).

In conclusion, based on Crime Concern's publications, it appears that their 'prevention' is based on giving advice through the consultancy services, involvement in developing community activity initiatives for youths 7-16 year olds, and promoting social crime prevention. Crime Concern is involved in the management of projects and continues to attract funding from government, charities and businesses. Now that a new government is in power, decisions will have to made by the new political leaders on whether Crime Concern will continue to do what is has been doing or whether its role should change.

The author suspects that the fact that Crime Concern's chairperson was replaced in 1992 by a non-Conservative, non-political figure, was to Crime

Concern's benefit in both the short and long term. Now Crime Concern could more convincingly appear independent of the Government. As a consequence, this could make them more trustworthy in terms of their aims and approach to practitioners. In the long term, by not appearing to be Conservative led, they have a much stronger chance of continuing to receive funding from the Home Office, no matter who is in power. In fact in the 1995 Annual Review, Crime Concern were described as an "independent crime prevention organisation" (Crime Concern, 1995a: 2) where as in past two Annual Reports they were simply described as a "national organisation" (Crime Concern, 1994, 1993b: back cover).

Crime Concern wants to be seen as a politically independent organisation with cross-party support. This is done by having a representative from each of the three major political parties sit on the Crime Concern Board. The reason for the desire to have all party support is that they have to work with local authorities run by the varying parties; they also have to contend with changes of political power at the local level.

In the 1995 Annual Report, the chairperson of Crime Concern announced his intention to stand down (Crime Concern, 1995a: 4). This is curious because according to one interviewee before this announcement, the Home Secretary wanted the former chairperson replaced. The chairperson is now Michael Hastings who was previously the vice chair for two years and BBC Parliamentary Liaison Officer. The author can imagine that if Michael Hastings were a Parliamentary Liaison Officer that he would have to get along well in all political circles. Having a chairperson from the media is also very likely to be beneficial to Crime Concern's publicity and consequently funding.

The National Association for the Care and Resettlement of Offenders (NACRO)

What is NACRO?

In 1966 NACRO replaced the National Association of Discharged Prisoners' Aid Societies (NADPAS). A pamphlet issued that year, entitled, "NACRO: An Organisation For The Prevention Of Crime" stated on the first page that "NACRO's purpose is to involve members of the community in crime prevention and the care, including the after care, of offenders" (NACRO, 1966: 1).

NACRO is a registered charity partly funded by grants from the Home Office and other government departments (e.g., Department of Health), and local authorities. Other contributions come from charitable trusts, companies, and donations and legacies from individual supporters. It is the "principal voluntary organization working for the care and resettlement of offenders" (NACRO, 1991) and is considered to be one of the first organisations interested in crime prevention outside of the police. Their work is however, broader than Crime Concern's in that they actively work with offenders and prisons.

The front cover of their pamphlet *What is NACRO?* states "NACRO helps people who have been in trouble with the law and those at risk of becoming so to deal with the problems they face and to be reaccepted into society without stigma" (NACRO, 1991).

In addition to providing resettlement services for ex-offenders, they have a Crime and Social Policy Section which incorporates community safety.

> NACRO's Crime and Social Policy section has responsibility for taking forward work in community safety. The section is responsible for a growing number of community safety initiatives, informing national and local opinion on community safety issues and helping to shape action. It can also offer a range of services to those involved in planning and delivering community safety such as local authorities, the police, the probation service, health authorities, voluntary organisations and community groups. Services include: Research, Monitoring and Evaluation, Briefings, Consultancy, and Project Development (NACRO, 1997: 2).

The role of this section is not to deliver programmes themselves, but rather to work with other agencies in a consultative capacity in servicing action at the local level.

Analysis of NACRO Publications

Since 1993/1994, the notion of preventing crime appears to be stressed more in their publications. For example, the *NACRO Directory 1994/1995* (NACRO, 1994b: 2), the first page of the 1993/1994 Annual Report (NACRO, 1994a), and the inside cover to the *NACRO Directory, January - June 1996* (NACRO, 1996b) all state: "NACRO is an independent voluntary organization working to prevent crime and promote the resettlement of offenders in the community".

The first paragraph of the chairman's introduction to the 1993/1994 Annual Report states "All NACRO's work has the same objective: within a framework of justice and fairness, to prevent crime, to reduce the amount of suffering, misery and fear caused by crime, and to reduce the number of victims of crime in the future" (NACRO, 1994a: 2). The first Section of the Annual Report describes how and why NACRO works. The first heading in this section is "preventing and reducing crime" (NACRO, 1994a: 3). The first paragraph then reads "The endeavour to prevent or reduce crime is therefore of the utmost importance. Dealing with crime after it has happened must always be a poor second best to taking the measures that will ensure it does not happen in the first place..." (NACRO, 1994a: 3).

Furthermore, the first section of the NACRO directory is called 'Crime Prevention and Community Safety' and states "NACRO aims to help prevent crime through services and projects which tackle the social and economic factors associated with crime as well as offering constructive alternatives for those most at risk of offending...." (NACRO, 1994b: 4).

Finally, NACRO NEWS published quarterly has had 'crime prevention and community safety' as the first heading in their 'Round Up' column since the summer of 1994 (Issues 13-16).

In the 1994/1995 Annual Review, crime prevention does not stand out as a separate heading within the report, but the front cover of the document has the phrases 'crime prevention', 'safer communities' and 'resettlement' in bold print. The themes within the actual report are: 'the whole person', 'inclusion', 'local', 'innovation', and 'achievements' (NACRO, 1995a).

In the 1995/96 Annual Report, the theme of prevention is once again emphasised. The publication is divided into 10 key messages about crime. They are:

1) Crime affects everyone
2) The Criminal justice system on its own cannot solve crime
3) Prevention is the best answer to crime
4) Prevention is more than locks and bolts
5) The key is to reduce youth crime
6) Offending can be reduced
7) Prison is for serious offenders
8) People are sent to prison as punishment not for punishment
9) The criminal justice system must be absolutely fair
10) Sensationalising crime makes matters worse (NACRO, 1996a).

Six of these ten themes are related to prevention. When asked whether this was a reflection of how resources within NACRO were divided, one interviewee stated, that the emphasis in the Annual Report on prevention was more of a "packaging thing. It was the best way of indicating the scope of the organisation".

As far as the ideology on the generators of crime goes, one leaflet which gives examples of the types of projects NACRO are involved in conveys the message that young people tend towards crime due to boredom and having "nothing to do" (NACRO 1994d: 1). This view is also transmitted in the 1994 (Summer) Newsletter (NACRO, 1994c). The newsletter, however, also acknowledges "that it is impossible to tackle crime without also tackling some of the contributory factors such as poor housing, low levels of education and training, unemployment and family stress" (NACRO, 1994c: 2).

NACRO's approach for preventing crime includes setting up and running activity programmes for youths, increasing employment opportunities and supporting tenants' associations. NACRO asserts that it can,

- help local authorities and other agencies to establish and manage community safety strategies;
- advise on methods of consulting and involving young people;
- advise organizations on setting up responses to car, cycle or motorcycle crime;
- advise on adventure activities and community holidays;
- provide training in youth work for volunteers and staff, etc. (NACRO 1994d: 5).

Thus, like Crime Concern, NACRO's crime prevention is about being a facilitator and manager for local initiatives. They also play the role of advisors and policy activists.

The quotations above illustrated how NACRO's image seemed to be emphasising crime prevention. One interviewee stated that in the summer of 1995, NACRO decided to reposition itself as a crime prevention organisation and that talks had taken place with Home Office officials and other ministers about it.

This was later confirmed in another interview. During the summer of 1995, the director of NACRO had meetings with Home Office officials and allegedly with Home Office Ministers regarding the role of NACRO vis à vis crime prevention. According to one Home Office official who met with the director, it was suggested that if the organisation's role in crime prevention were to develop, they should consider marketing it under a different heading. The words "care and resettlement of offenders", the author was told, are not consistent with Howard and Maclean's philosophy. In fact NACRO's funding from the Home Office was under threat.[30] According to the Home Office official, it was suspected that NACRO did not want to change its title and was just waiting and hoping for another government to come into power.

After these meetings had occurred, the author noted that the editorial to NACRO NEWS, Issue 18 somewhat confirmed the account of the Home Office official that NACRO would be sticking to its guns and was just waiting the Conservative government out, due to the fact that it mentions "the preparations for a general election within the next 18 months" (NACRO, 1996c: 1) and concludes with the following paragraph:

> Through its work NACRO has contributed to creating that level of understanding of what reduces crime. Now more than ever we shall need to stick to the beliefs that have sustained us since 1966: beliefs in prevention (rather than waiting until the crime has been committed and then responding), integration into society rather than exclusion, and reparation to the victim and society rather than punishment (NACRO: 1996c: 1).

Interestingly, the April-June 1996 issue of *NACRO NEWS* (NACRO, 1996d: 10, 11) announced that Vivien Stern, the director of NACRO for 19 years resigned on 3 May 1996 in order to give more time to Penal Reform International, and "in order to spend more time doing some independent thinking, writing and commentating on crime and criminal justice issues at home and abroad". Helen Edwards was officially made Chief Executive of NACRO in March 1997.

The author questions whether this resignation is partly due to frustrations with the Conservative (under Howard) political climate. Two excerpts of an interview with Vivien Stern printed in *NACRO NEWS*, Issue 19, illustrate the point:

---

[30] NACRO (1996d: 1) issue 19 addresses the fact that NACRO is experiencing funding restraints.

1) The Home Office in those days had a completely different view than it does now: it was interested in assisting NACRO to develop, wherever and with whoever, programmes that would help offenders and reduce crime (NACRO, 1996d: 10).
2) It's completely different now. Nowadays crime is a major political and social issue, and the ways of dealing with it are enormously important political questions that will affect the future of our democracy and the shape of our society (NACRO, 1996d: 11).

Are Crime Concern and NACRO in Competition vis à vis their Crime Prevention Role?

Prior to conducting the interviews, one couldn't help but wonder whether NACRO and Crime Concern were competitors. For example, like Crime Concern, NACRO undertakes consultancy work for local authorities and helps to set up and run projects - "either where funding has been identified or where assistance is needed to generate funding" (NACRO, 1994c: 6). As far as the crime prevention side of NACRO goes, they appear to be very similar to Crime Concern. This is not too alarming considering that Crime Concern's Chief Executive and Director of Field Operations both left NACRO to develop Crime Concern. In fact one of the ACPO crime prevention sub-committee minutes in 1992 mentioned that the subcommittee felt Crime Concern had adopted the strategy and tactics developed over the years by the police and NACRO.

In five interviews the question "Are NACRO and Crime Concern in competition?" was raised. The answer was in all cases "yes". According to the interviewees, the competition between the two did not become apparent until they both bid for the Safer Cities Projects, Phase II in 1993. In the end NACRO got 15 projects, Crime Concern got 14, and an organisation called the Society of Voluntary Associations (SOVA) got 3 projects.

One interviewee stated,

> we are competing on all kinds of things, for example, ... there are bits of charitable foundation money for doing research into crime prevention or community safety and we hear through the grapevine that <the other organisation> applies for many of the same things that we do ... we always run into each other in the hallway ... we are obviously pounding the same pavements.

Based on the publications of the two organisations, the 'crime prevention' work of both appeared to be very similar. NACRO however are not represented on any of the national committees examined in this research, and their potential role in crime prevention is not always appreciated. One senior Home Office official stated that they were involved in tertiary prevention. This image of theirs as only being involved in tertiary issues is their biggest drawback.

NACRO's title and consequential image that it portrays as being an organisation interested in offenders and prisons was discussed in a previous interview. The interviewee stated,

> for certain audiences it makes <NACRO> less credible as community safety practitioners because there is an erroneous view that the organisation is solely interested in offenders. ... We found that in some safer cities areas, for instance, the police will ask 'why is NACRO doing this? This programme is not about prisoners, it is about preventing crime. What do <NACRO> know about this?'. We also get these kinds of comments on steering committees and so on ... People look at the title and figure that sums it up.

Another Home Office official stated that NACRO's "natural place is on the offender and community development side". This same Home Office official stated,

> NACRO, although it does a bit on crime prevention, is basically seen <by the ministers> as dealing with offenders and the undeserving, soft on offenders, etc., etc. While there was a comfortable cohabitation with previous generations of Conservative ministers, the current lot had a big culture change with a vast shift to the right. I suppose <NACRO> were out on their ear.

Crime Concern have had a large advantage over NACRO in terms of crime prevention policy in that they are very well connected with the key players/organisations cited in this report. The Home Office official quoted above stated, "Maclean seems to get along very well with Whiskin, and I do not know whether it is because Crime Concern does things like Neighbourhood Watch etc., which ties in with Maclean's agenda". Another interviewee stated "Crime Concern, the Home Office and the Police have a better relationship than they have ever had". The Chief Executive of Crime Concern and the Chair to the ACPO sub-committee on crime prevention also get along well with Maclean and Howard.

Crime Concern is also well represented on crime prevention initiatives internationally (which NACRO is not), such as sitting on the Advisory Committee to the International Centre for the Prevention of Crime. NACRO's international ties tend to be with penal reform organisations.

In light of this information, it was questionable at the end of 1996 whether these two organisations would both continue to provide the same services within the field of crime prevention. At the time NACRO's funding from the Home Office was in question, but since then NACRO has received a grant of £80,000 from the Crime Prevention Agency as well as from other criminal policy sections and prisons.

Now that a new government is in power, things certainly look brighter for NACRO. One interviewee stated that the voluntary sector mirrored the commercial world and that competition within the crime prevention/ community safety domain was good. Crime Concern have however tried to create clear water between the work of the two organisations by for example, staying clear of the debate on juvenile justice systems, sentencing and the care and resettlement of offenders.

Within NACRO itself, there now appears to be more support for community safety than over the past few years. The fact that Crime Concern is more connected within the crime prevention field certainly does not hurt them, but neither does it mean that their future is indefinitely safeguarded. In fact Crime Concern and NACRO have worked together on some projects and this strand is being explored more carefully.

The new government will have to decide whether both organisations will continue to be funded or whether their roles will be differentiated. Will the labour government continue to support an initiative that was created by the Conservative government or will Crime Concern be remoulded into a 'Labour creation'?

Conclusion

This chapter examined the work of the two main national voluntary organisations affecting crime prevention policy in England and Wales. Crime Concern is the more recently formed organisation, having been launched in 1988. Although NACRO had been consulted several times regarding the set up of Crime Concern, the Conservative government wanted to create an organisation that 'they could control'.

This chapter brings out 3 issues.

1) The first is that although both organisations claim to be 'independent', they are not completely removed from politics. The main reason is that both receive funding from the Home Office, which is the responsibility of the Home Secretary.

Crime Concern was actually set up as a result of the Conservative party manifesto and its first chairperson was a Conservative party member who had lost his seat in the election. Although in 1992, the new chairperson was a non-Conservative supporter, Crime Concern's links with all political parties have been strong. The amount of influence that politics has on Crime Concern is questionable, especially since the second chairperson did resign as predicted in an interview. The author had been previously informed that this was the wish of the Home Secretary.

This does not mean that Crime Concern is run politically, but rather that Crime Concern and the Home Secretary have an influencing role in each other's work. For example, the 1995 Annual Review states that one of Crime Concern's aims is to "promote effective crime prevention measures to opinion formers, policy makers, budget holders, practitioners and sponsors with a view to securing more investment in practical crime prevention" (Crime Concern, 1995a: 2). The 1995 Annual Review also states that Nigel Whiskin's appointment to the National Crime Prevention Agency will be used to argue for:

- more investment to prevent crime by and against young people
- putting effective crime prevention measures in place on high crime estates
- extending the range of local partnerships and improving services to them (Crime Concern, 1995a: 4).

Being a member of the National Crime Prevention Agency put Crime Concern in a very strong position to influence crime prevention policy in England and Wales.

The question of politics also has a role to play with NACRO. Through various interviews it was stated that the Conservative government under Michael Howard did not want to give 'crime prevention' to NACRO since they were seen as not only a Labour organisation, but as activists. The fact that NACRO's Home Office contribution was in jeopardy also left one with the question of whether this was done for solely political reasons or whether it was an indication of the times (e.g., public attitudes towards the welfare state and of 'helping' offenders might have changed since 1966).

One could get the impression from these statements that under Howard NACRO was facing a slow death. One counter-argument is that most of the funding from the Home Office was put into the Single Regeneration Budget, which is essentially controlled by the Department of the Environment, and thus by a Member of Parliament other than the Home Secretary. Although the Department of the Environment is also 'Conservative', NACRO's strength has been in housing issues and rejuvenating estates, where Crime Concern is less active.

2) The second issue is one of the same people moving in the same circles or, in other words, the interconnectedness of the agencies. What essentially happens in the crime prevention field is that the same small circle of crime prevention specialists sit on each other's committees and have probably at some time worked together. Thus with the two organisations discussed in this chapter, one notes that both the Chief Executive and head of field operations at Crime Concern were recruited from NACRO and that the Director of NACRO sits on Crime Concern's Advisory Board. Interestingly, Crime Concern is not represented on any of NACRO's advisory committees. Two interviewees used the word "incestuous" to describe the world of crime prevention personnel.

3) The final issue to be raised is the role of the individual in making things happen. In particular, it is about Nigel Whiskin's role as chief executive of Crime Concern, in making the organisation what it is today. Nigel Whiskin is very well connected politically (to all political parties), and as stated earlier, got on well with the chairperson to ACPO's sub-committee on crime prevention, the Home Office and with the Home Secretary at the time. He is informed about crime prevention issues, having worked at NACRO for several years before taking up his current post. He not only knows the people 'that count' in England and Wales, but also internationally, as evidenced by the fact that he is on the advisory committee to the International Centre for the Prevention of Crime.

All of this helps Crime Concern in establishing itself as a professional organisation, and in getting corporate sponsorship. Crime Concern has taken a 'leadership' role in crime prevention, and as their 1995 Annual Review states, they have come to act "as a project manager, catalyst, consultant and capacity builder" (Crime Concern, 1995a: 2). These ingredients are all required within the field.

7 National Representation for Local Authorities

Introduction

The importance of local authorities in crime prevention is recognised in many forms (e.g., through the Morgan Report, Home Office Circulars, by the Police, Probation, and field research such as those done by Liddle and Gelsthorpe [1994 a,b,c], and Liddle and Bottoms [1991]). The subject of 'Local Authority and Government Schemes' was also a component of the Standard Crime Prevention Course provided at the Home Office Crime Prevention Centre in Stafford. While doing the research, the importance of local government in crime prevention was strongly emphasised.

Despite the recommendations of the Morgan Report, the previous Conservative government refused to accept a statutory role for local authorities in crime prevention. However, they did acknowledge that "local authorities have an important role in helping to create safer communities and reducing the fear of crime" (Home Office, 1996e: 9).

This chapter examines the Local Government Association (LGA) and the previous work of the Association of Metropolitan Authorities, the Association of County Councils and the Association of District Councils with respect to crime prevention policy. The role of community safety officers, and the National Community Safety Network are also reviewed. The National Community Safety Network has been gaining prominence over the past two years and has been consulted by Home Office officials about crime related policies.

The Local Government Association

In April 1997 the Association of Metropolitan Authorities (AMA), the Association of County Councils (ACC) and the Association of District Councils (ADC) were merged into one association called the Local Government Association. This association also represents the newly formed unitary authorities. This merger was strongly supported by the associations. For example the AMA stated, "The AMA believes that one Association would give the local government a more powerful voice" (AMA, 1994: 22).

The Local Government Association exists to "promote and protect the interests of its member authorities and the communities they serve in the constant round of negotiations that take place with central government, its departments and national organisations" (AMA, 1995a: 2; ACC, no date). "As an <association> view we have that little bit more clout with organisations like central government because we are not an individual <local authority>, we are more of a sizeable player" (Interview).

The Association's "guiding principle is that democratically elected local authorities know best about the needs and priorities of the areas they serve, and that as such local councils are an essential part of a democratic society" (AMA, 1994: 3; ADC, 1995b).

The association provides "guidance to members through bulletins, circulars and seminars, <carry> out research and development work which would be prohibitively expensive for a single or small group of authorities to undertake ..." (AMA, 1994: 3). The Association operates through a structure of panels and committees. Committees "provide an overall strategic framework" and panels "deal with day to day issues" (LGA, 1997c: 7).

No decision reached by the association is binding on individual member authorities. "All committee structures are composed of elected members only, except for those relating to the police" (Interview).

Although there is no statutory responsibility for crime prevention on local authorities at the moment, Schedule 2 of the Children Act 1989 states, "Every local authority shall take reasonable steps designed ... to encourage children within their area not to commit crime" (cited in AMA, 1993a: 21). The view of the Morgan Report is that this piece of legislation could be used as a precedent "for the way in which local authorities can be given statutory powers to enable them to play an important role in such multi-agency approaches" (Standing Conference on Crime Prevention, 1991: 29).

The main stimuli for the promotion of community safety have been Home Office Circular 8/1984 and the Morgan Report. Home Office Circular 8/84 "was a most important milestone in the development of the partnership approach" (AMA, 1993b: 14; Interviews). The Morgan Report was identified in the interviews as being the instigator for many community safety officers.

Developments related to crime prevention prior to 1997

In 1988, the Association of Metropolitan Authorities' Police Committee set up a Crime Prevention Working Party to investigate the current and potential activities of local authorities in crime reduction, including development of a lead role in establishing local strategies and partnerships (AMA, 1990: 4). They stated that crime had no single cause and therefore no single solution. Strategies therefore had to be broadly based and comprehensive (AMA, 1990: 9). "Situational policies alone will always prove to be inadequate" (AMA, 1990: 11).

Their report made 9 recommendations. Two of these recommendations were,

1) That local authorities under leadership of their chief executives should organise their crime reduction efforts more effectively, and develop appropriate structures and strategies in full participation and partnership with other local agencies, the private sector and general public (recommendation v); and

2) That local authorities should establish principal committees and appoint or nominate a principal officer with responsibility for crime reduction and community safety, backed by the appropriate degree of executive support (recommendation vii, AMA, 1990: 22).

In 1990 the Association of District Councils set up a working party of elected members to look at crime prevention for the first time. They produced a policy document called *Promoting Safer Communities* which explored "the unique contribution which district councils can make to crime prevention and community safety" (ADC, 1990: 3). The report stated that "it is of regret that a district council representative has not been included in membership of the <Morgan Report> Working Group" (ADC, 1990: 4). The report concluded, "The Association believes that because of their proximity to local communities, district councils are well-placed to implement crime prevention strategies and assess their effectiveness. It would go further, however, and suggest that they should take a leading role" (ADC, 1990: 16).

In December 1992, the Association of Metropolitan Authorities set up another working party examining Partnerships in Policing to consider how their district councils could work in partnership with local police forces to promote community safety (AMA, 1993b: 5). They stated,

The limitations of a sole reliance on the enforcement approach has led practitioners over the last decade to develop a broader-based approach which seeks to extend the concept of crime prevention into the community through social development. Although this approach encompasses enforcement and a 'locks and bolts' concern for physical crime prevention (otherwise known as the situational approach), it also seeks to address the fundamental personal and social patterns that can lead to chronic criminal behaviour; the causes as well as the symptoms of crime(AMA, 1993b: 11).

This approach is termed 'community safety'. The report states that community safety combines all those physical and psychological factors which contribute to social well being and the quality of community life (AMA, 1993b: 11). The report then provides examples of what some local authorities have done to combat crime and improve community safety within their area.

In 1993, the Working Party on Juvenile Justice within the Association of Metropolitan Authorities produced *Children and Trouble: A study of Juvenile Justice Issues for Local Government* (AMA, 1993a). They promoted community safety and stated, "Community safety at its best means preventive action and involves not only the Police and Probation Services, but Social Services, Education and Leisure and Recreation. Work with voluntary bodies in this field will be crucial for success" (AMA, 1993a: 48).

The working party made 37 recommendations, two of which are relevant for this research. They are:

1) We recommend that the appointment of Community Safety Officers in local government where none exist would be very useful (recommendation 31); and
2) We recommend that where there are community safety officers they have a juvenile justice role and where none, someone else should assume that role (recommendation 32; AMA, 1993a: 52).

In February 1994, the ADC held a conference on the theme of "Community Safety - Working in Partnership with the Police and the Public to Prevent Crime" (ADC, 1994a: i). Two hundred delegates attended from district councils, county councils, metropolitan and London boroughs and from the police service and police authorities (ADC, 1994a: i).

Furthermore, a working group within the ADC produced *Winning Communities: The role of housing in promoting community safety* (ADC, 1994b). The working group stated, "... crime prevention should feature prominently in both Housing Strategy Statements and Development Plans. Both documents must seek to establish a common set of aims, objectives and agreed approaches towards resolving these issues" (ADC, 1994b: 14).

In January 1995, the executive committee within the ADC set up a small sub-group of four elected members to look at policing and crime prevention matters specifically. "They come together as and when we need policy decisions outside of the executive committee" (Interview). The remit of the group includes "all issues relevant to the Association's policy on policing and community safety (crime prevention)" (ADC, 1995a).

The minutes of one AMA policy committee meeting on 12 September 1995 (item #15 [p 95 113]) examined community safety and protecting the public. The minutes state that the AMA was disappointed that the government did not accept recommendation v or many others in the Morgan Report. The minutes also point out that "the National Crime Prevention Board set up a few years ago by the Home Office and chaired by a minister has no nominated representative from the local authority associations in spite of approaches made for that purpose by the AMA" (AMA, 1995b: 2 [item 7]).

In December 1995 the AMA established a Community Safety Working Party which consisted of the AMA, the ADC, the ACC, the National Community Safety Network, Crime Concern, the probation service and the police service. Their terms of reference included the following two points:

1) To secure, on a long term basis, a position of influence for local government in the fields of community safety and crime prevention, including promotion of the case for a statutory duty.
2) To secure the most beneficial framework possible for local government to work in, including the appropriate financial and statutory support necessary for the delivery of the community safety function (LGA, 1997a: 9).

This working party's major accomplishments included commissioning a national survey of community safety initiatives and polices (with the Local Government Management Board), creating a 'Position Statement' outlining the case for a statutory role for local government in community safety, and creating a 'Manifesto' containing 58 proposals. The manifesto was produced to influence political parties in the run up to the election. The Proposals argued for the Morgan Report to be implemented. The proposals connected to this research include:

- Local authorities should be given a new power to promote and co-ordinate community safety in their areas. This would support a new duty to prepare and publish an annual *Community Safety Plan* to be deposited with the Home Secretary.
- The Community Safety Plan should be prepared in collaboration with the other key agencies who have an interest in community safety- the police authority, the police service, other statutory agencies (e.g., probation, magistrates, school governors, the health service, parish councils etc.) and the voluntary sector (e.g. NACRO, Victim Support, Crime Concern, Neighbourhood Watch, business, local community groups etc.).
- The National Crime Prevention Agency should be strengthened and turned into a body working at 'arms length' from Government to research, monitor and report on national crime patterns and trends; to co-ordinate the national crime prevention effort and to advise Government and the police on the future development of crime prevention policies. Local government should be guaranteed places on the Agency's board (LGA, 1997a: 47-48).

Community Safety within the LGA

According to one interviewee, the "LGA has decided community safety should be a top priority". Within the association's mission statement the promotion of "safe communities free from crime and vandalism" is cited (LGA, 1997c: 6). Within the LGA there are 7 panels, one of which is 'community safety'. This panel met for the first time in May 1997 where it was proposed that their terms of reference include:

- seek to secure a position of influence, and satisfactory policy framework, for local government in the field of community safety;
- define best practice and advise on effective local strategies to combat crime and enhance community safety;
- develop and maintain a high profile for community safety in the committees and other bodies of the LGA (LGA, 1997b: item 3).

The panel proposed to invite ACPO, ACOP, NACRO, Crime Concern and the Safe Neighbourhoods Unit to act as observers to the Panel. The Panel has defined community safety as follows:

> Community safety is defined as promoting the concept of community-based action to inhibit and remedy the causes and consequences of criminal, intimidatory and other related anti-social behaviour. Its purpose is to secure sustainable reductions in crime and fear of crime in local communities. Its approach is based on the formation of multi-agency partnerships between the public, private and voluntary sectors to formulate and introduce community-based measures against crime (LGA, 1997b: item 3).

The immediate priority of this panel will be in connection to the Crime and Disorder Bill. As one document states,

> The Queen's Speech announced a Crime and Disorder Bill which would address juvenile crime, anti-social disorder, racially motivated attacks and drink-related crime. The LGA understands that this Bill is likely to be introduced to Parliament in December 1997 and that it will be preceded by a White Paper. ... There is an immediate need for work to be progressed around this White Paper and the eventual Bill. (LGA, 1997b: item 7).

Other work that the Panel will be involved in include for example, working on a national information database on community safety initiatives, creating a national training organisation to pursue community safety education and training, working with Crime Concern on preventing crime in High Crime Neighbourhoods ([with the LGA's Housing Committee] LGA, 1997b: item 7).

The fact that a statutory power and duty will be placed in the Crime and Disorder Bill is of great significance for local government. By law, in order for the Local government to spend money on a project or issue, it must have a statutory power to do so. Up until now spending within 'community safety' matters has been born under other headings such as housing or other departments. The statutory power in essence gives the local authority the power to spend money in the domain. By having a duty within the statute, local authorities would be required to for example publish a community safety plan and carry out work to meet the plans targets. This duty is for example similar to the duty that local authorities must provide education for those between the ages of 5 and 16.

The Local Government Association appears to be very excited about this new Bill. One interviewee stated that what local authorities had done voluntarily (without statutory powers and duties) had gone as far as it could. Although some local authorities were very good in community safety, others were not so good. It is the latter that need to be forced to do more.

When asked whether this legislation would bring in more money for local authorities, the reply received was 'no'. The money will come through the same sources as it does now, such as the Single Regeneration Budget.

Local Community Safety Officers and the Creation of the National Community Safety Network

Local Community Safety Officers

The push for local community safety officers started with the recommendation from the Morgan Report that "shire counties in particular adopt a co-ordinating role when it comes to the multi-agency approach to crime prevention" (Interview). A few local councils had some form of community safety officers before the Morgan Report, but their number was few. District and Metropolitan councils are also taking an interest in appointing community safety co-ordinators.

> Although central government fell short of actually legislating in favour of local authorities having a community safety role, a very strong hint was dropped by the publication of the Morgan Report that perhaps it might be a good idea for those local governments not actually involved in crime prevention to develop some proposals in that direction (Interview).

Since the publication of the Morgan Report "most if not all shire counties have actually appointed a co-ordinator or if they have not done that, they have at least designated part of an officer's time towards becoming a kind of co-ordinating person for multi-agency crime reduction" (Interview).

> Local authorities, ... particularly county councils, are in a strong position to co-ordinate a range of other agencies. Obviously the police have got their

crime prevention role. ... I see my job as being co-ordinating the multi-agency side of things whereas the police role is to deliver the core crime prevention activity as laid down by the Home Office, by the Home Secretary and practised traditionally (Interview).

Generally speaking, the co-ordinators are responsible to some form of executive committee or group. The membership of these committees differs from area to area. The funding of the co-ordinators also comes from various sources. Some are paid for by the probation service, the county council, the district councils, police authorities, or commercial sources. Others have been seconded from their agencies (for example the probation or police service) for one half day a week or more.

When asked what background the co-ordinators generally came from the reply was as follows,

Probation officers definitely, police officers, senior road safety officers, a number of policy advisors, former safer cities personnel, very few social workers - they are the ones who spring to mind immediately. We may have one or two that come from academia who have studied criminology or whatever and found their way into it as a first job. At a guess there are probably more probation officers than anybody (Interview).

The co-ordinators "are almost always based in chief executives departments, sometimes in policy units, somewhere very central" (Interview). "You are in a way in a position of some influence, ... a fairly high profile position which is what Morgan was on about anyway" (Interview). The Morgan Report stated that the co-ordinator "should be at a level to command the confidence and support of senior management in local government and other agencies and have direct access to chief executives and the local police Commander" (Standing Conference on Crime Prevention, 1991: 6, recommendation xiii).

Normally, <community safety officers> are employed at quite a high level within the county council and you are on first name terms with just about everybody. It means that when the time comes to get something done, you know that if you pick up the telephone and ring a chief executive, of the district council for example, that you will get an appointment to go and see him. You will go and see him and you will chat about it and most probably you will come away with what it is you want (Interview).

With the new police authorities, in some counties,

> the community safety officer has been transferred either wholly or in part to the police authority ... there are a number of variations on the theme as to who co-ordinators now belong to. The vast majority have stayed very much within the local authority area (Interview).

The work that co-ordinators do varies from providing pamphlets and security packages for people who have just been burgled, to providing diversionary projects to "the outer edges of crime prevention, where traditional crime prevention leaves off and the social thing starts like outreach youth work, initiatives aimed at latchkey kids, ... and providing after school activities" (Interview). "Social services does the hands on stuff, but my job is to help identify where it would happen and ways that it could mesh with other activities that were going on there" (Interview).

When asked which agencies co-ordinators mostly deal with, the reply was "I would say police, probation, social services and district councils are probably pretty much on a par" (Interview).

One of the problems of being a local community safety officer is "finding out about successful projects from elsewhere" (Interview). This was one reason why a national network of community safety officers was formed: "we want to know more about what other people are doing" (Interview).

The National Community Safety Network

The beginnings of this network started just over five years ago when a meeting was held in Lincoln with a total of nine co-ordinators. That group continued to meet roughly every three to four months except that it grew in size. Because the number of persons attending what was originally intended to be a regional grouping increased so much, the idea of forming a national network for community safety officers was born. As it so happened, the chief executive of Lincolnshire county council was also chairman of the Association of County Chief Executives (ACCE), a professional body of senior local government officers. A meeting was held by the ACCE in February 1995 where "there was a big thumbs up about having a national network, ... a national working group was then set up" (Interview). "The main purpose of the community safety network is to facilitate local authority co-ordinators" (Interview).[31]

More and more people have been joining this network. In January 1996, the notion of paying members began. Every unit that wants to become a member pays a subscription fee of £50. The network is aimed at "community safety units, crime prevention partnerships, safer cities projects, and anybody who does what we feel is essentially a local authority based community safety activity" (Interview). The members will get a copy of the database (described below) and get to come to conferences at a knock-down price. So far, the National Community Safety Network held a conference in February 1996, in Surrey. A regional structure was proposed at this conference. In April 1997 another conference was held in Nottingham.

According to one interviewee, the network would like to copy the method used in Holland. This would consist of having a database which would include the names of co-ordinators across England and Wales, their telephone number and contact addresses, and about a half page description on what they are doing in their area and what they are comfortable to talk about.

"One of the most promising things that is coming out of it so far is that for the first time ever, local authority community safety officers <from the working group> are being invited to the Home Office to comment on national issues ... previously we had always been sidelined because we never really had a united voice" (Interview). "We are now being recognised nationally as being somebody who ought to be consulted about crime related policies" (Interview).[32]

The network was particularly pleased that it was recognised in the Home Office publication *Protecting the Public* (Home Office, 1996e). The document stated,

> The Government has welcomed the recent launch of a new National Network for Community Safety, which brings together local authority community safety and crime prevention practitioners across the country. The Home

---

[31] According to the interviewee, a Welsh association of community safety officers is also being formed. According to the interviewee the two networks are parallel isolated situations.

[32] A short article appearing in *Crime Prevention News* (October-December 1995: 4) confirms some of the information obtained above (see Home Office, 1995e).

Office has observer status on the steering committee of this body, which has considerable potential both to raise the profile of this important work within local authorities and to help those already engaged in it to learn from the experience of colleagues in other authorities (Home Office, 1996e: 9).

By April 1996, the credibility of the network was thought to have increased with links having been created with both ACPO and ACOP. Presently, national executive members of the network sit on the LGA's Community Safety Committee and the Home Office Training Needs Group. The network's aims have been identified as:

- promoting crime-related community safety as a key issue at National, Regional and Local level.
- promoting the exchange of information and ideas about crime-related community safety issues.
- establishing a framework for the development of Community Safety Officers.
- providing a united voice for consultation with central government.
- providing opportunity for joint development of initiatives, resources and training. (National Community Safety Network, no date).

Conclusion

This chapter examined the role of the local government association, the role of community safety officers/co-ordinators and the national network that was created for them. The chapter reviewed developments that have occurred in the past ten years related to community safety. The Local Government Association is now playing a major role in promoting a statutory power and duty for local authorities and the police in community safety for insertion into the Crime and Disorder Bill. This Bill should be out by the end of 1997.

This chapter also discussed how the appointment of community safety officers was boosted with the publication of the Morgan Report. Although it was not endorsed by the former Home Secretary, many local authorities decided to follow the report's recommendations. The co-ordinators found that they were working in isolation and not always aware of what other co-ordinators were doing across the country. Therefore, it was decided to form a network of co-ordinators that would keep them abreast of current initiatives. This network started taking subscribers early in 1996.

Two issues come out of this chapter. They are:

1) The politics of the previous central government were opposed to local authority control, thus making them less instrumental on policy issues. This is evidenced in the fact that local authority control over the police has been greatly reduced and given to the police services themselves and to the Home Secretary.

According to one interview, the previous Minister purposely did not approach the associations to ask for a representative on the new National Crime Prevention Agency since he knew they would give him a Labour party member. The result is that the associations, "always receive information second-hand which makes it difficult to make representations. We have to go through someone else to get our view heard ... psychologically you are always catching up ... you have to be reasonably proactive" (Interview). The author would argue that the Local Government Association (and the previous 3 associations) are quite proactive with respect to community safety.

Despite the refusal of the previous central government to accept recommendations made by the Morgan Report, many local authorities have continued to develop and promote crime prevention locally. Community safety officers have been appointed, and a national network for these co-ordinators has been created.

The LGA actively lobbied for a statutory responsibility and now that the Labour government is in power, the wording of the statute is in progress. The responsibility will, according to one interviewee, come without extra funding.

Although the LGA originally lobbied for local authorities to have statutory responsibility for community safety, the Crime and Disorder Bill will give responsibility to both local authorities and the police. Leadership groups will likely be formed with 2 or 3 members depending on the local government structure (in district council areas, there will be one police officer, one district council member and one county council member; in unitary areas, there will be one police officer and one unitary council member). This leadership group will likely have the responsibility to produce a Community Safety Strategy each year. In producing this strategy consultations will likely have to occur with local authority partnerships. These partnerships would for example consist of representatives from Probation, Social Services, Housing, Education, voluntary organisations and local business groups. However, care has to be taken that the

Community Safety Strategy does not conflict with, or just repeat what was said by local police authority strategies.

2) The role of the individual in making things happen, and having the right person in the right position at the right time is evidenced in this chapter. The community safety co-ordinator who managed to bring the national network to the forefront would according to Liddle and Bottoms (1991) and Liddle and Gelsthorpe (1994a) probably be described as a 'prime mover'. The role of individuals in the field is a factor of great significance as evidenced in Koch (1991). The co-ordinator in this research, was fortunate in that the Chief Executive of the County Council was also chairperson to the Association of County Council's executive committee which made it much easier to put the proposal of a national network forward. Had these ingredients not all been meshed together it could be questioned whether the same outcome would have occurred (e.g., having a national network for community safety officers).

8 Conclusion

This research investigated the structure of crime prevention policy-making and how it came to be what it is today. It aimed to answer three basic questions: (1) who influences crime prevention policy at the national level? (2) how is crime prevention at the national level structured? and (3) what role do the key organisations play in crime prevention, and what do they actually do?

The research examined the Home Office, the police service, the probation service, Crime Concern, NACRO, the Local Government Association and the National Community Safety Network. These were the agencies that were considered to be instrumental to crime prevention policy making in England and Wales. Publications disseminated from these organisations, as well as internal documents were analysed in order to understand both the role and meaning of crime prevention within them. Key participants in the national crime prevention policy making process were interviewed, which provided much insight on the relationships that exist amongst the various agencies.

This chapter examines the fourteen issues raised in chapter 1 and discussed throughout the research. An overall interpretation of how national crime prevention was structured, organised and determined in England and Wales between 1995 and 1997 is provided in the final commentary.

Review of the Issues

Issue 1: The Meaning of Crime Prevention

One of the problems within the domain of crime or criminality prevention is one of definition or conceptualisation. The author avoided defining any terms since one of the aims was to determine 'what is meant by crime prevention' within the field itself and especially in policy terms. This was determined through interviews and by analysing what was stated in various documents such as annual reports; training materials, and other sources disseminated through the agencies included in the research. The distinctive terms that the author came across most regularly in the interviews were: primary versus secondary versus tertiary prevention (e.g., see Brantingham and Faust, 1976); situational prevention versus social prevention, crime prevention versus criminality prevention, and crime prevention versus community safety where the latter was a much broader definition.

Although the author did not detect misuse of these terms in the interviews, a few of the publications were found to use the terminology in another context or, as with the *Operational Policing Review*, to use definitions that were contrary to those already accepted within the field.

Those interviewed from the Home Office, the police, and Crime Concern considered that crime prevention focused on primary and secondary prevention. Agencies involved in tertiary prevention were not considered to have a role in crime prevention policy. Within the probation service, the tertiary role was emphasised in the three most recent three year plans and from the respondents in Boroughville. This conforms with impressions of those interviewed that the probation service was involved in tertiary prevention.

However, the potential contribution of the probation service to primary and secondary prevention recognised by ACOP's crime prevention committee (or the lead officer for community safety within ACOP) was not widely acknowledged. The committee's hopes to influence national crime prevention policy and to publicise the manner in which the probation service could contribute to crime prevention policy was severely curtailed since Michael Howard and David Maclean were appointed.

The research confirmed that the type of crime prevention advocated by the Home Office and the police service is very much situational or, in other words, aimed at the crime event rather than the offender.

Criminality prevention, or focusing on the potential offender, was of little interest to the previous political masters. Those agencies that were considered to be concerned with criminality prevention had a minimal, if not non-existent, role in national crime prevention policy under Howard's reign. Thus, the probation service was no longer represented on the National Crime Prevention Agency; the recommendations made in the Morgan Report were ignored; the decision on whether or not to continue funding the Programme Development Unit was over ten months overdue; and NACRO's budget from the Home Office was questioned. Considering that £15 million was spent on CCTVs (78% of the crime prevention budget), not only is crime prevention situational, it is currently essentially about CCTVs.

One interviewee suggested that the Home Office and the police were one and the same as far as defining their boundaries within crime prevention. Their approaches were both centred around traditional situational crime prevention. In all the other organisations examined in this research a preference for the broader definition, community safety, was evident.

Issue 2: The Nature of Crime Prevention Policy Making

An observation made on more than one occasion was the fact that crime prevention was an incestuous environment. There are very few people within the field and all know each other or at least know of each other. Within the sphere of national policy making in 1995, there were literally one handful of individuals that could make things happen. These people were Nigel Whiskin, the Chief Executive of Crime Concern; Ian Chisholm, head of the Crime Prevention Unit;[33] John Stevens, Chairman of the ACPO sub-committee on Crime Prevention; Gloria Laycock, head of the Police Research Group; and David Maclean. Crime Prevention was therefore determined by a small number of people from the Home Office, the police and Crime Concern.

Now that some of these individuals have been replaced and a new government has come into power who will implement the Morgan Report, the focus of crime prevention policy will shift. Crime Concern still appears to be heavily influential but the other key players are still to be determined.

Around this handful of individuals there are other spheres of individuals whose names are highly recognised. For example, on the research front the name Ken Pease is continuously cited.

The end result of all this is that the same people sit on all the crime prevention related committees at the national level. Thus crime prevention policy is actually made and run by a very few select people. It is therefore the ideologies of these few people which are transferred into crime prevention policy. These few select people tend to discuss matters amongst

---

[33] In April 1996 Ian Chisholm left the Crime Prevention Agency and was temporarily replaced by Martin Narey who had previously been in charge of the co-ordination of computerisation in the Criminal Justice System. In September 1996, Richard Childs, an Assistant Chief Constable, took over as head of the Crime Prevention Agency.

themselves informally (e.g., outside of formal committee meetings) thus in a sense creating a sub-committee within each committee. According to one interviewee and the work of Crawford and Jones (1995), this is where most decisions get made. Based on this knowledge the significance of the individual in making things happen is obvious.

Issue 3: The Role of the Individual in Making Things Happen

The role of the individual is an important factor in not only national crime prevention policy but also in local crime prevention initiatives. In this research the significance of the individual was evidenced in most chapters. In chapter 2, the role of the individual politician was seen as important for policy. It was argued, for example, that it would be very unlikely that Home Office Circulars 8/84 and 44/90 would have been produced under Howard and Maclean's reign.

Chapter 3 demonstrated how the initiative and drive of individuals (along with seizing the right moment) led to significant changes within the Home Office. Ronald Clarke's determination and belief in situational crime prevention led to the establishment of the Crime Prevention Unit; Chris Nuttall's experience and beliefs led to the establishment of the Programme Development Unit; and finally Gloria Laycock's ambition led to the creation of the Police Research Group. These people firmly believed in something and were able to change the nature and structure of crime prevention within the country.

Chapter 4 demonstrated how John Stevens, a former chairperson to the ACPO sub-committee on crime prevention, opened up the sub-committee to include non-police members, and how relations improved between the police, Crime Concern and the Home Office including ministers under his chairmanship. The sub-committee progressed from a committee that had to ask to be represented on national committees/groups to one that was consulted in setting up the newly structured Crime Prevention Agency. According to those interviewed this was largely the result of John Stevens being an 'approachable' person.

Chapter 6 addressed the role of Nigel Whiskin, the Chief Executive of Crime Concern in making Crime Concern what it is today. Not only was Nigel Whiskin involved in setting up the Crime Prevention Agency, he was on the advisory committee of the 'International Conference for Crime Prevention Practitioners' held in Vancouver Canada from 31 March 1996 until 3 April 1996. Nigel Whiskin's character is said to be one that is able to get along with all political parties. This suggests that even though Crime Concern was set up by the Conservative Government, it is unlikely to be abolished under a new government. If anything it might be restructured.

Chapter 7 demonstrated how Peter Richardson came to organise the National Community Safety Network, in an attempt to decrease the likelihood of community safety officers and other practitioners within the field working in isolation. This network has now linked up with the Home Office, ACPO, ACOP, and the LGA in helping to prevent crime.

Interestingly, the significance of individuals in actually making things happen is something that is often brought up in crime prevention discussions. To date the author has not met an individual who does not believe that the personality of an individual running an initiative is of vital importance. It is an issue that is recognised, but not directly addressed in research. This research has therefore flagged up the issue as being a factor that can help explain how crime prevention works in terms of policy and practice.

Issue 4: The Extent of Political Ideology in Crime Prevention Policy

No matter who the Home Secretaries and ministers responsible for crime prevention have been between 1979 and 1997, all have been influenced by the political ideology of the Conservative Party. Very briefly this ideology was one based on more police, more prisons, and stiffer sentences. This is evidenced in every one of the Conservative Manifestos since 1979. The only differences between those in power has been the degree and manner in which these three issues have been advocated.

One senior Home Office official stated that ideology played a prominent part in policy and that crime prevention policy was "more political and irrational" than one might suspect: "It is rarely based on research but on what is thought by the individual minister to be popular to '*The Sun*' readers" (This latter comment was repeated in two further interviews with different individuals in other organisations).

The Conservative Party ideology is conveyed in research that has been disseminated from the Home Office Departments examined in this research (Issue 6 below).

The fact that criminality prevention was ignored in comparison to situational approaches coincided with the ideologies of Howard and Maclean. To use Cohen's (1985) term, an ideological contradiction was apparent with respect to Conservative party thinking vis à vis criminality prevention. Although the Government did acknowledge that "there is plenty of evidence from research here and in other countries that factors linked with offending include family background, experience at school and personality traits" (Home Office, 1996e: 10), their solution has been to set up the Ministerial Group on Juveniles to see what can be done. The author would argue that by reading the crime prevention literature (e.g., about the Cambridge Longitudinal Study on delinquency and the Perry Pre-School project) or in consulting with academics such as David Farrington, one could determine what should be done much more effectively than through a committee of ministers that have very little (if any) practical experience within the domain. Furthermore, if the Government really wanted to tackle criminality prevention, they would not have been so indecisive on funding the Programme Development Unit. Thus, although they acknowledge the need to focus on young people, they did very little about it.

Issue 5: The Influence of Politicians on Policy Making

The role of politicians on policy making is of great significance. Although all crime prevention ministers between 1979 and 1997 have been Conservative, their beliefs swayed from those who fell to the right of the Party and had a 'get tough on crime approach' to those who swayed more to the left and had a 'softer' approach to prevention. The fact that certain policy decisions were made can be largely explained by knowing who was in power at the time.

Thus in 1984 when Home Office Circular 8/84 was released, Douglas Hurd, considered a 'soft' Conservative member, was Minister of State. In the 1987 Conservative manifesto, Douglas Hurd was still in power and the following statement was made: "The origins of crime lie deep in society: in families where parents do not support or control their children; in schools where discipline is poor, and in the wider world where violence is glamorised and traditional values under attack" (Conservative Central Office, 1987: 55). This was the only such statement in all the Conservative manifestos since 1979.

When Home Office Circular 44/90 was released, the Morgan Report commissioned, and the Programme Development Unit approved, John Patten was the Minister of State. He has also been described as a 'soft Tory'.

When invitations for membership on the National Board for Crime Prevention were issued, Michael Jack was Minister of State. He was said to have believed that the probation service had a role to play in preventing crime and, therefore, invited the probation service to sit on the Board.

One senior Home Office official stated, "then there was that James Bulger murder and that really was I think surrounded by an uprush of right wing thinking about being tough on children who are criminals ...". The tragic death of James Bulger occurred in February 1993, and coincidentally on 28 May 1993 when there was a cabinet reshuffle, the new Home Secretary was announced as Michael Howard (Anonymous, 1993). Michael Jack was replaced by Charles Wardle, who was shortly replaced by David Maclean as having responsibility for crime prevention. Michael Howard's reputation was one of being 'tough on crime' and of belonging to the right of the Conservative Party.

When Michael Howard came into power as Home Secretary, he handed over the Safer Cities funding programme to the Department of the Environment. According to one senior Home Office official, before Howard's arrival, the Home Office was against the Department of the Environment running the Single Regeneration Budget. Coincidentally, Howard's previous position before becoming Home Secretary had been with the Department of the Environment. This is therefore another example of how the politician in power can change crime prevention policy.

This change had an effect on crime prevention policy in that the Home Office is no longer in control of which local programmes get funded. According to two Home Office officials, and two other interviews, the Department of the Environment very much focuses on "designing out crime" and "target hardening stuff". According to two Home Office officials there are ongoing arguments between the Home Office and Department of the Environment on how monies are being spent.

Howard and Maclean both affected crime prevention policy in that they encouraged Neighbourhood Watch, Street Watch, Neighbourhood Constables, and CCTVs as methods of preventing crime. They did not believe that the probation service had a role to play in crime prevention, and they were hesitant in funding the Programme Development Unit.

By the end of April 1996, no decision had been reached by the Minister concerning the Programme Development Unit's funding. To state that lack of funding should be considered as a reason for this delay is nonsense since in April 1996, the Minister agreed to provide funding to the International Crime Prevention Centre. This decision was made within three weeks, after the 'International Conference for Crime Prevention Practitioners' was held in Vancouver Canada (March 31-April 3, 1996).

The decision to delay the decision regarding the Programme Development Unit's funding was very much political.

Furthermore, Maclean wanted the Crime Prevention Agency to be headed by a senior police officer. Howard and Maclean were very much in favour of giving the police more control over crime prevention, and removing responsibility from local authorities. They rejected the recommendations made by the Morgan Committee, saying that crime prevention gets done without statutory obligations. It is extremely unlikely that any of the previous events mentioned under this issue would have occurred under the leadership of Howard and Maclean. This illustrates how individual politicians can influence crime prevention policy.

Issue 6: The Relationship Between Political Ideology and Practice & Research

Chapter 3 of this research suggested that the ideology of the Conservative Party has been transformed through Home Office Research. Since the 1980s, the proportion of research conducted on probation related issues dropped considerably. Research on police related matters has in the meantime received the largest proportion of research attention (based on number of publications and articles published by the Home Office departments examined in this research). Table 3.1 illustrated how the largest proportions of published research were conducted on (1) Police; (2) Courts and Sentencing; and (3) Prisons. The largest amounts of external research funding from the Research and Planning Unit from 1984/5 until 1994/5 were for research related to prisons (£2,934,100+) and Police (£1,943,671+ [see Table 3.2]). Within the Crime Prevention Unit (now known as the Crime Prevention Agency) and Police Research Group, the focus was on Situational Techniques and Policing. Youth targeted techniques received a minor amount of attention.

The findings above are consistent with Conservative party ideology whose emphasis was on police, prisons and stiffer sentences. Their focus was on 'individual responsibility', and opportunity reduction, as opposed to tackling the social-economic factors associated with crime.

Issue 7: Trends in Crime Prevention Policy Over the Past Fifteen Years

One advantage of not having a concrete definition set in stone is that the meaning of terms such as crime prevention and partnerships can be changed over time without explanation. Thus, crime prevention policy can change its focus without changing its terms. When crime prevention was first recognised by the Crime Policy Planning Unit around 1974, it focused on target hardening and attempting to reduce the opportunities for crime, as per Clarke and Mayhew (1980).

After the Crime Prevention Unit was created and after Home Office Circular 8/84, crime prevention expanded to include initiatives such as those in Kirkholt, the Five Towns Initiative, and Safer Cities. Since 1993, when the current Home Secretary and Minister came into office, the definition narrowed once again to include Neighbourhood Watch and CCTVs. Now that the Labour government are in power, the direction of crime prevention/community safety policy will change once again.

One change already is that the term 'community safety' is being employed reinforcing the notion that 'crime prevention' is of the police and Home Office in that it focuses on situational approaches. Community safety goes beyond situational approaches and includes factors listed under criminality prevention in this research. Unfortunately, the term 'community safety' is as yet not very clear.

Another trend that has occurred since 1984 is that politicians, in particular Michael Howard and David Maclean, have replaced the term 'multi-agency' with 'partnerships'. Not only have the terms changed, but so too has the meaning. This issue is somewhat connected to issue 4 discussed earlier in that individual politicians can change the direction and meaning of commonly utilised terms. In Home Office circulars 8/84 and 44/90, the notion of agencies working together to prevent crime was encouraged. In 1992, the Home Office Annual Report used the term partnership to refer to local statutory and voluntary agencies working with each other and with local people. Under Howard and Maclean, the definition of partnership narrowed to mean individuals and businesses helping the police. No mention was made of agencies. The emphasis was, to use King's (1989) words, on "consumerism, individualism and self-reliance". Technological anti-crime products are recommended.

Therefore, between 1984 and 1997 the meaning of partnership narrowed significantly from one which included statutory agencies to one that refers to individuals working with the police. The meaning of partnership will change once again under the Crime and Disorder Bill.

One factor to point out is that although the meaning of 'crime prevention' and 'partnership' changes over time, it does not necessarily mean that policy is advancing.

Issue 8: The Organisation of National Crime Prevention Policy

At the national level, the key organisations involved in crime prevention policy making between 1995 and 1997 were the Home Office, the police and Crime Concern. Although local authorities were not given statutory responsibility for crime prevention (or to use the Morgan Report's term, community safety), their role in local crime prevention initiatives was recognised (e.g., see Home Office, 1996e). The probation service used to be represented on the National Board for Crime Prevention, but their role in crime prevention policy making was severely curtailed within the current political climate.

Within the Home Office, the police service, and probation service, (sub) committees were set up to promote crime prevention within their respective organisations and outside. These committees included: the Ministerial Group on Crime Prevention, the Ministerial Group on Juvenile Crime, the ACPO sub-committee on crime prevention and the ACOP committee on crime prevention. The ministerial groups attempted to co-ordinate prevention amongst the various government departments; the ACOP committee promoted the role of crime prevention within its own organisation and ideally would have contributed to national crime prevention policy; and the ACPO sub-committee attempted to promote crime prevention both within the police service and outside.

Of the four, the only influential body for crime prevention policy was the ACPO sub-committee on crime prevention. The Ministerial Group on Crime Prevention had not met since July 1994, the Ministerial Group on Juvenile Crime had just been created, and the ACOP committee on crime prevention had been shunted out of the picture due to the beliefs of the previous political masters that probation does not have a part to play in crime prevention policy.

Between 1995 and 1997, the ACPO sub-committee on crime prevention became a leader in national crime prevention policy. This was largely due to its chairperson (see Issue 3). They opened up their membership to include non-police members, which made them appear more approachable. The newly appointed director of the Crime Prevention Agency was a member of this sub-committee.

Although one of the objectives of the sub-committee was to identify the causes of crime (which can be interpreted broadly or narrowly), another one of their objectives was "to continue to develop the situational approach to crime prevention, including target hardening through architectural liaison, design and technology" (see Figure 4.1). The objectives of this sub-committee did not conflict with Ministerial goals.

As stated earlier, the chairperson was heavily consulted in creating the National Crime Prevention Agency which illustrated the high level of influence on national crime prevention policy. The sub-committee's goal to influence crime prevention outside of the police service was realised at high levels in the last two years of the Conservative government.

Issue 9: The Prominence of Crime Prevention Within Each Agency

In examining the role of crime prevention, one observed that as the Morgan Report stated, "crime prevention is a peripheral concern for all agencies involved and a truly core activity for none of them" (Standing Conference on Crime Prevention, 1991: 3). Thus, if one examines Table 3.1 then one notices that crime prevention was not one of the top overall priorities of the Research and Planning Unit. Although crime prevention research was carried out in the Crime Prevention Unit, when the research arm became the Police Research Group, the focus changed to operational policing issues. The fact that the budget for the Programme Development Unit was under threat once again demonstrated a low priority for prevention.

Although various statements mention crime prevention (e.g., the Home Secretary's Key Objectives, the Statement of Objectives and Priorities for the Probation Service, and the Statement of Common Purpose and Values [ACPO, 1990]), little attention was provided to crime prevention in comparison to other issues.

Thus for example, in the Statement for Probation, prevention was mentioned under the heading 'Other work in the Community'. Although the Police Statement acknowledged that one of the purposes of the police was to prevent crime, the Police Probationer Training Foundation Course manual, and Her Majesty's Chief Inspectorate of Constabulary Annual Reports did not provide much attention to crime prevention. In fact most of the annual reports described crime prevention initiatives conducted by the Home Office and not the police. Furthermore, the *Operational Policing Review* (Joint Consultative Committee, 1990) defined primary, secondary and tertiary crime prevention in a manner that was inconsistent with commonly accepted definitions.

Within the Home Office, the prominence of crime prevention increased over the years. Although the Crime Prevention Unit was set up in 1983, it is Home Office Circular 8/84 that got the ball rolling in crime prevention outside of the Home Office. Even though crime prevention policy comes from the Home Office, the author would argue that it is not considered a core activity. In fact, the role of the Home Office in crime prevention seems to be diminishing. By giving the Safer Cities Phase II budget to the Single Regeneration Budget, the Home Office lost part of its control over crime prevention. Now that local authorities will have responsibility for community safety, the Home Office may loose even more control within the area. This could possibly be seen as an attempt to alleviate them from the responsibility for success or failure.

Although the Home Office has always advocated situational approaches to crime prevention, prevention policy has gone through trends. This could be a consequence of the lack of thought and research that was put into the initiatives before they even started. The current push for CCTV was, for example, not based on research but on individual convictions of what should be done to prevent crime.

One senior Home Office official stated, that one of the limits of the Home Office with regards to crime prevention was that they did not control the delivery mechanisms of crime prevention since this was done at a local level. However, one could argue against this statement by suggesting that the Home Office does in fact control delivery mechanisms in that they are at the moment providing funding for only CCTVs through the Challenge Competition. In order to receive any of this money at least an equal amount of money must be raised by the localities. By doing so, the Home Office are controlling the mechanisms for crime prevention to a certain degree. In a second interview, this same Home Office official stated, that by requesting an equal amount of funding to be raised locally, monies were being taken from other forms of prevention that might have otherwise been conducted. Although this latter point was not investigated in this research, it is something to consider.

Within the police service there is (based on the questionnaire results in Boroughville) agreement that police officers consider they do crime prevention work in their day-to-day activities. However, crime prevention receives little recognition in Her Majesty's Chief Inspectorate of Constabulary Annual Reports. The largest proportion of references made to crime prevention were about publicity campaigns and Neighbourhood Watch. The notions of repeat victimisation and CCTVs appeared for the first time in the 1994/95 Annual Report.

Although crime prevention is addressed in the *Police Probationer Training Foundation Course*, the Crime Prevention Standard Course offered by the Home Office Crime Prevention Centre is targeted to crime prevention officers and not to all police officers. Finally, the ACPO sub-committee on crime prevention is a sub-committee and not a full fledged committee, insinuating its position within policing matters.

Within the probation service, the majority of probation officers in Boroughville considered that they performed crime prevention work in their day-to-day activities. The largest proportion of officers stated this was done through supervisions. However the *National Standards for the Supervision of Offenders in the Community* published annually does not mention the role of probation in prevention. According to one interviewee, many probation areas are cutting back on crime prevention work due to 'tight budgets', demonstrating once again that it is not a core activity of the service. According to the most recent three year plan, the type of prevention advocated within the service is aimed at preventing re-offending while under supervision. This is consistent with the questionnaire results in Boroughville.

Crime Concern is an exception to the Morgan Report statement. Crime Prevention is a core activity of the organisation by the sole fact that all their work is based around the subject.

NACRO, however, has a very broad focus in which crime prevention is only one component. Although NACRO started out as being the only organisation outside of the police to be interested in crime prevention, their prominence appears to have been overshadowed by Crime Concern. If one uses a broad definition of crime prevention, then crime prevention can be considered to be a core activity of NACRO. However, NACRO has the reputation of focusing on tertiary prevention by focusing on offenders, which is not a component of current crime prevention policy. For this reason they are not universally accepted as being a key player in crime prevention policy. The core activities of NACRO are seen to be with the treatment and rehabilitation of offenders, a component not considered to be crime prevention within this government's ideology.

Since the Local Government Association was formed, one priority has been the wording of the Crime and Disorder Bill with regards to giving local authorities statutory responsibility for community safety. Community safety officers have also banded together to form the National Community Safety Network.

Issue 10: The Role of Each Agency in Crime Prevention Policy Making

Based on the research findings, the author concluded that the role of the Home Office is to advocate and publicise certain types of crime prevention through various policies, programmes, and research. The various types of crime prevention advocated are largely influenced by the political masters at the time.

The role of the police is to act as advisors at both a local and national level. In the previous political climate they were key advisors on crime prevention initiatives and were considered to be the lead agency in crime prevention at the national level. By suggesting that the police were key advisors does not imply that they were in control of crime prevention policy. Maclean and Howard promoted the police vis à vis crime prevention, but they still had the final say on how and what types of crime prevention got advocated or turned into policy. Police strategies for preventing crime were consistent with Home Office policy in that both focused on the target of crime rather than the potential offender.

Under the previous political masters, the role of the probation service in national crime prevention policy making was minimal. Their potential contribution to crime prevention policy lies with their experiences of dealing with offenders and determining the motivation and cause of offending from the offenders perspective.

Crime Concern are key advisors in national crime prevention policy making. Apart from the work they do in local communities, and of the recognition they have internationally, one of the main reasons why they have such an influential role in policy making is because Nigel Whiskin gets along well with the political masters. As stated earlier, the role of NACRO was minimal vis à vis national crime prevention policy under Howard and Maclean.

The role of local authorities and statutory agencies in national crime prevention policy was pushed aside under Howard and Maclean. Recommendations of the Morgan Committee to give local authorities statutory responsibility for crime prevention were rejected. This, however, did not stop many local authorities from employing community safety officers and incorporating crime prevention into current budgets. This move was supported by central government (e.g., see Home Office, 1996e).

Although one can accept that local authorities are in a key position to co-ordinate crime prevention by the sheer fact that they run departments such as housing, social services and education, one might question whether statutory responsibility is truly required in order for crime prevention to be more effective and efficient; or whether the desire for statutory responsibility is influenced by self-serving professional interests (see for example Cohen, 1985: chapter 3).

The definition of community safety still needs to be decided. Is it for example, "any good work" (as defined by Harvey et al., 1989: 85)? As Pease (1994: 687) stated, "the extreme vagueness of the Morgan Committee's definition of community safety gives no confidence that the revised definition will provide a satisfactory focus for the work".

Issue 11: Who Has Responsibility For Crime Prevention?

Based on the evidence provided in this research, the agency which was given responsibility for crime prevention by the Home Office under the Conservative government was undoubtedly the police. Until April 1996, the Crime Prevention Unit in the Home Office fell under the Police Department. Although the Unit was transferred to the Criminal Policy Directorate, it continued to be in the hands of the police.

The type of crime prevention advocated by the Home Office (or one should maybe say the politicians) was based on individuals helping the police through, for example, Neighbourhood Watch, Street Watch, and Neighbourhood Constables. Technology such as CCTVs was also advocated in order to help the police identify offenders and provide evidence that can help in prosecuting offenders. Furthermore, the *Police and Magistrates Court Act 1994* made policing less influenced by local authorities.

Finally, the type of crime prevention advocated by both the police service and Home Office is very much situational. The overall crime prevention strategies within each organisation are consistent with each other. In comparing the documentation amongst the agencies examined in this research, much more was said about crime prevention within the police service than for example the probation service or local authorities. In fact the Home Office Crime Prevention Centre run by police officers is the training centre for both police and non-police in crime prevention, suggesting once again that the police played the dominant role in crime prevention.

The fear within the ACPO sub-committee on crime prevention that the police will lose their leadership in crime prevention was unlikely under the Conservative government. The author now believes that given that local government will be given a statutory responsibility for community safety, the police could lose some of their primacy within the field. However, as Foucault (1969: 50-51) suggested, some individuals are accorded a status of competence and knowledge, and have through their profession the presumption that what they say is true. The author suggests that this is true of a police officer's crime prevention advice. Receiving advice from a police officer on how to prevent crime is probably more reassuring than receiving it from another source.

Issue 12: The Consistency Of National Instructions For Local Practice With National Practice

In examining crime prevention policy in England and Wales since 1979, one notices that as Ministers and Home Secretaries come and go, so to do crime prevention policies. Thus Home Office circulars 8/1984 and 44/1990, although widely recognised and acted upon at local levels, has not been practised at a national level. Within the Home Office itself, there is not an inter-departmental committee to co-ordinate crime prevention. It is all done informally.

Under Howard and Maclean, crime prevention was very narrowly defined. However, one gets the impression that at the local level much more is done than what was advocated by the politicians (e.g., CCTVs, Neighbourhood Watch, Street Watch and Neighbourhood Constables).

Issue 13: The Applicability Of Issues Raised At The National Level In This Research With Local Level Research Done By Others

The issues raised in this research are all connected to national policy making. However, based on discussions within local practitioners, it is very likely these issues also apply at the local level. The political mingling that goes on at all levels is something that is often left out of research evaluations.

This research, however, did find some common themes addressed in locally conducted research. It found, as did Crawford and Jones (1995), that within formally structured committees there is a sub-group which makes decisions amongst themselves in an informal setting. The findings also coincided with Liddle and Gelsthorpe's research that the Morgan Report is widely acknowledged at local levels. The role of the individual in being able to make things happen was addressed in Koch (1991).

Issue 14: The Consistency Of Perceived Roles Of Both Police And Probation Officers In Boroughville With National Findings

Although the findings from both police and probation officers in Boroughville are not generalisable to all of England, they were consistent with findings at the national level. Within the police service, the notion that crime prevention is about giving advice is evident at the national level. It is a theme that appeared in Her Majesty's Chief Inspector of Constabulary Annual Reports, in the Audit Commission report on Tackling Crime Effectively (1993), in the Operational Policing Review (Joint Consultative Committee, 1990: 9), and it was mentioned in the police probationer training manual which stated "often the action required will be straightforward and may simply consist of giving tactful advice to members of the public" (Home Office Central Planning Unit, 1991: 2/9/2).

Although the majority of police officers did perceive crime prevention as part of their day-to-day activities, this does not necessarily mean it takes up much of their time in comparison to other tasks. Even though crime prevention is part of their daily routine, it does not mean it has high priority. One must therefore be careful in how this information is used.

The findings from the probation service are also consistent with national findings. Thus, like the Central Council of Probation Committees (1987), the probation service's contribution to crime prevention is through supervisory activities. This would also be consistent with the key performance indicators in the two most recent three year plans for the probation service (Home Office, 1995m; 1996d).

These findings are thus an indication that national policy is at least somewhat consistent with local practice. In other words, although national policy making is political, it is not out of line with local practice. Further research would be required before firmer conclusions could be made about the extent to which national policy is consistent with local practice.

Final Commentary

So what does this all mean? In a nutshell, national crime prevention policy is very much centred on the individual Minister and Home Secretary. Within the previous political climate, Crime Concern, the police, and the Home Office were the key participants in national crime prevention policy. NACRO, the probation service, and local government as a statutory body for crime prevention were all disregarded (although voluntarily appointing community safety officers in local authorities was encouraged).

The more recent trend in crime prevention of focusing on individual responsibility is not unique to crime prevention policy. It could be considered as a reaction to much larger economic, political and social issues. As a result, technological situational approaches are advocated as opposed to funding initiatives related to criminality prevention.

In addition to crime prevention having a narrow focus at the national level, one comes to realise that crime prevention in England and Wales is really the result of a handful of key individuals. The decision making process itself in terms of directions to be taken tends to be done informally behind closed doors. As far as research goes, some reports are left unpublished by the Home Office, making it difficult to know on what basis decisions were made about certain policies. Previous crime prevention policy appears to have been based on the political masters' personal preferences and what they considered conforms to public opinion.

If crime prevention policy were based on the research it would be much broader than CCTV, Neighbourhood Watch, Street Watch and Neighbourhood Constable approaches. In fact these four approaches would not dominate policy due to the fact that research has not confirmed that these approaches are efficient methods of preventing crime.

In the United States of America (U.S.A.) studies such as those conducted by Pate (1986) on the effectiveness of foot patrols and Kelling et al., (1974) on the effectiveness of police patrol cars argued that adding more police in order to reduce crime was not an effective solution.

The Conservative government's approach to increase the use and length of imprisonment in England and Wales has also been demonstrated to be ineffective in the U.S.A. Penal policies were toughened in New York, Texas and California by increasing the use and length of imprisonment in an attempt to lower crime rates. However, rates of serious crime went up (Correctional Association of New York cited in Currie, 1985: 33-34). A study by the Correctional Association of New York in 1982 concluded "The state's new policies have been staggeringly expensive, have threatened a crisis of safety and manageability in the prison system, and have failed to reduce the rate of crime or even stop its increase" (Correctional Association of New York cited in Currie, 1985: 33).

If crime prevention policy were even slightly based on well known research, it would generally speaking focus on the work of Ken Pease, David Farrington, the Brantinghams and the work of Ronald Clarke. Since crime cannot be effectively tackled by the police and the criminal justice system, the main ingredient of the policy would be that it is an interdepartmental policy (e.g., with those departments represented on the Ministerial Group for Crime Prevention).

The policy would promote the research on repeat victimisation (e.g., see Farrell, 1992; Forrester et al., 1988; Forrester et al., 1990; Pease, 1991; Polvi et al., 1990; Lloyd et al., 1994; and Farrell and Pease, 1993). It would also consider providing more 'quality' nursery programmes such as the Perry Pre-School project (e.g., see Schweinhart and Weikart, 1993; Berrueta-Clement et al., 1984; Schweinhart, 1987) or the Carolina Abercedarian Project (Horacek et al., 1987). The policy would also emphasise the need to reduce the likelihood of antisocial behaviour by working with parents and even possibly by providing incentives to prevent some from becoming parents in the first place. David Farrington (1995: 958) concluded that "antisocial children tend to grow up into antisocial adults, and that antisocial adults tend to produce antisocial children". Thus providing incentives for antisocial adults or even adolescents not to conceive a child in the first place might be an economical solution. This would at minimum require the co-operation of Health, Education and Social Services.

The policy would continue to promote situational approaches and to explore new ones. However, the situational approach would not dominate over the approaches just described. The work of the Brantingham's would also be incorporated into town planning and building regulations.

Finally, the policy would encourage more evaluative research. Research from other fields such as the Health Sciences or Education might also be incorporated. The above description is only based on the criminological research. The author is certain that research conducted in other disciplines could have an impact on preventing crime.

One of the difficulties in doing this research was that every few months something within the 'crime prevention arena' changed. However, based on the findings of this research, it is fair to say that crime prevention policy (and probably policy in general) depends on who is in power and what their own convictions are. The next few years will prove to be very interesting within crime prevention policy, given the new government. Will the Crime and Disorder Bill change the direction of crime prevention policy in the future or will things basically remain the same?

References

Anderson, D., Chenery, S., and Pease, K. (1995) *Biting Back: Tackling Repeat Burglary and Car Crime*. Crime Detection & Prevention Series, Paper 58. London: HMSO.

Anonymous. (1993) "Editorial". *Crime Prevention News* July-September, London: Home Office: 2.

ACC. (no date) *Championing The County Cause: What The ACC Does And How It Works*. (Leaflet) London: ACC.

ACC. (1995) *Annual Report 1994-95*. London: ACC.

ACC/AMA. (1994) *Getting Started: Key Issues For New Police Authority Members*. London: ACC and AMA.

ACPO. (1990) *Statement of Common Purpose and Values*. Available in Home Office (1992c).

ACPO. (1995) *Crime Committee: ACPO Crime Strategy*. Unpublished paper received from ACPO sub-committee on crime prevention, 1995.

ACOP. (1995) *Annual Review*. London: ACOP.

ACOP. (1996) *Annual Report 1996/7*. London: ACOP.

ADC. (1990) *Promoting Safer Communities: A District Council Perspective*. London: ADC.

ADC. (1994a) *Joining Forces Against Crime*. London: ADC.

ADC. (1994b) *Winning Communities: The Role Of Housing In Promoting Community Safety*. London: ADC.

ADC. (1995a) *ADC Policing Working Group*. Minutes of meeting on Wednesday 11 January 1995.

ADC. (1995b) *ADC Publications List, September 1995*. London: ADC.

ADC. (1995c) *Annual Report 1994-1995*. London: ADC.

AMA. (1990) *Crime Reduction: A Framework For The Nineties?* London: AMA.

AMA. (1993a) *Children And Trouble: A Study Of Juvenile Justice Issues For Local Government*. London: AMA.

AMA. (1993b) *Local Authorities And The Police: Working In Partnership*. London: AMA/ALA/LBA

AMA. (1994) *About The AMA: Its Work, Its Organisation And Its Members, June 1994*. London: AMA.

AMA. (1995a) *Annual Report 1995*. London: AMA.

AMA. (1995b) *Community Safety: Protecting The Public*. Minutes of the Policy Committee Meeting on 12 September 1995, P95 113, item 15. London: AMA.

Audit Commission. (1990) *Effective Policing: Performance Review In Police Forces*. London: Audit Commission, Police Paper #8.

Audit Commission. (1993) *Helping With Enquiries: Tackling Crime Effectively*. London: Audit Commission, Police Paper #13.

Audit Commission. (1994) *Auditing Local Services*. London: Audit Commission.

Audit Commission. (1995) *Corporate Plan 1995-1998*. London: Audit Commission.

Audit Commission. (1996a) *Misspent Youth...Young people and crime*. London: Audit Commission.

Audit Commission. (1996b) *Streetwise: Effective police patrol*. London: Audit Commission.

Beccaria, C. (1963) *On Crimes And Punishments*. Originally published as *Dei delitti e delle pene*, 1764. Indianapolis: Bobbs-Merrill.

Bennett, T. (1990) *Evaluating Neighbourhood Watch*. Worcester, Great Britain: Billing & Sons Ltd.

Bennett, T., and Wright, R. (1984) *Burglars On Burglary*. Aldershot England: Gower Publishing Company.

Berrueta-Clement, J., et al. (1984) *Changed Lives: The Effects Of The Perry Preschool Program On Youths Through Age 19*. Michigan: The High/Scope Press.

Bottoms, A. E. (1990) "Crime prevention facing the 1990's". *Policing And Society*: *1*, 3-22.

Bottoms, A.E. (1995) "The philosophy and politics of punishment and sentencing". In Clarkson, C.M.V., and Morgan, R. (eds.) *The Politics Of Sentencing Reform*. Oxford: Clarendon Press, 17-49.

Bottoms, A.E., and Wiles, P. (1995) "Crime and insecurity in the city". In Fijnaut, C., et al. (eds.) *Changes In Society, Crime And Criminal Justice In Europe - Volume 1*. Antwerp: Kluwer.

Bottoms, A.E., and Wiles, P. (1996) "Understanding crime prevention in late modern societies". In Bennett, T (ed.) *Preventing Crime And Disorder: Targeting Strategies And Responsibilities*. Cambridge: Institute of Criminology, 1-41.

Brantingham, P., and Brantingham, P. (1981) *Environmental Criminology*. Beverly Hills: Sage Publications.

Brantingham, P., and Brantingham, P. (1984) *Patterns In Crime*. New York: Macmillan.

Brantingham, P., and Brantingham, P. (1991) *Environmental Criminology*. Prospect Heights, IL: Waveland Press.

Brantingham, P., and Brantingham, P. (1993) "Environment, routine and situation: toward a pattern theory of crime". In Clarke, R., and Felson, M. (eds.) *Routine Activity And Rational Choice*. London: Transaction Publishers, 259-294.

Brantingham, P., and Faust, F. (1976) "A conceptual model of crime prevention". *Crime And Delinquency*: *22*, 284-296.

Bright, J. (1991) "Crime prevention: the British experience". In Stenson, K., and Cowell, D. (eds.) *The Politics Of Crime Control*. London: Sage Publications, 62-86.

Brittan, S. (1975) "The economic contradictions of democracy". *British Journal Of Political Science*: 5(1), 129-159.

Brown, B. (1995) *CCTV In Town Centres: Three Case Studies*. Crime Detection and Prevention Series Paper 68. London: Home Office.

Buck, M. (1983) "What's in it for us? - The police perspective". In Anonymous. *Crime Prevention Diversion: Corporate Action With Juveniles*. Proceedings of a Conference on 'Crime Prevention', Albany Hotel, Birmingham, 4-6 December 1983.

Cain, M. (1973) *Society And The Policeman's Role*. London: Routledge & Kegan Paul.

Canadian Council on Social Development. (1989) *Crime Prevention Through Social Development: A Discussion Paper For Social Policy Makers And Practitioners*. Ottawa.

Central Council of Probation Committees. (1987) *Crime Prevention: A Role For Probation Committees*. London: Working Party on Crime Prevention.

Central Council of Probation Committees. (1990) *Probation: The Key To Change*. Working Party Report. London: Central Council of Probation Committees.

Clarke, R. (1980) "Situational crime prevention: theory and practice". *British Journal Of Criminology*: 20(2), 136-147.

Clarke, R. (ed.) (1992) *Situational Crime Prevention: Successful Case Studies*. New York: Harrow and Heston Publishers.

Clarke, R., and Cornish, D. (eds.) (1983) *Crime Control In Britain: A Review of Policy Research*. State University of New York Press.

Clarke, R.V. and Cornish, D.B. (1985) "Modelling offenders' decisions: a framework for policy and research". In Tonry, M., and Morris, N. (eds.) *Crime And Justice: An Annual Review Of Research, 6*. Chicago: University of Chicago Press.

Clarke, R., and Mayhew, P. (1980) *Designing Out Crime*. London: HMSO.

Cohen, L., and Felson, M. (1979) "Social change and crime rate trends: a routine activities approach". *American Sociological Review*: 44, 588-608.

Cohen, S. (1985) *Visions Of Social Control*. Cambridge: Polity Press.

Committee of Inquiry on the Police. (1979) *Report III: The Structure And Role Of Police Staff Associations*. London: HMSO.

Conger, J.J., and Miller, W.C. (1966) *Personality, Social Class And Delinquency*. New York: Wiley.

Conservative Central Office. (1979) *Conservative Manifesto 1979*. London: McCorquodale Printer Ltd.

Conservative Central Office. (1983) *The Conservative Manifesto 1983*. London: McCorquodale Printers Ltd.

Conservative Central Office. (1987) *The Conservative Manifesto 1987*. London: McCorquodale Confidential Print Ltd.
Conservative Central Office. (1992) *The Best Future For Britain: The Conservative Manifesto 1992*. Derby: Bemrose U.K. Ltd.
Conservative Central Office. (1993) *Conservative Party News: The Rt Hon. Michael Howard QC MP, Wednesday 6 October, 1993*. 400/93.
Conservative Central Office. (1995) *Conservative Party News: The Rt Hon. Michael Howard QC MP, Thursday 12 October, 1995*. 478/95.
Cornish, D., and Clarke, R. (eds.) (1986) *The Reasoning Criminal: Rational Choice Perspectives On Offending*. New- York: Springer-Verlag.
Cornish, D.B., and Clarke, R. (1987) "Understanding crime displacement: an application of rational choice theory". *Criminology*: 25, 933-947.
Correctional Association of New York. (1982) *The Prison Population Explosion in New York State: A Study of Its Causes and Consequences with Recommendations for Change*.
Crawford, A., and Jones, M. (1995) "Inter-agency co-operation and community-based crime prevention: some reflections on the work of Pearson and colleagues". *British Journal Of Criminology*: 35(1), 17-33.
Crime Concern. (no date) *Making Communities Safer: Crime Concern*. Swindon: Crime Concern.
Crime Concern. (1989) *Crime Concern Annual Review 1988/89*. Swindon: Crime Concern.
Crime Concern. (1990) *Crime Concern: Introduction*. Swindon: Crime Concern.
Crime Concern. (1992) *Crime Concern Annual Review 1992*. Swindon: Crime Concern.
Crime Concern. (1993a) *About Crime Concern*. Swindon: Crime Concern.
Crime Concern. (1993b) *Crime Concern Annual Review 1993: Homing In On Crime*. Swindon: Crime Concern.
Crime Concern. (1994) *Annual Review 1994: Towards A Safer Britain*. Swindon: Crime Concern.
Crime Concern. (1995a) *Crime Concern 1995: Annual Review*. Swindon: Crime Concern.
Crime Concern. (1995b) *The Prevention of Criminality: A briefing paper for crime prevention partnerships*. Briefing Paper 2. Swindon: Crime Concern.
Crime Concern. (1996a) *1996 Annual Review*. Swindon: Crime Concern.
Crime Concern. (1996b) *On the Right Track: Diverting young people from crime in rural areas*. Report on the conference held on 24 June 1996 in Nottingham. Swindon: Crime Concern.
Crime Concern. (1997a) *Crime Against small business: facing the challenge*. Briefing Paper 5. Swindon: Crime Concern.
Crime Concern. (1997b) *The National Crime Prevention and Community Safety Awards 1997*. Swindon: Crime Concern.

Croft, J. (1978) *Research In Criminal Justice*. Home Office Research Study No. 44. London: HMSO.
Croft, J. (1982) "Planning". *Research Bulletin*: *14*, 5-6. Home Office Research and Planning Unit. London: Home Office.
Currie, E. (1985) *Confronting Crime: An American Challenge*. New York: Pantheon Books.
Dishion, T. (1990) "The peer context of troublesome child and adolescent behavior". In Leone, P. *Understanding Troubled And Troubling Youth*. London: Sage Publications, 128-153.
Duplock, R. (1993) *Crime Prevention And The Children Act 1989*. MPhil Short Thesis Presented to the Institute of Criminology, University of Cambridge, June 1993.
Ekblom, P. (1993) "Proximal circumstances: towards a discipline of crime prevention through a mechanism-based classification". London: Home Office Research and Planning Unit.
Ekblom, P. (1996) "Safer Cities and residential burglary: a summary of evaluation results". *European Journal Of Criminal Policy And Research*: March 1996.
Ekblom, P., and Pease, K. (1995) "Evaluating crime prevention". In Tonry, M., and Farrington, D. (eds.). *Building A Safer Society: Strategic Approaches To Crime Prevention*. Crime and Justice Series, Volume 19. London: The University of Chicago Press, 585-662.
Farrell, G. (1992) "Multiple victimisation: its extent and significance". *International Review of Victimology*, *2*, 89-111.
Farrell, G., and Pease, K. (1993) *Once Bitten, Twice Bitten: Repeat Victimisation and its Implications for Crime Prevention*. Crime Prevention Unit Paper 46. London: Home Office.
Farrington, D. (1989a) "Implications of longitudinal studies for social prevention". *Canadian Journal Of Criminology*: *31*(4), 453-463.
Farrington, D. (1989b) *Implications Of Criminal Career Research For The Prevention Of Offending*. Paper given at the British Criminology Conference, Bristol, July 1989.
Farrington, D. (1994) "Early developmental prevention of juvenile delinquency". *Criminal Behaviour and Mental Health*: *4*, 209-227.
Farrington, D. (1995) "The twelfth Jack Tizard memorial lecture. The development of offending and antisocial behaviour from childhood: Key findings from the Cambridge study in delinquent development". *Journal of Child Psychiatry*: *36*(6), 929-964.
Ford, R. (1995) "Howard launches anti-crime agency". *The Times*: September 4, 1995: 6.
Forrester, D., Chatterton, M., and Pease, K. (1988) *The Kirkholt Burglary Prevention Project, Rochdale*. Crime Prevention Unit Paper 13. London: Home Office.

Forrester, D., Frenz, S., O'Connell, M., and Pease, K. (1990) *The Kirkholt Burglary Prevention Project: Phase II*. Crime Prevention Unit Paper 23. London: Home Office.

Foucault M. (1969) *The Archaeology Of Knowledge*. Translated by A.M. Sheridan Smith, 1972. London: Routledge.

Geraghty, J. (1991) *Probation Practice In Crime Prevention*. Crime Prevention Unit Paper 24. London: Home Office.

Goldstein, H. (1979) "Improving policing: a problem-oriented approach". *Crime And Delinquency*: (April), 234-258.

Graham, J. (1990) *Crime Prevention Strategies In Europe And North America*. Helsinki Institute for Crime Prevention and Control Finland, HEUNI No. 18: United Nations.

Graham, J., and Bennett, T. (1995) *Crime Prevention Strategies In Europe And North America*. Helsinki Institute for Crime Prevention and Control Finland, HEUNI No. 28: United Nations.

Hamilton-Smith, N. (1994) *Crime Concern: An Examination Of The Goals, Strategies And Activities Of A Crime Prevention Organisation*. Short MPhil Thesis presented to the Institute of Criminology, University of Cambridge, June 1994.

Harris, R. (1992) *Crime, Criminal Justice And The Probation Service*. London: Tavistock/Routledge.

Harvey, L., Grimshaw, P., and Pease, K. (1989) "Crime prevention delivery: the work of crime prevention officers". In Morgan, R., and Smith, D. (eds.) *Coming To Terms With Policing: Perspectives On Policy*. London: Routledge, 82-96.

Heal, K. (1992) "Changing perspectives on crime prevention: the role of information and structure". In Evans, D., Fyfe, N., and Herbert, D. (eds.) *Crime, Policing And Place: Essays In Environmental Criminology*. London: Routledge, 257-271.

Heal, K., and Laycock, G. (1988) "The development of crime prevention: issues and limitations". In Hope, T., and Shaw, M. (eds.) *Communities And Crime Reduction*. London: HMSO, 236-245.

Hirschi, T., and Hindlelang, M. J. (1977) "Intelligence and delinquency: a revisionist view". *American Sociological Review*: 42, 571-587.

Hirst, J. (1993) *Royal Commission Research Papers: A Policing Perspective*. Police Research Series No. 6. London: Home Office Police Department.

Hogwood, B. (1992) *Trends In British Public Policy*. Buckingham: Open University Press.

Home Office. (1965) *Report Of The Committee On The Prevention And Detection Of Crime* (Cornish Committee). London: Home Office.

Home Office. (1980) *Report Of Her Majesty's Chief Inspector Of Constabulary 1979*. London: HMSO.

Home Office. (1981) *Report Of Her Majesty's Chief Inspector Of Constabulary 1980*. London: HMSO.

Home Office. (1982) *Report Of Her Majesty's Chief Inspector Of Constabulary 1981*. London: HMSO.
Home Office. (1983a) *The Crime Prevention Centre*. Stafford: Home Office Crime Prevention Centre.
Home Office. (1983b) *Report Of Her Majesty's Chief Inspector Of Constabulary 1982*. London: HMSO.
Home Office. (1984a) *Crime Prevention*. Home Office Circular 8/1984. London: Home Office.
Home Office. (1984b) *The Probation Rules 1984*. Statutory Instrument 1984 No. 647. London: Home Office.
Home Office. (1984c) *Probation Service In England And Wales: Statement Of National Objectives And Priorities*. London: Home Office.
Home Office. (1984d) *Report Of Her Majesty's Chief Inspector Of Constabulary 1983*. London: HMSO.
Home Office. (1985a) *The Government's Expenditure Plans 1985-86 To 1987-88*. Volume II, CM 9428-II. London: HM Treasury HMSO.
Home Office. (1985b) *Report Of Her Majesty's Chief Inspector Of Constabulary 1984*. London: HMSO.
Home Office. (1986) *Report Of Her Majesty's Chief Inspector Of Constabulary 1985*. London: HMSO.
Home Office. (1987) *Report Of Her Majesty's Chief Inspector Of Constabulary 1986*. London: HMSO.
Home Office. (1988) *Report Of Her Majesty's Chief Inspector Of Constabulary 1987*. London: HMSO.
Home Office. (1989) *Report Of Her Majesty's Chief Inspector Of Constabulary 1988*. London: HMSO.
Home Office. (1990a) *Crime, Justice And Protecting The Public: The Governments Proposals For Legislation*. London: HMSO.
Home Office. (1990b) *Crime Prevention: The Success Of The Partnership Approach*. Home Office Circular 44/90. London: Home Office.
Home Office. (1990c) *Partnership In Crime Prevention*. London: HMSO.
Home Office. (1990d) *Report Of Her Majesty's Chief Inspector Of Constabulary 1989*. London: HMSO.
Home Office. (1990e) *Supervision And Punishment In The Community: Framework For Action*. CM 966. London: HMSO.
Home Office. (1991a) *Annual Report 1991: The Government's Expenditure Plans 1991-92 To 1993-94 For The Home Office And The Charity Commission*. CM 1509. London: HMSO.
Home Office. (1991b) *Her Majesty's Chief Inspector Of Constabulary Annual Report 1990*. London: HMSO.
Home Office. (1992a) *Annual Report 1992: The Government's Expenditure Plans 1992-93 To 1994-95 For The Home Office And The Charity Commission*. CM 1909. London: HMSO.

Home Office. (1992b) *Her Majesty's Chief Inspector Of Constabulary Annual Report 1991*. London: HMSO.
Home Office. (1992c) *National Standards For The Supervision Of Offenders In The Community*. London: Home Office.
Home Office. (1992d) *The Probation Service: Three Year Plan For The Probation Service 1993-1996*. London: HMSO.
Home Office. (1993a) *Annual Report 1993: The Government's Expenditure Plans 1993-94 To 1995-96 For The Home Office And The Charity Commission*. CM 2208. London: HMSO.
Home Office. (1993b) *A Practical Guide To Crime Prevention For Local Partnerships*. Report prepared for the Home Office by Crime Concern. London: Home Office.
Home Office. (1993c) *Crime Prevention: Background Brief*. Issued in January 1993 from the Home Office Crime Prevention Unit.
Home Office. (1993d) *Her Majesty's Chief Inspector Of Constabulary Annual Report 1992*. London: HMSO.
Home Office. (1993e) *HM Inspectorate Of Probation, Annual Report 1992-1993*. London: Home Office.
Home Office. (1993f) "New National Board and Ministerial Group". *Crime Prevention News*: April - June, 3. London: Home Office.
Home Office. (1994a) *Annual Report 1994: The Government's Expenditure Plans 1994-95 To 1996-97 For The Home Office And The Charity Commission* CM 2508. London: HMSO.
Home Office. (1994b) *Guidelines For Street Watch Schemes*. London: Home Office.
Home Office. (1994c) *Her Majesty's Chief Inspector Of Constabulary Annual Report 1993*. London: HMSO.
Home Office. (1994d) *HM Inspectorate Of Probation, Annual Report 1993-1994*. London: Home Office.
Home Office. (1994e) *Partners Against Crime*. London: Home Office.
Home Office. (1994f) *The Probation Service: Three Year Plan For The Probation Service 1994-1997*. London: HMSO.
Home Office. (1994g) *Research And Planning Unit Programme*. London: Home Office Research and Statistics Department, 1993-1994.
Home Office. (1994h) *Research And Planning Unit Programme 1994-1995*. London: Home Office Research and Statistics Department.
Home Office. (1994i) *Your Practical Guide To Crime Prevention*. London: Home Office.
Home Office. (1995a) *Annual Report 1995: The Government's Expenditure Plans 1995-96 To 1997-98 For The Home Office And The Charity Commission*. CM 2808. London: HMSO.
Home Office. (1995b) *The Civil Service Year Book 1996*. London: HMSO.

Home Office. (1995c) *Closed Circuit Television Challenge Competition 1996/97: Bidding Guidance*. London: Home Office.
Home Office. (1995d) *Crime Prevention Media Pack.* November 1995. London: Home Office.
Home Office. (1995e) "Crime reduction network launched". *Crime Prevention News*: October - December, 4.
Home Office. (1995f) *Her Majesty's Chief Inspector Of Constabulary Annual Report 1994/95*. London: HMSO.
Home Office. (1995g) *HM Inspectorate Of Probation, Annual Report 1995*. London: Home Office.
Home Office. (1995h) *Home Office Crime Prevention Centre: Aims & Objectives*. Unpublished document provided by the Home Office Crime Prevention Centre.
Home Office. (1995i) *Home Office Programme Development Unit, Grants For Innovative Projects 1995: Reducing Criminality*. Letter dated 19 April 1995 from Christine Lehman, Programme Development Unit to those that might be interested in receiving a grant.
Home Office. (1995j) *National Standards For The Supervision Of Offenders In The Community*. London: Home Office Probation Service Division.
Home Office. (1995k) "Outcome of the Senior Management Review: Part 1". *Home Office Review: 4* (27 October 1995). London: Home Office.
Home Office. (1995l) *Preventing Crime Into The Next Century: Michael Howard*. Home Office News Release 260/95, 22 November 1995.
Home Office. (1995m) *The Probation Service: Three Year Plan For The Probation Service 1995-1998*. London: Home Office.
Home Office. (1996a) *Annual Report 1996: The Government's Expenditure Plans 1996-97 To 1998-99 For The Home Office And The Charity Commission*. CM 3208. London: HMSO.
Home Office. (1996b) *Her Majesty's Chief Inspectorate of Constabulary Annual Report 1995/96*. London, The Stationery Office.
Home Office. (1996c) *Ministers Launch New Approach To Tackle Juvenile Crime*. Home Office News Release 014/96, 18 January 1996.
Home Office. (1996d) *The Probation Service: Three Year Plan For The Probation Service 1996-1999*. London: Home Office Probation Service Division.
Home Office. (1996e) *Protecting The Public: The Government's Strategy On Crime In England And Wales*. CM 3190. London: HMSO.
Home Office. (1996f) *Research Bulletin, Issue 38*. London: Home Office Research and Statistics Directorate.
Home Office. (1997a) *Annual Report 1997: The Government's Expenditure Plans 1997-1998 to 1999-2000*. CM3608. London: HMSO.
Home Office. (1997b). *Her Majesty's Inspectorate of Probation Annual Report 1996*. London: Home Office.
Home Office. (1997c) *Preventing Children Offending: A consultation document*. CM3566. London: Home Office.

Home Office. (1997d) *New Ministerial Group on Youth Crime Meets.* Home Office News Release 165/97, 9 July 1997.

Home Office. (1997e) *The Three Year Plan For The Probation Service, 1997-2000.* London: Home Office.

Home Office Central Planning Unit. (1991) *Police Probationer Training: Foundation Course, Second Edition.* Police Training Support.

Home Office Crime Prevention Centre. (1995) *The 10 Principles Of Prevention.* Unpublished document provided by the Crime Prevention Centre.

Home Office Crime Prevention Unit. (1996) *Crime Prevention Expenditure.* Unpublished table. Parts of this table are published in Home Office (1997a: 46).

Horacek, H., et al., (1987) "Predicting school failure and assessing early intervention with high-risk children". *Journal of the American Academy of Child and Adolescent Psychiatry, 26,* 293-327.

Howard, M. (1996) "Crime Watch". *New Scientist*: 6/13 January 1996, 47.

Jeffery, C.R. (1971) *Crime Prevention Through Environmental Design.* Beverly Hills: Sage Publications.

Johnston, L. (1996) "Policing diversity: the impact of the public-private complex in policing". In Leishman, F., Loveday, B., and Savage, S. (eds.) *Core Issues In Policing.* London: Longman, 54-70.

Joint Consultative Committee. (1990) *Operational Policing Review.* Surbiton: Police Federation of England and Wales.

Jones, T., Newburn, T., and Smith, D. (1994) *Democracy & Policing.* London: Policy Studies Institute.

Judd, C., Smith, E., and Kidder, L. (1991) *Research Methods In Social Relations: International Edition.* (6th Edition). Orlando Florida, U.S.A.: Holt, Rinehart and Winston Inc.

Kelling, G., Pate, T., Dieckman, D., and Brown, C. (1974) *The Kansas City Preventive Patrol Experiment: A Technical Report.* Police Foundation, U.S.A.

King, M. (1989) "Social crime prevention à la Thatcher". *The Howard Journal*: 28(4), 291-312.

Koch, B. (1991) *The Prince George Community Social Development Board: A Case Study Of Municipal Inter-Agency Crime Prevention.* Master of Arts Thesis Submitted to the University of Ottawa, September 1991.

Koch, B. (1996) *National Crime Prevention Policy in England and Wales 1979-1995.* PhD thesis submitted to The Institute of Criminology, University of Cambridge, December 1996.

Kolvin, I., et al. (1990) *Continuities Of Deprivations.* Avebury: ESRC/DHSS Studies in Deprivation and Disadvantage, No 15.

Labour Party. (1997) *new Labour because Britain deserves better.* London.

Lavrakas, P., and Bennett, S. (1988) "Thinking about the implementation of citizen and community anti-crime measures". In Hope, T., and Shaw, M. (eds.) *Communities And Crime Reduction.* London: Home Office and Planning Unit, 221-235.

Laycock, G., and Heal, K. (1989) "Crime prevention: the British experience". In Evans, D., and Herbert, D. (eds.) *The Geography Of Crime*. London: Routledge, 315-330.

LGA. (1997a) *Crime: the local solution, current practice*. London: LGA and Local Government Management Board.

LGA. (1997b) *Meeting of the Community Safety Panel: 28 May 1997*. Minutes for members of the LGA Community Safety Panel. London: LGA.

LGA. (1997c) *The national voice for local communities*. London: LGA.

Liddle, M., and Bottoms, A. (1991) *Implementing Circular 8/84 - A Retrospective Assessment Of The Five Towns Crime Prevention Initiative*. Unpublished Report submitted to the Home Office by the Institute of Criminology, University of Cambridge.

Liddle, M., and Gelsthorpe, L. (1994a) *Crime Prevention And Inter-Agency Co-operation*. Crime Prevention Unit Series, paper No. 53. London: Home Office.

Liddle, M., and Gelsthorpe, L. (1994b) *Inter-Agency Crime Prevention: Further Issues*. Supplementary Paper to Crime Prevention Unit Series Paper No. 52 and 53. London: Home Office.

Liddle, M., and Gelsthorpe, L. (1994c) *Inter-Agency Crime Prevention: Organising Local Delivery*. Crime Prevention Unit Series, Paper No. 52. London: Home Office.

Lloyd, S., Farrell, G., and Pease, K. (1994) *Preventing Repeated Domestic Violence: A Demonstration Project on Merseyside*. Crime Prevention Unit Paper 49. London: Home Office.

Lodge, T.S (1974) "The founding of the Home Office Research Unit". In Hood, R. (ed.) *Crime, Criminology And Public Policy: Essays In Honour Of Sir Leon Radzinowicz*. London: Heinemann Educational Books Ltd, 11-24.

Loveday, B. (1994a) *The Competing Role Of Central And Local Agencies In Crime Prevention Strategies*. May 1994. University of Central England Business School.

Loveday, B. (1994b) *Ducking And Diving: The Construction Of Government Policy For Police And Criminal Justice In The 1990s*. June 1994. University of Central England Business School.

Loveday, B. (1996) "Crime at the core?". In Leishman, F., Loveday, B., and Savage, S. (eds.) *Core Issues In Policing*. London: Longman, 73-100.

Maclean, D. (1995a) "Consolidation and community: two key concerns for the new police authorities". *County News, Association Of County Councils*: 88(6), 8.

Maclean, D. (1995b) "Crime prevention workshop". *Police Review*: 1 December 1995, 26-27.

Martinson, R. (1974) "What works? - questions and answers about prison reform". *Public Interest*: Spring, 22-54. Also In Martinson, R., Palmer, T., and Adams, S. (1976) *Rehabilitation, Recidivism, And Research*. New Jersey, U.S.A.: National Council on Crime and Delinquency, 7-39.

Matthews, R., and Young, J. (1992) "Reflections on realism". In Young, J., and Matthews, R. (eds.) *Rethinking Criminology: The Realist Debate*. London: Sage Publications, 1-23.

Matza, D. (1964) "The positive delinquent". In *Delinquency And Drift*. Toronto: Wiley, 1-32.

Maynard, W. (1994) *Witness Intimidation: Strategies For Prevention*. Crime Detection & Prevention Series, Paper 55. London: Home Office.

McCord, J. (1979) "Some child-rearing antecedents of criminal behavior in adult men". *Journal Of Personality And Social Psychology: 37*, 1477-1486.

McLaughlin, E., and Muncie, J. (1994) "Managing the criminal justice system". In Clarke, J., Cochrane, A., and McLaughlin, E. (eds.) *Managing Social Policy*. London: Sage Publications, 115-140.

McLellan, D. (1986) *Ideology*. Minneapolis: University of Minnesota Press.

Mueller, G.O.W. (1990) "Whose prophet is Cesare Beccaria? An essay on the origins of criminological theory". In Laufer, W., and Adler, F. (eds.) *Advances In Criminological Theory: Volume Two*. London: Transaction Publishers, 1-14.

NACRO. (1966) *NACRO: An Organisation For The Prevention Of Crime 1966*. London: NACRO.

NACRO. (1988) *NACRO Factsheet: The Probation Service*. London: NACRO.

NACRO. (1991) *What Is NACRO?* London: NACRO.

NACRO. (1993) *NACRO Factsheet: Police*. London: NACRO.

NACRO. (1994a) *NACRO Annual Report 1993/1994*. London: NACRO.

NACRO. (1994b) *NACRO Directory 1994/1995*. London: NACRO.

NACRO. (1994c) *NACRO NEWS: 13*. London: NACRO.

NACRO. (1994d) *Reducing Youth Crime*. London: NACRO.

NACRO. (1995a) *1994/1995 NACRO*. London: NACRO.

NACRO. (1995b) *NACRO NEWS: 14*. London: NACRO.

NACRO. (1995c) *NACRO NEWS: 15*. London: NACRO.

NACRO. (1995d) *NACRO NEWS: 16*. London: NACRO.

NACRO. (1996a) *10 Key Messages About Crime: NACRO Annual Report 1995/1996*. London: NACRO.

NACRO. (1996b) *NACRO Directory, January - June 1996*. London: NACRO.

NACRO. (1996c) *NACRO NEWS: 18*. London: NACRO.

NACRO. (1996d) *NACRO NEWS: 19*. London: NACRO.

NACRO. (1997) *NACRO and Community Safety*. London: NACRO.

National Community Safety Network. (no date) *Membership Application, National Community Safety Network*.

Newman, O. (1972) *Defensible Space: Crime Prevention Through Urban Design*. New York: MacMillan.

Normandeau, A., and Leighton, B. (1990) *A Vision Of The Future Of Policing In Canada: Police Challenge 2000*. Ottawa: Solicitor General Canada.

O'Connor, J. (1973) *The Fiscal Crisis Of The State*. New York: St. James's Press.

Oldfield, D. (ed.) (1995) *PRG In Focus: An Introduction To The Police Research Group*. London: Police Research Group. London: Home Office.

Pate, A. (1986) "Experimenting with foot patrol: the Newark experience". In Rosenbaum, D. (ed.). *Community Crime Prevention: Does It Work?* London: Sage Publications, 137-156.

Pease, K. (1991) "The Kirkholt project: preventing burglary on a British public housing estate". In Clarke, R. (ed.). *Situational Crime Prevention: Successful Case Studies*. New York: Harrow and Heston.

Pease, K. (1994) "Crime prevention". In Maguire, M., Morgan, R., and Reiner, R (eds.) *The Oxford Handbook Of Criminology*. Oxford: Clarendon Press, 659-703.

Polvi, N., Looman, T., Humphries, C., Pease, K. (1990) "Repeat break and enter victimisation: time course and crime prevention opportunity". *Journal of Police Science and Administration*, 17, 8-11.

Reiss, A.J. (1986) "Why are communities important in understanding crime?" In Reiss, A.J. and Tonry, M. (eds.) *Communities And Crime*. Chicago: University of Chicago Press.

Rock, P. (1990) *Helping Victims Of Crime*. Oxford: The Clarendon Press.

Rock, P. (1994) "The social organization of a Home Office initiative". *European Journal of Crime, Criminal Law and Criminal Justice*: 2(2), 141-167.

Rosenbaum, D. (1988) "Community crime prevention: a review and synthesis of the literature". *Justice Quarterly*: 5, 323-395.

Ruggiero, V. (1992) "Realist criminology: a critique". In Young, J., and Matthews, R. (eds.) *Rethinking Criminology: The Realist Debate*. London: Sage Publications, 123-140.

Rutter, M., and Giller, H. (1983) *Juvenile Delinquency: Trends And Perspectives*. Markham: Penguin Books.

Savage, S., and Charman, S. (1996) "Managing change". In Leishman, F., Loveday, B., and Savage, S. *Core Issues In Policing*. London: Longman, 39-53.

Schweinhart, L.J. (1987) "Can preschool programs help prevent delinquency?" In Wilson, J.Q. and Loury, G.C. (eds.) *Families, Schools And Delinquency Prevention*. Volume III of 'From Children To Citizens'. New York: Springer Verlag.

Schweinhart, L.J. and Weikart, D.P. (1993) *A Summary Of Significant Benefits: The High/Scope Perry Pre-School Study Through Age 27*. Ypsilanti/Michigan: High/Scope Press.

Shaw, C.R., and McKay, H.D. (1969) *Juvenile Delinquency And Urban Areas* (revised edition). Chicago: University of Chicago Press.

Sherman, J. (1996) "Labour intends to cut spending on welfare benefits". *The Times*: 8 May 1996, 11.

Skogan, W. G. (1990) *Disorder And Decline: Crime And The Spiral Of Decay In American Neighbourhoods*. New York: The Free Press.

Smith, L., and Laycock, G. (1985) *Reducing Crime: Developing The Role Of Crime Prevention Panels*. Crime Prevention Unit Series, Paper No. 2. London: Home Office.

Standing Conference on Crime Prevention. (1991) *Safer Communities: The Local Delivery Of Crime Prevention Through The Partnership Approach*. London: HMSO.

Stern, P. (1979) *Evaluating Social Science Research*. New York: Oxford University Press.

Sutherland, E., and Cressey, D. (1955) *Criminology*. Philadelphia: Lippincott.

Sutton, M. (1996) *Implementing Crime Prevention Schemes In A Multi-Agency Setting: Aspects Of Process In The Safer Cities Programme*. Home Office Research Studies. London: HMSO.

Sykes, G., and Cullen, F. (1992) *Criminology, Second Edition*. U.S.A: Harcourt Brace Jovanovich College Publishers.

Tarling, R. (1993) "The Research and Planning Unit of the Home Office (England and Wales)". *European Journal On Criminal Policy And Research*: *1-4*, 139-142.

Tarling, R. (1995) "Foreword". In Maung, Natalie Aye *Young People, Victimisation And The Police: British Crime Survey Findings On Experiences And Attitudes Of 12 To 15 Year Olds*. Home Office Research Study No. 140. London: HMSO.

Taylor, I. (1992) "Left realist criminology and the free market experiment in Britain". In Young, J., and Matthews, R (eds.) *Rethinking Criminology: The Realist Debate*. London: Sage Publications, 95-122.

Thomas, T. (1990) "Multi-agency policing: a review of a Danish experiment in multi-agency co-operation". *Policing*: *6*, 582-585.

Tilley, N. (1991) *Opportunity Knocks!-Crime Prevention And The Safer Cities Story*. Paper presented at the Social Policy Association Annual Conference, Nottingham University, 9-11 July 1991.

Tuck, M. (1987) "Tom Lodge, CBE". *Research Bulletin*: *23*, 5. Home Office Research and Planning Unit. London: Home Office.

Tuck, M. (1988) "Crime prevention: a shift in concept". In Graham, J. (ed.) *Research Bulletin*: *24*. London: Home Office Research and Planning Unit.

Tuck, M. (1989) "Is criminology any use?" *Research Bulletin*: *26*, 5-8. Home Office Research and Planning Unit. London: Home Office.

Utting, D., Bright, J., and Henricson, C. (1993) *Crime And The Family: Improving Child-Rearing And Preventing Delinquency*. Occasional Paper 16. Family Policy Studies Centre.

van Dijk, J., and de Waard, J. (1991) "A two-dimensional typology of crime prevention projects; with bibliography". *Criminal Justice Abstracts*: September 1991, 483-503.

Vold, G. and Bernard, T. (1986) *Theoretical Criminology, Third Edition*. New York: Oxford University Press.

Wadsworth, M. (1979) *Roots Of Delinquency*. Oxford: Martin Robertson.

Walklate, S. (1996) "Community and crime prevention". In McLaughlin, E., and Muncie, J. (eds.) *Controlling Crime*. London: Sage Publications.

Waller, I. (1989) *Current Trends In European Crime Prevention: Implications For Canada*. Ottawa: Department of Justice Canada.

Waller, I. (1991) *Introductory Report: Putting Crime Prevention On The Map*. Produced for the International Conference on Urban Safety, Drugs, and Crime Prevention; November 18-20 1991, Paris.

Ward, M. (1995) "Cameras fail to beat street crime". *New Scientist*: 23/30 December, 4.

Wardle, C. (1993) "Crime Prevention Minister". *Crime Prevention News*: October - December, 3. London: Home Office.

Weatheritt, M. (1986) *Innovations In Policing*. London: Croom Helm.

West, D.J. (1982) *Delinquency: Its Roots, Careers And Prospects*. London: Heinemann.

West, D.J., and Farrington, D. (1973) *Who Becomes Delinquent?* London: Heinemann.

West, D.J., and Farrington, D. (1977) *The Delinquent Way Of Life*. London: Heinemann.

Wharf, B. (1989) "Implementing Achieving Health for All". *Canadian Review of Social Policy*: 24, 42-48.

Wilson, J. Q. (1975) *Thinking About Crime*. New York: Basic Books.

Wolfgang, M.E., et al. (1972) *Delinquency In A Birth Cohort*. Chicago: University of Chicago Press.

Appendices

Appendix I: Examples Of Crime Prevention Done By Police Officers

"Code Book"

Advice to Victims: This category specifically stated that advice was provided to victims/complainants, or, stated that advice was given at the scene of a crime. Examples include: "at scene of crime, advice is always given" "advice re: security at burglaries", "advising victims on security precautions", "advice at scenes where crime has been committed", "giving advice at scenes of crime".

Other Advice: This category did not specify whether advice was given specifically to victims, nor did it specify that it was provided after an incident. Advice was, however, provided. Examples include: "advice given to house owners routinely", "giving advice", "advising public on preventative measures that they can take", "advice on home and personal security", "advice on home and car security".[1]

Patrol: This included
   a) foot, bicycle and car patrols,
   b) being a visible deterrent whether it be the police vehicle or uniform, and

---

[1] Note: The following example would be grouped both under 'Advice to victims' and 'Other advice': "crime prevention advice on telephone prior to or after offence". In this case advice is specifically given to victims, but also to others.

c) police presence. These three were grouped together since one infers the other.

Examples include: "normal uniform patrol work", "preventative patrol", "general patrol has some deterrent value by high visibility in problem areas", "preventative patrol, by being in uniform or on foot or in a vehicle deters some offenders", "presence in crime areas", "being seen in crime areas in uniform", "police presence prevents much crime - whether it be against property or the person".

Neighbourhood Watch: This included responses which specifically stated "Neighbourhood Watch" and three responses which mentioned helping with property marking. Examples include: "start up neighbourhood watches", "neighbourhood watch liaison", "neighbourhood watch launches", "initiate neighbourhood watch schemes", "marking of property".

Arrest: This included responses related to arrest, prosecution, applying the law/enforcement, and incapacitation. Examples include: "applying the law", "arrest/prosecution of offenders", "by arresting and convicting offenders", "arrest criminals", "prosecute offenders".

Stop Checks: This included stop checks of people and vehicles. The term 'stop check/search' or 'questioning suspected persons' was used in the responses, as opposed to just 'checking'. It was felt, for example, that there was a difference between checking whether a vehicle might have left its doors unlocked and formally stopping a vehicle to check its contents/occupants. Examples include: "stop/check vehicles/persons", "PACE 1984 stop searches", "stop/search", "regularly stop checking known criminals and suspected persons", "questioning suspected persons".

Schools: This included talks/visits to schools. Examples include: "school visits", "promote crime prevention displays at school fetes", "liaison with schools", "school visits (primary) from time to time", "schools".

Giving Information to Colleagues: This category involved giving information to colleagues. Responses included: "briefing other officers", "advice to colleagues", "disseminate intelligence so that operational officers can act on it".

Talking To or Informing Members of the Public: This category made no mention of the word advice thus potentially enabling an exchange of information to the benefit of both parties. This category also excludes questioning suspect persons. Examples include: "consultation with shopkeepers", "personal safety talks aimed at women", "by talking to groups", "talking with youths", "various talks and specific crime evenings and weeks", "general info to public and local community groups", "informing the public", "speak to people/public on a day to day basis when the opportunity arises".

Household/Business Surveys: This category mentioned conducting surveys. Examples include: "home crime prevention surveys at request of house holder", "domestic surveys of private houses for crime prevention", "home and property surveys", "house surveys", "home and business security surveys".

Multi-Agency Schemes: This category included responses which suggested a relationship with more than one agency. The term liaison was not enough to enable a response to fit into this category. For example the response "liaison with schools" was not included in this category since it did not suggest a liaison with more than one agency, or necessarily an ongoing relationship. Responses included: "multi-agency crime prevention strategies/partnership schemes", "interagency discussion of policy/community problems" (this response was also coded under "setting policies" and "Inter-agency liaison and projects").

Security/Checks: In this category no mention is made whether advice is given. There is also no indication of contact with "humans". It is not clear whether checks are made in passing or whether the police have been specifically asked to conduct a 'security survey'. This group also differs from stop checks in that no mention is made of stopping vehicles or persons. Examples include: "checking vehicles and shops for security", "during course of duty you spot anything that you feel is vulnerable to criminals", "check factories/workshops/ car parks", "house security, car security", "security of premises" and "insecurities cars and buildings".

Facilitating Crime Prevention Strategies: This category includes responses relating to the management of crime prevention in general. Examples include: "by directing staff towards the aim of crime prevention" (this response was also coded under managing resources), "managing the collective approach to crime prevention for the whole sub-division" (this response was also coded under "managing resources"), "supervising strategies and creating strategies to enhance local crime prevention plans", "organization of crime prevention initiatives".

Press Releases to Inform Public: This category includes responses related to the media, in particular the newspapers. Responses include: "liaison with press", "info given to press about current crime initiatives", "press release to warn of crime trends".

Cautioning First Time Offenders: This category includes giving formal cautions to first time offenders. Responses include: "Counselling at time of administering cautions" and "by use of properly issued warnings and cautions to deter offenders from re-offending".

Police/Observations: This category includes observing potential criminals without their knowledge. Responses include: "collating information on known active criminals", "by proactive policing e.g., observation", "observation and stop/checks to deter potential crime" (this response was also coded under "stop checks"), "plain clothes observation", "pro-active-plain clothes", "observations in plain clothes".

Setting Policies: This category includes responses related to policy-making. Responses included: "it is my job to set policies geared towards crime prevention", "interagency discussion of policy/community problems" (this response was also coded under "multi-agency schemes").

Managing Resources: This category includes responses related to management in general, rather than those directly related to crime prevention, as cited under "facilitation of crime prevention". Responses included: "managing the collective approach to crime prevention for the whole sub-division" (this response was also coded under "facilitating crime prevention strategies"), "managing resources to target active criminals to try and impact on the crime rate", "I direct uniform patrols to areas subject to burglaries, car crime, etc.", "by directing staff towards the aim of crime prevention" (this response was also coded under "facilitating crime prevention strategies").

Other: This category includes single responses that did not fit under any of the preceding heading, or responses which were too general to draw conclusions on what was meant exactly. Examples include: "direct measures", "crime prevention officer" (no other information was provided), "fitting police alarms", "hand out crime stoppers letters", "dealing with offenders" and "community policing" (no further explanation/definition was provided) "probation", "encourage relevant CS projects".

Appendix II: Examples Of Crime Prevention Done By Probation Officers

"Code Book"

Detention: This category mentioned the role of bail hostels. Responses included: "by offering bail beds to people who would otherwise live close to victims" and "ensuring residents on hostel premises after curfew - reduces risk of night-time burglaries etc."

Supervisions: This category included individual work which challenged an offender's perspective on crime. It also included those replies which specifically mentioned supervisions. Examples include: "individual supervision with clients can prevent crime in both short and long term", "challenging offending behaviour/supervision", "work with individual offenders", "supervision work with offenders which identifies changes that they will make in order to stop offending", "by discussing various issues with clients to help them see that crime is not worth the consequences".

Multi-Agency Involvement: This category mentioned the terms multi-agency or partnership. Responses included: "multi-agency planning", "in partnership with the local council", "multi-agency role".

Welfare Assistance: This category includes helping offenders with substance misuse, employment, housing, or education. Examples include: "try to sort out problems (e.g., alcohol, drug misuse, employment etc.) that may lead to offending behaviour", "assistance regarding accommodation/employment/ substance misuse. General welfare work", "help them to find work, training or education therefore need to offend diminishes", "work with Housing Providers", "assist offenders into employment education or training".

Management: This category includes examples tied to management. Responses included: "resource management directed towards crime prevention activities", "as part of strategic planning", "supervision of staff who have contact with clients".

Other: This category included responses that did not fit under any of the preceding headings or responses which were too general to draw conclusions on what was meant exactly. Examples include: "all our work in the criminal field contributes towards crime prevention"; "just being on probation", "encourage relevant CS projects".